SUBROGATION AND MARSHALLING

This innovative and thought-provoking book studies how subrogation and marshalling should be understood in private law.

Subrogation and marshalling are legal rules which give a person new rights with prima facie the same content as someone else's extinguished rights. Explaining why the law does this has proven difficult. This book argues that key to understanding subrogation is the distinctive form of the rights that it creates. The form of rights created reflects a particular role in ensuring interpersonal justice: subrogation's role is to properly distribute the burden of debts. Taking this model, the book goes on to resolve persistent controversies in the case law, including when subrogation should occur, what rights it should create, the relationship between subrogation and marshalling, and whether subrogation is a remedy for unjust enrichment.

Volume 47 in the series Hart Studies in Private Law

Subrogation and Marshalling

Rory Gregson

•HART•
OXFORD • LONDON • NEW YORK • NEW DELHI • SYDNEY

HART PUBLISHING

Bloomsbury Publishing Plc

Kemp House, Chawley Park, Cumnor Hill, Oxford, OX2 9PH, UK

1385 Broadway, New York, NY 10018, USA

29 Earlsfort Terrace, Dublin 2, Ireland

HART PUBLISHING, the Hart/Stag logo, BLOOMSBURY and the Diana logo are trademarks of Bloomsbury Publishing Plc

First published in Great Britain 2024

A catalogue record for this book is available from the British Library.

A catalogue record for this book is available from the Library of Congress.

Library of Congress Control Number: 2024940202

ISBN: HB: 978-1-50996-922-7
ePDF: 978-1-50996-924-1
ePub: 978-1-50996-923-4

Typeset by Compuscript Ltd, Shannon

PREFACE

This book was inspired by a series of four UK Supreme Court decisions in five years, in which the members of the Court were split over whether or not subrogation is a remedy for unjust enrichment.[1] As yet, there is no developed explanation of how the modern law of subrogation could be understood outside the law of unjust enrichment. This book fills that gap.

The key to understanding subrogation, and the central argument of the book, is that subrogation describes the creation of a distinctive form of rights: C's new rights have prima facie the same content as X's extinguished rights. This distinctive form of rights reflects a distinctive justification: subrogation's role is to properly distribute the burden of debts. In turn, this distinctive justification dictates that subrogation is governed by different rules, and is available in different circumstances, compared to other legal remedies. In short, subrogation has a unique form and a unique role to play in ensuring interpersonal justice. It cannot be reduced to being one of many remedies for unjust enrichment.

This focus on form determines the book's scope in two ways. First, there are two types of subrogation – subrogation to subsisting rights and subrogation to extinguished rights – and works on subrogation typically address both. But these two types of subrogation create different forms of rights, so analysing them together causes more confusion than illumination. Each type of subrogation must be understood on its own terms and so this book only concerns subrogation to extinguished rights. Second, having defined subrogation as a particular form of rights, it is possible to find other examples of this form of rights which travel under different names. For instance, a focus on form reveals that the equitable doctrine of marshalling creates rights of the subrogation form, and so marshalling should be understood as an example of subrogation.

To advance these arguments, the book will be structured as follows. Part I, comprising Chapters 1 and 2, serves as the introduction. Chapter 1 defines

[1] *Menelaou v Bank of Cyprus UK Ltd* [2015] UKSC 66, [2016] AC 176; *Investment Trust Companies v Revenue and Customs Commissioners* [2017] UKSC 29, [2018] AC 275 [49] (Lord Reed); *Swynson Ltd v Lowick Rose LLP* [2017] UKSC 32, [2018] AC 313; *Prudential Assurance Co Ltd v Revenue and Customs Commissioners* [2018] UKSC 39, [2018] 3 WLR 652 [69] (Lord Reed, Lord Hodge, and Lord Mance).

subrogation, outlining the key features of the form of rights created by subrogation. Chapter 2 then introduces six controversies which surround subrogation and which the book seeks to resolve:

1. Is subrogation justified?
2. Is subrogation a remedy for unjust enrichment?
3. Is subrogation redundant?
4. When should subrogation occur?
5. What rights should subrogation create?
6. What is the relationship between subrogation and marshalling?

Part II comprises Chapters 3 to 7 and considers whether subrogation is redundant according to the law as it stands. It is often said that subrogation is (at least sometimes) redundant because it duplicates a 'direct unjust enrichment claim'. On this view, subrogation's form is unimportant and it is interchangeable with direct unjust enrichment claims. Part II argues that this is mistaken. Close analysis of the cases reveals that rules which govern direct unjust enrichment claims do not govern subrogation. In particular:

- Chapter 3 shows that subrogation is not governed by the rules which determine whether there was an enrichment in a direct claim.
- Chapter 4 shows that subrogation is not governed by the rules which determine whether that enrichment was at the claimant's expense in a direct claim.
- Chapter 5 shows that subrogation is not governed by the rules which determine whether an enrichment was unjust in a direct claim.
- Chapter 6 shows that while the change of position defence applies to most direct claims, there is no authority for it applying to subrogation.
- Chapter 7 shows that subrogation and direct claims have different effects.

Part II therefore concludes that subrogation and direct claims are governed by different rules; subrogation is available in different circumstances and has a different effect compared to direct claims. Accordingly, subrogation does not duplicate a direct claim and subrogation is not redundant.

Part III, comprising Chapters 8 to 11, then turns to consider what the law ought to be as a matter of principle, addressing the controversies over whether subrogation is justified, when it should occur, what rights it should create, and its relationship with marshalling. Chapter 8 argues that many previous attempts to justify subrogation are unsuccessful because they fail to justify the particular form of rights created by subrogation.

Chapter 9 considers the relationship between subrogation and tracing. It rejects the popular idea that the justification for trusts over traceably acquired rights can also justify subrogation to traceably discharged debts. The two take different forms, and so any attempt to justify a trust over a traceably acquired right struggles to explain the different form of rights created by subrogation.

Instead, Chapter 10 argues that subrogation's distinctive form reflects a distinctive justification: subrogation is justified by ensuring that the burden of debts are distributed as they should be. It then considers, in light of this justification, when subrogation should occur and what rights it should create.

Chapter 11 considers the relationship between subrogation and marshalling. It argues that marshalling is an example of subrogation, but with a different justification to other instances of subrogation. Marshalling is justified by preventing a private party determining the distribution of assets on insolvency. This different justification dictates that marshalling is available in different circumstances, compared to other instances of subrogation.

The controversy over whether subrogation is a remedy for unjust enrichment cuts across the division between what the law is and what the law ought to be, and so it is addressed by both Parts II and III. Part II argues that subrogation is not a remedy for unjust enrichment in the sense that it duplicates a direct unjust enrichment claim. Part III argues that, once the justification for subrogation is understood, ideas of unjust enrichment are a dangerous distraction which have misled the courts.

Chapter 12 concludes by summarising the book's answers to the six questions posed in Chapter 2.

ACKNOWLEDGEMENTS

This book builds on my doctoral thesis at the University of Oxford. My first thanks are therefore due to my supervisor, Rob Stevens. I have been fortunate to have been taught by many outstanding teachers, but none better than Rob. I have been inspired by his ability to make the complex simple and the simple nuanced, and above all by his ability to animate a dry technical problem by locating it within a coherent vision of what private law ought to be.

Chapters 4 to 6 are adapted from my MPhil thesis, which was co-supervised by Rob Stevens and Fred Wilmot-Smith. I could not have hoped for a better mentor than Fred, who has been generous with his time and advice, continuing to guide my career and comment on my work long after the end of his formal appointment as my supervisor. I constantly aspire to hold myself to his rigorous standards.

The ideas of the book are stronger for the searching criticism of my MPhil examiners (Lord Burrows and Charles Mitchell), Confirmation of Status assessors (Ben McFarlane and William Swadling), and DPhil examiners (Ben McFarlane and Lionel Smith). The central idea of this book – that subrogation describes the creation of a particular form of rights – comes from feedback that Ben gave me during my Confirmation of Status, though it took me many years to realise the import of what he had told me.

I am grateful to the Arts and Humanities Research Council, Balliol College, and the Clarendon Fund for funding my MPhil and DPhil studies. I learned much from discussing this project with Mindy Chen-Wishart, Lorren Eldridge, Katie Johnston, Tim Liau, Nick McBride, Tim Pilkington, Helen Scott, Ben Spagnolo, Andreas Televantos, and Alex Waghorn.

The book also owes much to my two spells in Cambridge, first as an undergraduate and then as a Fellow of Trinity College. I thank Stephen Watterson – whose brilliant undergraduate lectures first got me interested in subrogation – and David Ibbetson – who gave me the confidence to pursue a doctorate.

Finally, this book would not have been possible without the love and laughter of those with whom I shared my life as a doctoral student: Gareth, Jacob, Clara, Conni, and Carole.

SUMMARY CONTENTS

PART I
INTRODUCTION

PART II
IS SUBROGATION REDUNDANT?

PART III
IS SUBROGATION JUSTIFIED?

CONTENTS

PART II
IS SUBROGATION REDUNDANT?

PART III
IS SUBROGATION JUSTIFIED?

LIST OF TABLES

TABLE OF CASES

England and Wales

Australia

Canada

Ireland

Scotland

South Africa

United States

TABLE OF STATUTES

PART I

Introduction

1

What is Subrogation?

I. Two Forms of Subrogation

The key to understanding subrogation and marshalling, and the central argument of this book, is that subrogation describes the creation of a particular form of rights. It is therefore appropriate to begin by identifying the defining features of this form.

Professor Mitchell distinguished two types of subrogation, which he initially called 'simple' and 'reviving' subrogation,[1] and which he later called 'subrogation to subsisting rights' and 'subrogation to extinguished rights'.[2] The two types of subrogation create rights of different forms.

Subrogation to subsisting rights allows C to exercise and obtain the benefit of X's rights against D. The best-known example is the subrogation of insurers. If I negligently crash my car into yours, the law of torts gives you a right to compensation for the damage, and so you could sue me. But in practice that is not what you would do. Instead, you would contact your insurer, who would pay for the repairs to your car. In effect, then, your insurer would pay for loss which I caused. To put this right, your contract with your insurer provides that your insurer can exercise and take the benefit of your right to recover damages from me. Your insurer can sue me, in your name, to recover its loss.[3] Your insurer is said to be subrogated to your subsisting right against me.

[1] C Mitchell, 'The Law of Subrogation' [1992] *LMCLQ* 483, 485–92; C Mitchell, *The Law of Subrogation* (Oxford, Clarendon Press, 1994) 4–7.

[2] C Mitchell and S Watterson, *Subrogation: Law and Practice* (Oxford, OUP, 2007) paras 1.04–1.10; C Mitchell, P Mitchell and S Watterson, *Goff and Jones: The Law of Unjust Enrichment* (London, Sweet & Maxwell, 2022) para 19-45. See also *Ibrahim v Barclays Bank Plc* [2011] EWHC 1897 (Ch), [2011] 2 CLC 589 [7] (Vos J); *Alliance Bank JSC v Aquanta Corp* [2011] EWHC 3281 (Comm), [2012] 1 Lloyd's Rep 181 [21] (Burton J). For an explanation for this change in language, see C Mitchell, 'Subrogation: Persistent Misunderstandings' in A Burrows and Lord Rodger of Earlsferry (eds), *Mapping the Law: Essays in Memory of Peter Birks* (Oxford, OUP, 2006) 106–11.

[3] *Esso Petroleum Co Ltd v Hall Russell & Co Ltd (the Esso Bernicia)* [1989] AC 643 (HL); *Lord Napier and Ettrick v Hunter* [1993] AC 713 (HL).

As this example illustrates, subrogation to subsisting rights often[4] – though not always[5] – occurs because the parties contracted for it. As a result, most questions about subrogation to subsisting rights can be answered by the parties' contract and the law of contract.[6] This form of subrogation is not what this book is about.

By contrast, subrogation to extinguished rights (sometimes called equitable subrogation[7]) occurs when X had rights against D and these rights were extinguished.[8] Subrogation to extinguished rights means giving C new rights against D, which prima facie have the same content as X's extinguished rights against D.[9] These new rights are C's, and so C must sue D using their own name and not X's.

The classic example is *Butler v Rice*.[10] Mrs Rice owned a house subject to a bank's charge. Acting behind his wife's back, Mr Rice asked Butler for a loan to pay off the bank's charge. Butler thought that Mr Rice owned the house, so agreed to the loan in exchange for a mortgage over the house. Butler therefore paid the loan monies to Mr Rice, who paid the bank, discharging the bank's charge. When Mrs Rice discovered the arrangement, she refused to execute a mortgage in favour of Butler. On the face of it, then, Butler was unsecured.

However, the court held that because Butler's loan had been used to pay off the bank's charge, Butler was subrogated to the bank's extinguished charge. In other words, Butler acquired a new charge with the same content as the charge that the bank used to have. This meant that Butler was secured after all.

Subrogation to extinguished rights occurs in many different factual contexts. Watterson groups them into three categories: 'common liability' cases,

[4] *Banque Financière de La Cité SA v Parc (Battersea) Ltd* [1999] 1 AC 221 (HL) ('*BFC*') 231E–H (Lord Hoffmann); A Tettenborn, *The Law of Restitution in England and Ireland* (London, Cavendish, 2002) paras 2-41–2-44; Mitchell and Watterson (n 2) para 1.08; R Merkin and J Steele, *Insurance and the Law of Obligations* (Oxford, OUP, 2013) 106–15.

[5] Mitchell and Watterson (n 2) paras 1.07–1.09; A Burrows, *The Law of Restitution* (Oxford, OUP, 2011) 165–66; A Burrows, *A Restatement of the English Law of Unjust Enrichment* (Oxford, OUP, 2012) 175–77; Mitchell, Mitchell and Watterson (n 2) para 21–04.

[6] *BFC* (n 4) 231E–H (Lord Hoffmann).

[7] *Investment Trust Companies v Revenue and Customs Commissioners* [2017] UKSC 29, [2018] AC 275 ('*ITC*') [49] (Lord Reed); *Swynson Ltd v Lowick Rose LLP* [2017] UKSC 32, [2018] AC 313 [18]–[34] (Lord Sumption).

[8] *Burston Finance Ltd v Speirway Ltd* [1974] 1 WLR 1648 (Ch) 1652B (Walton J); *Cheltenham & Gloucester Plc v Appleyard* [2004] EWCA Civ 291 [25] (Neuberger LJ); *Menelaou v Bank of Cyprus UK Ltd* [2015] UKSC 66, [2016] AC 176 ('*Menelaou* (SC)') [39] (Lord Clarke), [83] (Lord Neuberger), [111] (Lord Carnwath); *ITC* (n 7) [49] (Lord Reed); *Swynson* (n 7) [18] (Lord Sumption); Mitchell and Watterson (n 2) paras 1.05, 3.01; Mitchell, Mitchell and Watterson (n 2) para 39–01.

[9] *Day v Tiuta International Ltd* [2014] EWCA Civ 1246 [43] (Gloster LJ); Mitchell and Watterson (n 2) paras 3.15–3.18, 8.05–8.31; Mitchell, Mitchell and Watterson (n 2) paras 7-70, 39-11, 39-37–39-48. JA Dieckmann, 'The Province of Subrogation Determined: Some Corrections – a Functional Analysis of the Guarantor's Right to Derivative Recourse, Comprising a Critique of the Restitutionary Thesis' (2012) 20 *ERPL* 989, 1000–01. For this notation of the parties, see eg Burrows, *Restitution* (n 5) 145.

[10] *Butler v Rice* [1910] 2 Ch 277 (Ch).

'misappropriation' cases, and 'lending' cases.[11] In common liability cases, C pays X, discharging C and D's common debt to X.[12] In misappropriation cases, money held on trust for C is paid to X without C's consent, discharging D's debt to X.[13] In lending cases, like *Butler*, C's loan to D (or a fourth party) is paid to X, discharging D's debt to X.

Across these varied contexts, subrogation to extinguished rights is always non-contractual: it occurs 'by operation of law' and not because then parties contracted for it.[14] Mitchell and Watterson explain that if the parties want C to acquire X's rights then they can choose to transfer X's rights by assignment. Subrogation to extinguished rights is therefore 'an unnecessary complication' which parties 'never contract' for.[15] Consequently, questions about subrogation to extinguished rights cannot be resolved by the terms of a contract or the relatively settled law of contract. Subrogation to extinguished rights is therefore less understood than contractual subrogation and subrogation to subsisting rights.[16]

Because subrogation to subsisting rights and subrogation to extinguished rights create completely different forms of rights, analysing them together causes more confusion than illumination. This book only concerns subrogation to extinguished rights, which it calls 'subrogation' for short, and it excludes subrogation to subsisting rights. This allows the book to investigate the lesser understood form of subrogation in greater depth.

II. Subrogation Defined

Subrogation, then, describes the creation of a particular form of rights: C's new rights have prima facie the same content as X's extinguished rights. Three aspects of this definition require further elaboration.

[11] S Watterson, 'Subrogation' in G Virgo and S Worthington (eds), *Commercial Remedies: Resolving Controversies* (Cambridge, CUP, 2017) 452–54. See also Burrows, *Restitution* (n 5) 145; Mitchell, Mitchell and Watterson (n 2) para 39–01.

[12] eg *Niru Battery Manufacturing Co v Milestone Trading Ltd (No 2)* [2004] EWCA Civ 487, [2004] 1 CLC 882.

[13] eg *Boscawen v Bajwa* [1996] 1 WLR 328 (CA).

[14] *BFC* (n 4) 231E (Lord Hoffmann).

[15] Mitchell and Watterson (n 2) para 3.01.

[16] *Challenger Managed Investments Ltd v Direct Money Corp Pty Ltd* [2003] NSWSC 1072 [50] (Bryson J); *Swynson Ltd v Lowick Rose LLP* [2015] EWCA Civ 629, [2016] 1 WLR 1045 ('*Swynson* (CA)') [47] (Davis LJ).

A. Same Content

First, C's rights have the same content as X's extinguished rights.[17] So if X's rights against D were secured, then so too are C's new rights against D. If X had equitable security, then subrogation gives C equitable security.[18] If X had legal security, then subrogation gives C legal security.[19] Similarly, if X's rights had priority in the event of D's insolvency, then C's new rights have the same preferential status.[20] D's new debt to C can be no greater than D's extinguished debt to X,[21] and D's new debt to C incurs interest at the same rate as D's extinguished debt to X.[22]

B. Prima Facie

However, the idea that C's new rights have the same content as X's extinguished rights is only a 'prima facie' position, which can be modified by other considerations.[23] For instance, where C voluntarily[24] becomes D's creditor, subrogation will give C no more than it bargained for.[25] Thus, if C agreed to make an unsecured loan to D, then subrogation will not give C security, even if X's rights were secured.[26] Here, subrogation departs from the starting point that C's new rights have the same content as X's extinguished rights.

[17] *Filby v Mortgage Express (No 2) Ltd* [2004] EWCA Civ 759 [63] (May LJ); *Day* (n 9) [43] (Gloster LJ).

[18] *Butler* (n 10); *Menelaou* (SC) (n 8).

[19] *Castle Phillips Finance v Piddington* (1995) 70 P & CR 592 (CA) 602 (Peter Gibson LJ); *Appleyard* (n 8) [23], [69]–[74] (Neuberger LJ); *Primlake Ltd v Matthews Associates (No 2)* [2009] EWHC 2774 (Ch) [17](c), [27] (Jeremy Cousins QC); *Anfield (UK) Ltd v Bank of Scotland Plc* [2010] EWHC 2374 (Ch), [2011] 1 WLR 2414, [6], [40] (Proudman J).

[20] *Hodgson v Shaw* (1834) 3 My & K 183, 40 ER 70; *Re M'Myn* (1886) 33 ChD 575 (Ch) 578 (Chitty J); *Re Lord Churchill* (1888) 39 ChD 174 (Ch); *Re Lamplugh Iron Ore Co Ltd* [1927] 1 Ch 308 (Ch). cf *Copis v Middleton* (1823) Turn & R 224, 37 ER 1083; *Re Bell Lines Ltd* [2006] IEHC 188, revd on a different point [2010] IESC 15; *Re Dalma No 1 Pty Ltd* [2013] NSWSC 1335.

[21] *Equity & Law Home Loans Ltd v Prestidge* [1992] 1 WLR 137 (CA) 144E–H (Mustill LJ); *Appleyard* (n 8) [43] (Neuberger LJ); *Day* (n 9) [43] (Gloster LJ).

[22] *Western Trust & Savings Ltd v Rock* (1993-02-26) (CA); *Castle Phillips* (n 19) 602 (Peter Gibson LJ); *Filby* (n 17) [63]–[67] (May LJ); *Appleyard* (n 8) [76]–[77] (Lord Neuberger MR).

[23] Mitchell and Watterson (n 2) para 8.12; Mitchell, Mitchell and Watterson (n 2) paras 7-70, 39-11.

[24] *Mayhew v Crickett* (1818) 2 Swans 185, 191, 36 ER 585, 587 (Lord Eldon LC); *Duncan Fox & Co v North & South Wales Bank* (1880) 6 App Cas 1 (HL); *Boscawen* (n 13) 338B–340A (Millett LJ); *Insol Funding Co Ltd v Cowlam* [2017] EWHC 1822 (Ch) [120] (Master Bowles).

[25] eg *Re Wrexham Mold & Connah's Quay Railway Co* [1899] 1 Ch 440 (CA); *Paul v Speirway* [1976] Ch 220 (Ch) 233B (Oliver J); *BFC* (n 4) 235D (Lord Hoffmann), 237H (Lord Clyde), 242F–G (Lord Hutton); *Appleyard* (n 8) [38], [41] (Neuberger LJ); *Swynson* (n 7) [31]–[34] (Lord Sumption) [86] (Lord Mance).

[26] *Paul* (n 25).

C. New Rights

Because of this, subrogation is distinct from a transfer or legal assignment, which give C rights with identical content to those X used to have.[27] Instead, subrogation gives C new rights with prima facie the same content as X's extinguished rights. In *Banque Financière de la Cité SA v Parc (Battersea) Ltd* ('*BFC*'), Lord Hoffmann explained:

> the phrase 'keeping the charge alive' needs to be handled with some care. It is not a literal truth but rather a metaphor or analogy. In a case in which the whole of the secured debt is repaid, the charge is not kept alive at all. It is discharged and ceases to exist. … When judges say that the charge is 'kept alive' for the benefit of the plaintiff, what they mean is that his legal relations with a defendant … are regulated as if the benefit of the charge had been assigned to him. It does not by any means follow that the plaintiff must for all purposes be treated as an actual assignee of the benefit of the charge ….[28]

Similarly, in *Day v Tiuta International Ltd*, Gloster LJ said:

> [C] does not actually acquire the creditor's interest, but rather obtains a new and independent equitable security interest which prima facie replicates the creditor's old interest. Subrogation does not effect an actual assignment of the discharged creditor's rights to the subrogated creditor. What subrogation means in this context is that the subrogated creditor's legal relations with a defendant … are regulated as if the benefit of the charge had been assigned to him. This means that the claimant does not necessarily occupy exactly the same position as the discharged creditor in every respect. Whilst these new rights often mirror the characteristics and content of the rights which were previously held by the creditor, and cannot be greater than those rights, they need not resemble them in every respect.[29]

Many of the metaphors which surround subrogation are therefore misleading.[30] The cases sometimes say that C 'step[s] into the shoes of' X,[31] or that X's rights are

[27] JE Penner, *Property Rights: A Re-Examination* (Oxford, OUP, 2020) ch 6.

[28] *BFC* (n 4) 236D–G (citation omitted).

[29] *Day* (n 9) [43].

[30] *Niru Battery* (n 12) [63] (Clarke LJ); P Birks, *An Introduction to the Law of Restitution* (Oxford, Clarendon Press, 1989) 95–98; C Rotherham, *Proprietary Remedies in Context* (Oxford, Hart Publishing, 2002) 246; C Rotherham, 'Subrogation' in S Hedley and M Halliwell (eds), *The Law of Restitution* (London, Butterworths, 2002) para 8.4; Mitchell and Watterson (n 2) paras 3.07, 3.10–3.18; C Mitchell, 'Unjust Enrichment' in A Burrows (ed), *English Private Law* (Oxford, OUP, 2013) para 18.280; C Mitchell, 'Unjust Enrichment' in A Burrows (ed), *Principles of the English Law of Obligations* (Oxford, OUP, 2015) para 3.280; Mitchell, Mitchell and Watterson (n 2) para 39–06.

[31] *Patten v Bond* (1889) 60 LT 583 (Ch) 585–86 (Kay J); *Swynson* (n 7) [62] (Lord Mance).

'kept alive' for C,[32] or that C is treated 'as having had an assignment to him of [X]'s rights'.[33] Some courts have denied subrogation because X's rights have been extinguished and so there are no rights for C to be subrogated to.[34] This makes sense if one takes these metaphors literally: there are no shoes for C to step into; there are no rights to be kept alive for C; there are no rights to assign to C.

However, the courts now recognise that C does not acquire X's rights, but rather C acquires new rights with prima facie the same content as X's extinguished rights.[35] Consequently, the metaphors should not be taken literally,[36] and, as Millett LJ observed, the 'discharge of [X's rights] is certainly not a bar to subrogation …; it is rather a precondition'.[37]

Subrogation therefore has a dual character. On the one hand, it gives C rights which prima facie have the same content as X's extinguished rights. But on the other hand, C's rights are new; they are not a transfer of X's rights.

Occasionally these two aspects of subrogation's form are in tension. For instance, the limitation period applicable to rights created by subrogation is unresolved.[38] On the one hand, C's rights may have the same limitation period as X's extinguished rights, reflecting that subrogation gives C rights with prima facie the same content as X's extinguished rights. On the other hand, rights created by subrogation may have their own distinct limitation period, reflecting that they are new rights and not a transfer of X's rights.

The same point is evident in Mitchell and Watterson's approach to the priority of security interests created by subrogation.[39] On the one hand, they say that, against pre-existing interests, C's new rights have the same priority as X's extinguished rights. On the other hand, the priority of C's rights against interests which arise subsequently should be determined on the basis that subrogation gave C new equitable rights at the moment all the elements of C's subrogation claim existed.

[32] *Chetwynd v Allen* [1899] 1 Ch 353 (Ch) 357 (Romer J); *Butler* (n 10) 282–83 (Warrington J).

[33] *Burston* (n 8) 1652B (Walton J).

[34] *Re Diplock* [1948] 1 Ch 465 (CA) 548–549 (Lord Greene MR, Wrottesley and Evershed LJJ); *Capital Finance Co Ltd v Stokes* [1969] 1 Ch 261 (CA) 279E, 280A–B (Harman LJ), 280G–81A (Sachs LJ).

[35] *BFC* (n 4) 236D–G (Lord Hoffmann); *Day* (n 9) [43] (Gloster LJ); Birks, *Introduction* (n 30) 95–98; Mitchell and Watterson (n 2) paras 3.07, 3.10–3.18, 8.05–8.31; C Mitchell, 'Unjust Enrichment' in A Burrows (ed), *English Private Law* (Oxford, OUP, 2013) para 18.279; C Mitchell, 'Unjust Enrichment' in A Burrows (ed), *Principles of the English Law of Obligations* (Oxford, OUP, 2015) para 3.279; Mitchell, Mitchell and Watterson (n 2) paras 7-70, 39-11, 39-47–39-58.

[36] *BFC* (n 4) 236D–G (Lord Hoffmann).

[37] *Boscawen* (n 13) 340G.

[38] *Grove Park Properties v Royal Bank of Scotland Plc* [2018] EWHC 3618 (Comm); Mitchell and Watterson (n 2) paras 7.137–7.162.

[39] Mitchell and Watterson (n 2) paras 8.61–8.106; S Watterson, 'Subrogation, Priority Disputes and Rectification: Mapping a Route Through the Thicket' [2016] *RLR* 1; Mitchell, Mitchell and Watterson (n 2) paras 39-70–39-89.

This again reflects the tension inherent in subrogation's dual character: on the one hand C's rights prima facie have the same content as X's extinguished rights; on the other, C's rights are new.

III. Subrogation's Aliases

Having defined subrogation as giving C new rights which prima facie have the same content as X's extinguished rights, it is possible to identify examples of this form of rights which travel under different names.

A. Recoupment and Contribution

Recoupment and contribution are good examples. These doctrines apply where C and D are both obliged to pay the same debt to X. If C pays X, then the debt of both C and D is discharged. D is then obliged to pay C to the extent that D ought to have borne the burden of paying the debt to X. If D ought to have borne the burden of paying the whole debt, then C has a right to 'reimbursement' or 'recoupment' against D.[40] If D ought to have borne the burden of paying only some of the debt, then C has a right to 'contribution' against D.[41]

C's right to recoupment or contribution is an example of subrogation because this right has prima facie the same content as X's extinguished right against D. So, if X's rights had priority in the event of D's insolvency, then C's right to reimbursement or contribution has the same preferential status.[42] Similarly, if X's rights were secured, then so too is C's right to reimbursement or contribution.[43]

B. Marshalling

Subrogation has a controversial relationship with another equitable doctrine, that of marshalling. Sometimes, marshalling is described as an example of subrogation.[44]

[40] eg *Brook's Wharf & Bull Wharf Ltd v Goodman Bros* [1937] 1 KB 534 (CA).
[41] Civil Liability (Contribution) Act 1978, s 1(1); cf s 2(2).
[42] *Hodgson v Shaw* (1834) 3 My & K 183, 191 40 ER 70, 73 (Lord Brougham LC).
[43] *Yonge v Reynell* (1852) 9 Hare 809, 68 ER 744; *Forbes v Jackson* (1882) 19 ChD 615 (Ch). cf *Cochrane v Cochrane* (1985) 3 NSWLR 403 (NSWSC) 405D–G (Kearney J).
[44] *Chase Corporation (Australia) Pty Ltd v North Sydney Brick and Tile Co Ltd* (1994) 35 NSWLR 1 (NSWSC) 25B–C (Cohen J); Mitchell, *The Law of Subrogation* (n 1) 143; C Mitchell, 'Book Review'

Sometimes, marshalling is described as 'akin to subrogation'.[45] At other times, marshalling and subrogation are distinguished and analysed separately.[46]

Marshalling is a complicated doctrine and it will be examined in detail in Chapter 11. For present purposes, the core case of marshalling can be illustrated by the following example. Say D owes £1m to X, secured over two properties, Whiteacre and Blackacre, which are each worth £1m. D also owes £1m to C who has security over Whiteacre, ranking behind X's security. However, C does not have security over Blackacre. This is illustrated by the following diagram.

WHITEACRE	**BLACKACRE**
Value £1m	Value £1m
X's first charge for £1m	X's first charge for £1m
C's second charge for £1m	

If D is solvent, then both creditors can be paid. The problem arises if D is insolvent.[47] If X chooses to realise its security over Blackacre, then C can realise its security over Whiteacre and so both creditors will be paid. However, if X chooses to realise its security over Whiteacre, then X's right to £1m will exhaust Whiteacre (which is only worth £1m), leaving C unsecured. C would then compete with D's unsecured creditors and so may not be paid in full. As such, X's choice of which security to realise can affect whether or not C will be paid.

Marshalling prevents X's choice prejudicing C. If X chooses to realise its security over Whiteacre, then C 'can look to the other property to satisfy the debt owed to him'.[48] In other words, C acquires security over Blackacre with the same characteristics as X's extinguished security.[49] Marshalling therefore fits the definition of

[2000] *LMCLQ* 589, 590; JD Heydon, MJ Leeming and PG Turner, *Meagher, Gummow and Lehane's Equity: Doctrines and Remedies* (Chatswood NSW, Butterworths, 2015) para 11–020.

[45] *Highbury Pension Fund Management Co v Zirfin Investments Ltd* [2013] EWHC 238 (Ch), [2014] Ch 359 [15] (Norris J).

[46] *Re Dent Co* [2016] EWHC 2650 (Ch), [2017] Ch 422 [26], [29]–[30] (Norris J); SR Derham, 'Set-Off Against an Assignee' (1991) 107 *LQR* 126, 131–32; C Hare, 'Marshalling Marshalling' in PS Davies, S Douglas and J Goudkamp (eds), *Defences in Equity* (Oxford, Hart Publishing, 2018) 242.

[47] *National Crime Agency v Szepietowski* [2013] UKSC 65, [2014] AC 338 [32] (Lord Neuberger).

[48] ibid [31] (Lord Neuberger). See also *Aldrich v Cooper* (1803) 8 Ves Jun 382, 32 ER 402; *Ex p Kendall* (1811) 17 Ves Jun 514, 520, 34 ER 199, 201 (Lord Eldon LC); *Webb v Smith* (1885) 30 ChD 192 (CA) 200 (Cotton LJ); *Re Bank of Credit and Commerce International SA (No 8)* [1996] Ch 245 (CA) 271F–H (Rose LJ); *Re Bank of Credit and Commerce International SA (No 8)* [1998] AC 214 (HL) 230H–31B (Lord Hoffmann); *Szepietowski* (n 47) [1]–[2], [31]–[32] (Lord Neuberger).

[49] In Australia, C only acquires this security once there is a court order giving effect to marshalling: *Commonwealth Trading Bank v Colonial Mutual Life Assurance Society Ltd* (1970) 26 FLR 338 (Tas SC);

subrogation: it gives C new rights with the same content as X's extinguished rights. Marshalling is indeed an example of subrogation.

C. Imputed Intention

Also examples of subrogation are some cases in which courts rely on imputed intention to give priority to a lender's security interest. *Equity & Law Home Loans v Prestige* is representative.[50] Mr Prestidge and Mrs Brown purchased a house, which was registered in Mr Prestidge's name. Part of the purchase price came from X's £30,000 loan to Mr Prestidge, which was secured by a charge over the property. However, Mr Prestidge intended to 'cheat' Mrs Brown.[51] Without Mrs Brown's knowledge, Mr Prestidge borrowed £43,000 from C, secured by a new charge over the house. Mr Prestidge used £30,000 of C's loan to repay X's loan, extinguishing X's charge. Mr Prestidge 'pocketed' the remaining £13,000 and defaulted on C's loan.[52] C sought possession of the house. Mr Prestidge conceded that he held the house on trust for Mrs Brown,[53] and Mrs Brown argued that her beneficial interest had priority over C's charge.

Giving the judgment of the Court of Appeal, Mustill LJ explained that Mrs Brown had consented to X's charge as it was necessary for the house to be purchased in the first place.[54] Mustill LJ imputed to Mrs Brown the intention to consent to the replacement of X's charge with C's, 'whether [Mrs Brown] knew about it or not, provided that it did not change [her] position for the worse'.[55] Accordingly, C had priority over Mrs Brown to the extent of £30,000.[56]

Mustill LJ explained that he imputed this intention to Mrs Brown because it was 'common sense'[57] and:

> Any other answer would be absurd, for it would mean that if Mr. Prestidge had in good faith and without the knowledge of [Mrs Brown] transferred the mortgage to another

Chase (n 44) 18G–21B (Cohen J); *Sarge Pty Ltd v Cazihaven Homes Pty Ltd* (1994) 34 NSWLR 658 (NSWSC) 664D–65G (Young J).

[50] *Prestidge* (n 21). See also *Bristol and West Building Society v Henning* [1985] 1 WLR 778 (CA); *Paddington Building Society v Mendelsohn* (1985) 50 P & CR 244 (CA).

[51] *Prestidge* (n 21) 140G (Mustill LJ).

[52] ibid 141D (Mustill LJ).

[53] ibid 142E (Mustill LJ).

[54] ibid 144B.

[55] ibid 144B–C.

[56] ibid 144E–H (Mustill LJ).

[57] ibid 144B–C.

> society in order, say, to obtain a more favourable rate of interest, she would suddenly receive a windfall in the shape of the removal of the encumbrance which she had intended should be created in consequence of a transaction which could not do her any harm and of which she was entirely ignorant.[58]

The problem with this reasoning is that the remortgage which actually took place was designed to 'cheat'[59] Mrs Brown and so, had she been aware of it, she would not have consented to it. As a result, Mustill LJ's reliance on Mrs Brown's intention seems fictional. As Lord Kerr put it in *Jones v Kernott*:

> The reason that I question the aptness of the notion of imputing an intention is that, in the final analysis, the exercise is wholly unrelated to ascertainment of the parties' views. It involves the court deciding what is fair in light of the whole course of dealing with the property. That decision has nothing to do with what the parties intended, or what might be supposed would have been their intention had they addressed that question.[60]

Instead, as Dixon suggests, the case is an example of subrogation,[61] even though the court did not use this language. C acquired a new charge with prima facie the same content as X's extinguished charge. X's extinguished charge for £30,000 had priority over Mrs Brown's beneficial interest, and so C's new charge had priority over Mrs Brown's beneficial interest only to the extent of £30,000.

In short, *Prestidge* sails under false colours. The Court relied upon the fiction of imputed intention, but the result is better understood as an example of subrogation.

IV. A Remedy?

Subrogation is often described as a remedy.[62] By contrast, in his textbook, Lord Burrows prefers to call subrogation a 'process or means of getting to particular rights or remedies'. This is because C does not seek subrogation against D, but subrogation 'to particular rights and remedies' against D.[63]

[58] ibid 143H.

[59] ibid 140G (Mustill LJ).

[60] *Jones v Kernott* [2011] UKSC 53, [2012] 1 AC 776 [74].

[61] M Dixon, 'Equitable Co-Ownership: Proprietary Rights in Name Only?' in E Cooke (ed), *Modern Studies in Property Law, Volume 4* (Oxford, Hart Publishing, 2007) 37.

[62] eg *BFC* (n 4); *Menelaou* (SC) (n 8); *Swynson* (n 7) [18] (Lord Sumption); G Virgo, *The Principles of the Law of Restitution* (Oxford, OUP, 2015) 636; Mitchell, Mitchell and Watterson (n 2) para 39–01.

[63] Burrows, *Restitution* (n 5) 146. See also Mitchell and Watterson (n 2) para 1.01 'process'; Burrows, *Restatement* (n 5) 172 'process or means'; J Palmer, 'Unjust Enrichment, Proprietary Subrogation and

The word 'remedy' is used to mean different things. Birks identified five different meanings of the word, three of which were synonymous with the word 'right'.[64] Given that subrogation describes the creation of a particular form of rights, in this sense Lord Burrows is right that subrogation is a 'process or means of getting to particular rights or remedies'.[65]

By contrast, Smith and Zakrzewski each define a remedy as a court order.[66] Whether subrogation is a remedy in this sense turns on whether subrogation gives C rights as soon as X's rights are extinguished (and a court order merely declares C's rights which have already arisen) or whether a court order is needed to give C rights of the subrogation form (and before the court order C merely has a power to demand that a court order subrogation). This mirrors debates elsewhere in private law over whether, before a court order, claimants have a right or merely a power to sue.[67] For many purposes, the answer does not matter and the arguments of this book are consistent with either view. In England and Wales, subrogation gives C rights as soon as X's rights are extinguished, and a court order merely confirms the rights that have already arisen.[68] On this view, subrogation creates a particular form of rights, and not a remedy in Smith and Zakrzewski's sense.

Ultimately, the substance of subrogation is giving C new rights with prima facie the same content as X's extinguished rights. This substance does not change whether or not the word 'remedy' is defined in a way that captures subrogation. Thus, in *Menelaou v Bank of Cyprus UK Ltd*, Lord Neuberger stated that it 'seems to me questionable whether a sharp distinction can satisfactorily be drawn between a process and a remedy, but the point has no effect on the outcome of this case'.[69] This book occasionally refers to subrogation as a 'remedy' because this is the language in common usage. However, nothing is intended to turn on this.

Unsatisfactory Explanations' (2016) 28 *Singapore Academy of Law Journal* 955, para 16 'mechanism'; N Tamblyn, 'Separating Unjust Enrichment and Subrogation' (2017) 44 *Exeter LR* 1, 4.

[64] P Birks, 'Rights, Wrongs, and Remedies' (2000) 20 *OJLS* 1.

[65] Burrows, *Restitution* (n 5) 146.

[66] R Zakrzewski, *Remedies Reclassified* (Oxford, OUP, 2009) 43; SA Smith, *Rights, Wrongs, and Injustices* (Oxford, OUP, 2019) 6.

[67] SA Smith, 'A Duty to Make Restitution' (2013) 26 *Canadian Journal of Law and Jurisprudence* 157; NB Oman, 'Why There Is No Duty to Pay Damages: Powers, Duties, and Private Law' (2011) 39 *Florida State ULR* 137; Smith, *Rights, Wrongs, and Injustices* (n 66) ch 7; S Steel and R Stevens, 'The Secondary Legal Duty to Pay Damages' (2020) 136 *LQR* 283.

[68] *Boscawen* (n 13) 342B–D (Millett LJ); *Halifax Plc v Omar* [2002] EWCA Civ 121, [2002] 2 P&CR 26 [81]–[84] (Jonathan Parker LJ); *Day* (n 9) [42] (Gloster LJ). cf S Watterson; 'Modelling Subrogation as an "Equitable Remedy"' (2016) 2 *CJCCL* 609. In Australia, security is only created by the doctrine of marshalling once there is a court order: *Commonwealth Trading Bank* (n 49); *Chase* (n 44) 18G–21B (Cohen J); *Sarge* (n 49) 664D–65G (Young J).

[69] *Menelaou* (SC) (n 8) [96].

2

Six Controversies

I. Introduction

This chapter introduces six interlocking controversies which surround subrogation, and which this book seeks to resolve:

1. Is subrogation justified?
2. Is subrogation a remedy for unjust enrichment?
3. Is subrogation redundant?
4. When should subrogation occur?
5. What rights should subrogation create?
6. What is the relationship between subrogation and marshalling?

II. Is Subrogation Justified?

Chapter 1 defined subrogation as giving C new rights with prima facie the same content as X's extinguished rights. The most fundamental controversy surrounding subrogation is whether there is any justification for creating rights of this unusual form. C might deserve rights against D but why should these rights have prima facie the same content as X's extinguished rights?[1]

Answering this question has proven difficult. Subrogation used to rest on two fictions. The first fiction was that X's rights are 'kept alive' for C,[2] or that C is

[1] *Menelaou v Bank of Cyprus UK Ltd* [2015] UKSC 66, [2016] AC 176 ('*Menelaou* (SC)') [109] (Lord Carnwath); P Jaffey, *The Nature and Scope of Restitution* (Oxford, Hart Publishing, 2000) 270; C Rotherham, *Proprietary Remedies in Context* (Oxford, Hart Publishing, 2002) 245, 248.

[2] *Chetwynd v Allen* [1899] 1 Ch 353 (Ch) 357 (Romer J); *Butler v Rice* [1910] 2 Ch 277 (Ch) 282–83 (Warrington J).

treated 'as having had an assignment to him of [X]'s rights'.[3] The second fiction was that the parties intended this.[4] These fictions purported to explain the relationship between C's rights and X's.

However, C's new rights do not have exactly the same content as X's extinguished rights; this is only a prima facie position which may be departed from.[5] For this reason, subrogation is distinct from assignment. Furthermore, if the parties intended C to acquire X's rights, then they could choose to transfer X's rights by assignment. As Mitchell and Watterson note, subrogation is therefore 'an unnecessary complication' which parties 'never contract' for.[6] Consequently, the courts have correctly rejected both fictions. Instead, they now recognise that subrogation occurs by operation of law, and gives C new rights with prima facie the same content as X's extinguished rights.[7]

Once these fictions are excised, some doubt that it is possible to justify the form of rights created by subrogation. Birks wrote that subrogation 'is in the nature of a metaphor which can be done without',[8] and in *Menelaou v Bank of Cyprus UK Ltd* Lord Carnwath agreed.[9] The Constitutional Court of South Africa rejected a subrogation claim because:

> For [subrogation] to succeed, the Court would have to create an entirely new contract between [C] and [D]. But how? What would be the payments and the repayment period? At what interest rate? What forfeiture and cancellation and other provisions? … The whole matter is impossible. … [T]he Court 'cannot make a contract between [C] and [D]'.[10]

In light of the difficulties in justifying subrogation, one Australian judge said that:

> it is enough to see subrogation as an entitlement which equity accords to [C], firmly established by judicial decisions notwithstanding that a satisfactory doctrinal basis is difficult to identify ….[11]

[3] *Burston Finance Ltd v Speirway Ltd* [1974] 1 WLR 1648 (Ch) 1652B (Walton J).

[4] *Patten v Bond* (1889) 60 LT 583 (Ch) 586 (Kay J); *Butler* (n 2) 282–83 (Warrington J); *Ghana Commercial Bank v Chandiram* [1960] AC 732 (PC) 745 (Lord Jenkins); *Orakpo v Manson Investments Ltd* [1978] AC 95 (HL) 104G–05C (Lord Diplock).

[5] See ch 1, s II(B) above.

[6] C Mitchell and S Watterson, *Subrogation: Law and Practice* (Oxford, OUP, 2007) para 3.01.

[7] *Banque Financière de La Cité SA v Parc (Battersea) Ltd* [1999] 1 AC 221 (HL) ('*BFC*') 231D–32B, 236D–G (Lord Hoffmann), 241D (Lord Hutton); *Day v Tiuta International Ltd* [2014] EWCA Civ 1246 [43] (Gloster LJ).

[8] P Birks, *An Introduction to the Law of Restitution* (Oxford, Clarendon Press, 1989) 93.

[9] *Menelaou* (SC) (n 1) [117]. See also [109].

[10] *Absa Bank Ltd v Moore* [2016] ZACC 34 [43]–[44] (Cameron J).

[11] *Challenger Managed Investments Ltd v Direct Money Corp Pty Ltd* [2003] NSWSC 1072 [50] (Bryson J).

This is unsatisfactory: the justification for subrogation matters.[12] On the one hand, if there is no good justification for subrogation, then it should be abolished. On the other hand, if there is a good justification for subrogation, then that justification should condition when subrogation occurs and the content of the rights that subrogation creates. Accordingly, identifying the justification for subrogation can help decide novel cases, and there is an argument for reforming the law where it does not fit its justification.

III. Is Subrogation a Remedy for Unjust Enrichment?

This closely links to a second controversy over whether subrogation is a remedy for unjust enrichment. In England and Wales, the modern orthodoxy, amongst both judges and academics, is that subrogation is a remedy for unjust enrichment.[13] However, some commentators dissent from this view,[14] the High Court of Australia has rejected it,[15] and in three recent cases the UK Supreme Court has started to reconsider its position.

First, in *Menelaou v Bank of Cyprus UK Ltd*, while Lord Clarke treated subrogation as a remedy for unjust enrichment,[16] Lord Carnwath was 'less convinced …

[12] K Barker, 'Understanding the Unjust Enrichment Principle in Private Law: A Study of the Concept and Its Reasons' in JW Neyers, M McInnes and SGA Pitel (eds), *Understanding Unjust Enrichment* (Oxford, Hart Publishing, 2004) 95–96.

[13] *Boscawen v Bajwa* [1996] 1 WLR 328 (CA) 335C–F (Millett LJ); *BFC* (n 7) 228C–F (Lord Steyn), 231H (Lord Hoffmann), 238H (Lord Clyde); *Menelaou* (SC) (n 1) [37], [49]–[50] (Lord Clarke), [78]–[99] (Lord Neuberger); *Investment Trust Companies v Revenue and Customs Commissioners* [2017] UKSC 29, [2018] AC 275 ('*ITC*') [49] (Lord Reed); *Swynson Ltd v Lowick Rose LLP* [2017] UKSC 32, [2018] AC 313 [19], [22], [30] (Lord Sumption), [55]–[90] (Lord Mance); Birks, *Introduction* (n 8) 93–97, 191–92; C Mitchell, *The Law of Subrogation* (Oxford, Clarendon Press, 1994); A Tettenborn, *The Law of Restitution in England and Ireland* (London, Cavendish, 2002) paras 2-22–2-39; C Mitchell, *The Law of Contribution and Reimbursement* (Oxford, OUP, 2003) paras 1.12, 14.02; Mitchell and Watterson (n 6) para 3.02; B McFarlane, *The Structure of Property Law* (Oxford, Hart Publishing, 2008) 303–04; A Burrows, *The Law of Restitution* (Oxford, OUP, 2011) 144; A Burrows, *A Restatement of the English Law of Unjust Enrichment* (Oxford, OUP, 2012) 173; C Mitchell, P Mitchell and S Watterson, *Goff and Jones: The Law of Unjust Enrichment* (London, Sweet & Maxwell, 2022) para 39–01.

[14] Jaffey (n 1) 273; S Hedley, *A Critical Introduction to Restitution* (London, Butterworths, 2001) 329; S Hedley, *Restitution: Its Division and Ordering* (London, Sweet & Maxwell, 2001) 119–148; Rotherham, *Proprietary Remedies in Context* (n 1) 250–51; C Rotherham, 'Subrogation' in S Hedley and M Halliwell (eds), *The Law of Restitution* (London, Butterworths, 2002) para 8.10; SB Midwinter, 'Subrogation Finds Some "Well-Settled Principles"' [2003] *LMCLQ* 6; M Leeming, 'Subrogation, Equity, and Unjust Enrichment' in J Glister and P Ridge (eds), *Fault Lines in Equity* (Oxford, Hart Publishing, 2012) 40–43; G Virgo, *The Principles of the Law of Restitution* (Oxford, OUP, 2015) 637; TRS Cutts, 'Modern Money Had and Received' (2018) 38 *OJLS* 1, 25.

[15] *Bofinger v Kingsway Group Ltd* [2009] HCA 44, (2009) 239 CLR 269 [85]–[98].

[16] *Menelaou* (SC) (n 1) [18], [37], [49]–[50].

of the case for "rationalising" the older cases "through the prism of unjust enrichment"'.[17] Instead, he treated subrogation as 'a claim to a property right'.[18] Lord Neuberger primarily followed Lord Clarke's unjust enrichment approach[19] but was 'attracted to the view that [subrogation] could be justified on the alternative basis of an orthodox proprietary claim rather than on unjust enrichment'[20] and to this extent agreed with Lord Carnwath.[21] The two remaining members of the Court agreed with both Lord Clarke and Lord Neuberger.[22]

Next, in *Swynson Ltd v Lowick Rose LLP*, Lord Sumption stated that 'it would be unwise to … try to fit the subrogation cases into any broader category of unjust enrichment. It is in many ways sui generis.'[23] Most recently, in *Prudential Assurance Co Ltd v Revenue and Customs Commissioners*, Lord Mance, Lord Reed, and Lord Hodge – giving the joint judgment of the Supreme Court – stated obiter that 'subrogation … is arguably based on a different principle'.[24] In sum, in less than three years, six Justices of the UK Supreme Court questioned the orthodoxy that subrogation is a remedy for unjust enrichment.

In order to evaluate whether subrogation is a remedy for unjust enrichment, it is important to be clear what this means. It is generally assumed that there are two consequences of subrogation being a remedy for unjust enrichment: first, that a claim for subrogation raises the unjust enrichment questions; and second, that subrogation is redundant.[25] Each consequence will now be examined in turn.

First, it is uncontroversial that:

> a court must first ask itself four questions when faced with a claim for unjust enrichment as follows. (1) Has [D] been enriched? (2) Was the enrichment at [C]'s expense? (3) Was the enrichment unjust? (4) Are there any defences available to [D]?[26]

[17] ibid [108].
[18] ibid.
[19] ibid [61]–[99].
[20] ibid [59].
[21] ibid [100]–[104].
[22] ibid [141] (Lord Kerr and Lord Wilson).
[23] *Swynson* (n 13) [30].
[24] *Prudential Assurance Co Ltd v Revenue and Customs Commissioners* [2018] UKSC 39, [2018] 3 WLR 652 [68].
[25] M Cleaver, 'Equitable Subrogation in Australia and England' (2018) 29 *Journal of Banking and Finance Law and Practice* 34, 46; Pablo Letelier, 'A Wrong Turn? Reconsidering the Unified Approach to Unjust Enrichment Claims' (2020) 136 *LQR* 121.
[26] *Benedetti v Sawiris* [2013] UKSC 50, [2014] AC 938 [10] (Lord Clarke). See also *BFC* (n 7) 227A–B (Lord Steyn); *Menelaou* (SC) (n 1) [18] (Lord Clarke); *ITC* (n 13) [24], [41] (Lord Reed); *Swynson* (n 13) [110] (Lord Neuberger); *Samsoondar v Capital Insurance Company Ltd* [2020] UKPC 33, [2021] 2 All ER 1105 [18] (Lord Burrows); Birks, *Introduction* (n 8) 7; Burrows, *Restitution* (n 13) 27; Burrows, *Restatement* (n 13) 25; Mitchell, Mitchell and Watterson (n 13) para 1-14. cf *Skandinaviska Enskilda Banken AB (Publ) v Conway* [2019] UKPC 36, [2019] 3 WLR 493 [80] (Lord Reed).

Those who say that subrogation is a remedy for unjust enrichment say that a court ought to ask these four questions when faced with a subrogation claim.[27] Indeed, the first judicial endorsement of the idea that unjust enrichment claims should be analysed by asking the four questions came in the subrogation case of *Banque Financière de la Cité SA v Parc (Battersea) Ltd* ('*BFC*').[28]

Second, the idea that subrogation is a remedy for unjust enrichment is often followed by the idea that subrogation 'duplicat[es]'[29] a 'direct unjust enrichment claim' on the same facts, and therefore subrogation is 'redundant'.[30] This is a complex idea so it will be treated as a separate, third, controversy.

IV. Is Subrogation Redundant?

There are three variants of the idea that subrogation is redundant. From broadest to narrowest, these are:

1. Subrogation always duplicates a direct unjust enrichment claim.
2. Subrogation to personal rights always duplicates a direct unjust enrichment claim.
3. In common liability cases, subrogation to personal rights duplicates the rights created by recoupment or contribution.

Each variant will now be explained in turn.

A. Subrogation Always Duplicates a Direct Claim

The broadest of the three variants is that subrogation always duplicates a 'direct' unjust enrichment claim. A 'direct' claim seems to be one decided without relying

[27] *BFC* (n 7) 234B–G (Lord Hoffmann); *Niru Battery Manufacturing Co v Milestone Trading Ltd (No 2)* [2004] EWCA Civ 487, [2004] 1 CLC 882 ('*Niru Battery* (CA)') [56] (Clarke LJ); *Menelaou v Bank of Cyprus Plc* [2013] EWCA Civ 1960, [2014] 1 WLR 854 ('*Menelaou* (CA)') [27] (Floyd LJ); *Sandher v Pearson* [2013] EWCA Civ 1822 [9] (Arden LJ); *Menelaou* (SC) (n 1) [18] (Lord Clarke); *Swynson* (n 13) [56] (Lord Mance), [110] (Lord Neuberger); Mitchell and Watterson (n 6) paras 3.02–3.03; Burrows, *Restitution* (n 13) 145; S Watterson, 'Modelling Subrogation as an "Equitable Remedy"' (2016) 2 *CJCCL* 609, 618–19, 669–70; Mitchell, Mitchell and Watterson (n 13) para 39-25.

[28] *BFC* (n 7) 226G–28D (Lord Steyn), 234B–G (Lord Hoffmann).

[29] *Menelaou* (CA) (n 27) [59] (Moses LJ); Burrows, *Restitution* (n 13) 147.

[30] Mitchell and Watterson, (n 6) paras 3.08, 8.32; C Mitchell, 'Unjust Enrichment' in A Burrows (ed), *English Private Law* (Oxford, OUP, 2013) para 18.280; C Mitchell, 'Unjust Enrichment' in A Burrows (ed), *Principles of the English Law of Obligations* (Oxford, OUP, 2015) para 3.280; Mitchell, Mitchell and Watterson (n 13) para 39–02.

on subrogation; it is direct in the sense that it gives C new rights without the detour into defining these rights by reference to X's extinguished rights.[31] Proponents of this view say that in all cases subrogation duplicates a direct claim, so subrogation is always redundant.

For example, Birks wrote that:

> within the law of restitution [subrogation] really adds nothing to the number of techniques already identified. It is in the nature of a metaphor which can be done without.[32]

In *Menelaou*, Lord Carnwath agreed.[33] This view can be represented as follows:

<table>
<tr><th></th><th>Common liability cases</th><th>Misappropriation and lending cases</th></tr>
<tr><td>Subrogation to personal rights</td><td colspan="2" rowspan="2">Subrogation 'adds nothing' and 'can be done without'</td></tr>
<tr><td>Subrogation to proprietary rights</td></tr>
</table>

As the previous chapter explained, Birks was certainly right that there are 'metaphor[s]' associated with subrogation 'which can be done without'.[34] In fact, Palmer suggests that:

> It would be best to abandon the terminology of subrogation in order to place greater emphasis on the task of identifying the explanation for the particular rights that [C] is given in any of the cases that have traditionally been considered to fall within … subrogation.[35]

But even once the fictions are gone and the word 'subrogation' is expunged, there still remains a group of cases in which the law gives C new rights with prima facie the same content as X's extinguished rights. Birks would still be unhappy. He was

[31] Birks, *Introduction* (n 8) 191–92; Hedley, *Restitution* (n 14) 142; Burrows, *Restitution* (n 13) 147.
[32] Birks, *Introduction* (n 8) 93.
[33] *Menelaou* (SC) (n 1) [117]. See also [109]; Tettenborn, (n 13) paras 2-37–2-38.
[34] See ch 1, s II(C) above.
[35] J Palmer, 'Unjust Enrichment, Proprietary Subrogation and Unsatisfactory Explanations' (2016) 28 *Singapore Academy of Law Journal* 955, para 17 (footnotes omitted). See also para 60; *Re Wrexham Mold & Connah's Quay Railway Co* [1899] 1 Ch 440 (CA) 447 (Lindley MR); *BFC* (n 7) 238A (Lord Clyde); Hedley, *Restitution* (n 14) 142–43; Rotherham, *Proprietary Remedies in Context* (n 1) 246–48; Rotherham, 'Subrogation' (n 14) paras 8.5–8.7; Burrows, *Restitution* (n 13) 146; Burrows, *Restatement* (n 13) 172.

not just arguing that the fictions should be abolished or that subrogation should be renamed. He was arguing that the rights themselves were redundant; that giving C rights with prima facie the same content as X's extinguished rights 'adds nothing' to the other remedies for unjust enrichment.[36]

Part II of this book argues that this is not true. Subrogation is available in different circumstances and has a different effect compared to direct unjust enrichment claims. Accordingly, subrogation does not duplicate a direct claim, and so subrogation is not redundant. This builds on the work of a number of other commentators, who have argued that subrogation and direct claims are governed by different rules.[37] Indeed, Hedley made this argument as early as 2001.[38]

B. Subrogation to Personal Rights Always Duplicates a Direct Claim

Compared to Birks, Mitchell and Watterson's monograph on subrogation took a more nuanced position. They suggested that subrogation to personal rights duplicates 'a direct … claim in unjust enrichment'[39] whereas subrogation to proprietary rights does not:

> In principle, [C]'s position should be improved by [subrogation] only in cases where [X]'s rights were proprietary. A claimant who is entitled to subrogation should always also have a direct personal claim of his own, making [subrogation to X]'s personal rights redundant. The courts have sometimes failed to recognize this, or have chosen to ignore it, and have permitted [C] to 'acquire' extinguished personal rights while simultaneously denying them direct claims. This is incoherent and self-contradictory. … [D]iscrepancies of this kind cannot be justified once it is recognized that [C]'s direct personal claim to restitution and his claim to be subrogated to [X]'s personal rights rest on a common basis.[40]

[36] Birks, *Introduction* (n 8) 93. See also 7, 93–97, 191–92, 399; Jaffey, (n 1) 271 fn 65.

[37] S Watterson, 'Subrogation' in G Virgo and S Worthington (eds), *Commercial Remedies: Resolving Controversies* (Cambridge, CUP, 2017) 439–48; Cutts (n 14) 22–25.

[38] Hedley, *Restitution* (n 14) 119–48.

[39] Mitchell and Watterson (n 6) para 8.32.

[40] ibid paras 3.08, 8.32. See also C Mitchell, 'Subrogation: Persistent Misunderstandings' in A Burrows and Lord Rodger of Earlsferry (eds), *Mapping the Law: Essays in Memory of Peter Birks* (Oxford, OUP, 2006) 111–12; Mitchell and Watterson (n 6) paras 3.19–3.24; 8.32–8.38; C Mitchell, 'Unjust Enrichment' in A Burrows (ed), *English Private Law* (Oxford, OUP, 2013) para 18.280; C Mitchell, 'Unjust Enrichment' in A Burrows (ed), *Principles of the English Law of Obligations* (Oxford, OUP, 2015) para 3.280; Mitchell, Mitchell and Watterson (n 13) paras 39-02–39-03; Virgo, *The Principles of the Law of Restitution* (n 14) 655.

On this view, 'the same limits' apply to 'subrogation to [X]'s personal rights' as apply to 'a direct personal claim in unjust enrichment'.[41] Furthermore, subrogation to proprietary rights is different only because it gives C proprietary rights; in all other respects the authors presented subrogation to proprietary rights as governed by the same rules as subrogation to personal rights and direct claims. In his textbook, Burrows took the same position,[42] which can be represented as follows:

	Common liability cases	**Misappropriation and lending cases**
Subrogation to personal rights	Subrogation to personal rights duplicates a direct unjust enrichment claim	
Subrogation to proprietary rights		

If subrogation and direct claims are governed by the same rules, then the rules which govern direct claims also govern subrogation. For example, Mitchell, Mitchell, and Watterson state that:

> As an equitable remedy designed to reverse unjust enrichment, a [subrogation] claim … may be defeated or limited by any defence or bar that will defeat or limit any cause of action in unjust enrichment. These include [the defence] of change of position ….[43]

Some authors also reason in the opposite direction: because subrogation and direct claims are governed by the same rules, the rules which govern subrogation must also govern direct claims. For example, in some subrogation cases, the only sense in which an enrichment comes at C's expense is that it would not have accrued '"but for" [a] defective transfer from C's wealth'.[44] Birks therefore argued that this was the test for whether an enrichment comes at C's expense in direct claims.[45]

Leading cases also support the idea that subrogation (to personal rights) duplicates a direct unjust enrichment claim. In *BFC*, Lord Steyn said that 'on

[41] Mitchell and Watterson (n 6) para 8.32.

[42] Burrows, *Restitution* (n 13) 148–167, 446. See also Tettenborn (n 13) para 2–37; P Birks, *Unjust Enrichment* (Oxford, OUP, 2005) 297–98.

[43] Mitchell, Mitchell and Watterson (n 13) para 39–38. See also Mitchell and Watterson (n 6) paras 7.01, 7.68, 8.07; Watterson, 'Modelling Subrogation as an "Equitable Remedy"' (n 27) 619, 671.

[44] S Watterson, '"Direct Transfers" in the Law of Unjust Enrichment' (2011) 64 CLP 435, 465.

[45] Birks, *Unjust Enrichment* (n 42) 96–98 cited by Mitchell and Watterson (n 6) para 5.15 fn 22. See also Watterson, 'Direct Transfers' (n 44) 458–59, 464–66.

an application of established principles of unjust enrichment [C is] entitled to succeed .... But, if it were necessary to do so, I would reach the same conclusion in terms of the principles of subrogation'.[46]

In *Menelaou*, Moses LJ stated that there 'is, as Professor Burrows suggests, no need to duplicate the reasoning in relation to both unjust enrichment and subrogation; the answer should be the same: see per Lord Steyn in [*BFC*]'.[47] Lord Clarke suggested that many of the rules governing subrogation are the same as those which govern direct claims. When deciding whether D was enriched at C's expense, he engaged with the debate over when D is enriched at C's expense for the purposes of a direct claim.[48] He stated that the unjust factor in subrogation cases is usually either mistake or failure of consideration[49] and these are unjust factors in direct claims too. Obiter, he suggested that subrogation is susceptible to the change of position defence[50] which also applies to direct claims.

In *Swynson*, Lord Neuberger recognised that C claimed to be 'subrogated to [X]'s [personal] claim against [D]',[51] but then did not mention subrogation again and dismissed C's claim because there was 'no good reason for upholding the present unjust enrichment claim given that it is not within the normal scope of such claims'.[52] Both Lord Mance and Lord Neuberger applied the rules for direct claims laid down by the Supreme Court in *Investment Trust Companies v Revenue and Customs Commissioners* ('*ITC*').[53]

In short, the prevailing view is that subrogation is governed by the same rules as direct claims in unjust enrichment, except possibly for the rules determining whether C is entitled to personal or proprietary rights. Subrogation (to personal rights) therefore duplicates a direct claim in unjust enrichment and is redundant.

Again, Part II of the book will argue that this is not true. Subrogation and direct claims are governed by different rules. Subrogation is therefore available in different circumstances, and has a different effect, compared to direct claims. Accordingly, subrogation (to personal rights) does not duplicate a direct claim and so subrogation (to personal rights) is not redundant.

[46] *BFC* (n 7) 228C–D.
[47] *Menelaou* (CA) (n 27) [59] citing *BFC* (n 7) 228 (Lord Steyn); Burrows, *Restitution* (n 13) 147.
[48] *Menelaou* (SC) (n 1) [27]–[32].
[49] ibid [21] (citations omitted).
[50] ibid [36].
[51] *Swynson* (n 13) [94].
[52] ibid [120].
[53] ibid [56], [58], [67], [89] (Lord Mance), [114]–[115], [117], [120] (Lord Neuberger), citing *ITC* (n 13).

C. Subrogation Duplicates Recoupment and Contribution

The broad claims that subrogation (to personal rights) *always* duplicates a direct unjust enrichment claim should not be confused with the narrow claim that subrogation to personal rights *in common liability cases* duplicates recoupment or contribution. For example, Burrows writes that 'often the resort to subrogation is unnecessary because the same reasoning on unjust enrichment that triggers subrogation ought also to trigger the direct remedy of recoupment or contribution'.[54] Similarly, Mitchell and Watterson suggest that in common liability cases:

> subrogation is essentially a *supplementary* remedy, available on the same basis, and awarded on the same facts, as an award of contribution or reimbursement. Hence if [X]'s rights against [D] were merely personal rights then subrogation is not generally needed because it cannot give [C] anything more than he already possesses, viz a personal claim against [D].[55]

This argument may be represented as follows:

	Common liability cases	**Misappropriation and lending cases**
Subrogation to personal rights	Subrogation duplicates recoupment and contribution	
Subrogation to proprietary rights		

In fact, Chapter 1 argued that rights of recoupment and contribution are examples of subrogation, rather than its duplicates.[56] Furthermore, even if subrogation duplicates recoupment and contribution, it does not follow that subrogation is redundant in all cases for two reasons.

First, the labels of recoupment and contribution are generally only applied to personal rights.[57] If C is given proprietary rights, then the label of subrogation tends to be used. Accordingly, subrogation to proprietary rights does not duplicate

[54] Burrows, *Restitution* (n 13) 148. See also 149, 167, 446; A Burrows, '"At the Expense of the Claimant": A Fresh Look' [2017] RLR 167, 182.

[55] Mitchell and Watterson, (n 6) para 6.15 (original emphasis).

[56] See ch 1, s III(A) above.

[57] Rotherham, 'Subrogation' (n 14) para 8.2; Mitchell and Watterson (n 6) paras 3.08, 6.15; Burrows, *Restitution* (n 13) 149; Mitchell, Mitchell and Watterson (n 13) para 39–30.

recoupment and contribution. As a result, subrogation is not redundant in the bottom row of the table above.

Second, the labels of recoupment and contribution are only used in cases where C and D owed a common debt to X.[58] By contrast, subrogation is not limited to these cases and is also awarded in misappropriation and lending cases.[59] As a result, the argument that subrogation duplicates recoupment and contribution does not prove subrogation redundant in misappropriation and lending cases. In other words, subrogation is not redundant in the right-hand column of the table above.

In sum, recoupment and contribution are best understood to be examples of subrogation. In this sense, subrogation to personal rights sometimes duplicates recoupment or contribution. However, subrogation is available on a wider range of facts, and is often more advantageous, compared to recoupment or contribution. Consequently, even though subrogation sometimes duplicates recoupment or contribution, it does not follow that subrogation is redundant.

D. Summary

It is generally assumed that there are two consequences of subrogation being a remedy for unjust enrichment: first, that a court faced with a subrogation claim ought to ask the four unjust enrichment questions; and second, that subrogation is redundant.

When judges and scholars write that subrogation is 'redundant'[60] or 'duplicat[ive]',[61] they slip between different claims. Sometimes they make the broad claim that subrogation (to personal rights) always duplicates a 'direct' unjust enrichment claim, and so subrogation (to personal rights) is redundant. Part II will show that this is not true. But on other occasions, judges and scholars make the narrow claim that subrogation to personal rights in common liability cases duplicates recoupment and contribution. This is correct, but only because recoupment and contribution are examples of subrogation, and this does not prove that subrogation is redundant.

[58] Mitchell, *The Law of Contribution and Reimbursement* (n 13) paras 1.11, 6.02, 6.18.

[59] Burrows, *Restitution* (n 13) 145; Watterson, 'Subrogation' (n 37) 452–54; Mitchell, Mitchell and Watterson (n 13) para 39–01. These types of cases are introduced in ch 1, s I above.

[60] Mitchell and Watterson (n 6) paras 3.08, 8.32; C Mitchell, 'Unjust Enrichment' in A Burrows (ed), *English Private Law* (Oxford, OUP, 2013) para 18.280; C Mitchell, 'Unjust Enrichment' in A Burrows (ed), *Principles of the English Law of Obligations* (Oxford, OUP, 2015) para 3.280; Mitchell, Mitchell and Watterson (n 13) para 39–02.

[61] *Menelaou* (CA) (n 27) [59] (Moses LJ); Burrows, *Restitution* (n 13) 147.

V. When Should Subrogation Occur?

In light of the previous three controversies, it is unsurprising that there is also controversy over when subrogation should occur.[62] Before the courts treated subrogation as a remedy for unjust enrichment, subrogation occurred in certain established categories of cases.[63] For example, if C stood surety for D's debt to X and C paid X, discharging D's debt to X, then C would be subrogated to X's extinguished rights against D.[64] Beyond the established categories, the availability of subrogation was 'ill-defined and obscure'.[65]

In the leading House of Lords decision of *Orakpo v Manson Investments Ltd* in 1977, Lord Salmon gave the following unhelpful guidance:

> The test as to whether the courts will apply the doctrine of subrogation to the facts of any particular case is entirely empirical. It is, I think, impossible to formulate any narrower principle than that the doctrine will be applied only when the courts are satisfied that reason and justice demand that it should be.[66]

In a famous passage, Lord Diplock said that:

> there is no general doctrine of unjust enrichment recognised in English law. What it does is to provide specific remedies in particular cases of what might be classified as unjust enrichment in a legal system that is based upon the civil law. There are some circumstances in which the remedy takes the form of 'subrogation,' but this expression embraces more than a single concept in English law. It … takes place by operation of law in a whole variety of widely different circumstances … and appear[s] to defeat classification except as an empirical remedy to prevent a particular kind of unjust enrichment.
>
> This makes particularly perilous any attempt to rely upon analogy to justify applying to one set of circumstances which would otherwise result in unjust enrichment a remedy of subrogation which has been held to be available for that purpose in another and different set of circumstances.[67]

Subsequently, however, the House of Lords changed direction. In 1991, in *Lipkin Gorman v Karpnale Ltd*, the House recognised the principle of unjust enrichment.[68]

[62] Rotherham, 'Subrogation' (n 14) para 8.8; Birks, *Unjust Enrichment* (n 42) 298; Cleaver (n 25) 55.
[63] *Re TH Knitwear (Wholesale) Ltd* [1988] 1 Ch 275 (CA) 284D (Slade LJ).
[64] *Duncan Fox & Co v North & South Wales Bank* (1880) 6 App Cas 1 (HL) 10–13 (Lord Selborne LC); *Re TH Knitwear* (n 63) 284D (Slade LJ).
[65] *Re TH Knitwear* (n 63) 284F (Slade LJ). *Duncan Fox* (n 64) 13–14 (Lord Selborne LC); *Re TH Knitwear* (n 63) 284D–H (Slade LJ).
[66] *Orakpo* (n 4) 110D–E. See also 112D–E (Lord Edmund-Davies).
[67] ibid 104C–G.
[68] *Lipkin Gorman v Karpnale Ltd* [1991] 2 AC 548 (HL) 578E (Lord Goff).

In 1998, in *BFC*, the Law Lords stated that subrogation is a remedy for unjust enrichment.[69] Following *BFC*, subrogation is not limited to the established categories,[70] and is sometimes said to occur whenever a party is unjustly enriched by the discharge of X's rights at C's expense.[71]

This is illustrated by *Niru Battery Manufacturing Co v Milestone Trading Ltd (No 2)*.[72] There, X was a victim of a fraud which was caused by C's negligent misrepresentation, and which left D unjustly enriched at X's expense. X obtained judgment against C and D. C owed X a duty to compensate X for the losses caused by its negligence, while D owed X a duty to make restitution of its unjust enrichment at X's expense. C and D were therefore jointly and severally indebted to X under a court judgment. C paid the whole of the judgment, discharging both parties' debt to X. C then sought to be subrogated to X's extinguished rights against D.

Moore-Bick J (at first instance) and Clarke LJ (giving the judgment of the Court of Appeal[73]) held that D ought to have borne the burden of the common liability.[74] D was therefore unjustly enriched at C's expense, and so C was subrogated to X's extinguished rights against D.[75]

Moore-Bick J said that 'the categories of cases in which the remedy of subrogation might be available' were not restricted,[76] so subrogation could be awarded even though there was 'no reported case in which a tortfeasor has obtained … subrogation against a party liable only in restitution'.[77]

On appeal, Clarke LJ affirmed that conclusion.[78] He said that 'subrogation is appropriate in much wider circumstances than'[79] a limited number of 'recognised

[69] *BFC* (n 7) 228C–F (Lord Steyn), 231H (Lord Hoffmann), 238H (Lord Clyde).

[70] ibid 228B–F (Lord Steyn), 229B–D, 236H–37D (Lord Hoffmann), 237G–38A (Lord Clyde), 242F–H (Lord Hutton); *Menelaou v Bank of Cyprus Plc* [2012] EWHC 1991 (Ch) [20] (David Donaldson QC); *Menelaou* (SC) (n 1) [45]–[51] (Lord Clarke) [84]–[99] (Lord Neuberger); Theresa Villiers, 'A Path Through the Subrogation Jungle: Whose Right is it Anyway?' [1999] *LMCLQ* 223, 225; Tettenborn, *Restitution* (n 13) para 2–36; Burrows, *Restitution* (n 13) 145, 148, 166, 446; Burrows, *Restatement* (n 13) 173; Watterson, 'Modelling Subrogation as an "Equitable Remedy"' (n 27) 669–70. cf *Insol Funding Co Ltd v Cowlam* [2017] EWHC 1822 (Ch) [119]–[127] (Master Bowles).

[71] Tettenborn, (n 13) para 2–36; Burrows, *Restitution* (n 13) 148, 166, 446; Burrows, *Restatement* (n 13) 173; Watterson, 'Modelling Subrogation as an "Equitable Remedy"' (n 27) 669–70.

[72] *Niru Battery Manufacturing Co v Milestone Trading Ltd (No 2)* [2003] EWHC 1032 (Comm), [2003] 2 All ER (Comm) 365 ('*Niru Battery* (QB)') affd *Niru Battery* (CA) (n 27); Burrows, *Restitution* (n 13) 145, 446.

[73] *Niru Battery* (CA) (n 27) [81] (Sedley LJ), [90] (Butler-Sloss P).

[74] *Niru Battery* (QB) (n 727) [55] (Moore-Bick J); *Niru Battery* (CA) (n 27) [50] (Clarke LJ).

[75] *Niru Battery* (QB) (n 72) [28]–[56] (Moore-Bick J); *Niru Battery* (CA) (n 27) [22]–[65], [80] (Clarke LJ).

[76] *Niru Battery* (QB) (n 72) [31].

[77] ibid [30].

[78] *Niru Battery* (CA) (n 27) [52]–[56].

[79] ibid [56].

categories of case'[80] and that 'the correct approach today is to ask' the four unjust enrichment questions.[81]

Orakpo's 'empirical' test was opaque and uncertain,[82] and the attempt to improve on it is welcome. Nevertheless, there remains confusion over what C must prove in order to be entitled to subrogation.[83] This is for two reasons.

First, while the idea that subrogation is a remedy for unjust enrichment is the current orthodoxy, it remains controversial.[84] If the doubts are justified and the idea that subrogation is a remedy for unjust enrichment falls away, then so too does the idea that subrogation occurs whenever a party is unjustly enriched by the discharge of X's rights at C's expense.[85]

Second, even if subrogation is a remedy for unjust enrichment, saying that subrogation occurs 'whenever a party is unjustly enriched by the discharge of X's rights at C's expense' is not specific enough to determine when subrogation occurs. As Lord Reed explained in *ITC*, this formulation provides:

> no more than broad headings for ease of exposition[:] … not … legal tests, but … sign-posts towards areas of inquiry involving a number of distinct legal requirements. In particular, the words 'at the expense of' do not express a legal test; and a test cannot be derived by exegesis of those words, as if they were the words of a statute.[86]

As the previous section showed, there is controversy over whether subrogation is governed by the same legal tests as a 'direct' unjust enrichment claim. If subrogation is not governed by the same rules as direct claims, then it is unclear what rules do govern subrogation and so it is unclear when subrogation occurs.

The continuing controversy over when subrogation should occur can be illustrated by three leading House of Lords and Supreme Court decisions: *Banque Financière de la Cité SA v Parc (Battersea) Ltd* ('*BFC*');[87] *Menelaou v Bank of Cyprus UK Ltd*;[88] and *Swynson Ltd v Lowick Rose LLP*.[89]

[80] ibid [52].
[81] ibid [56].
[82] Birks, *Introduction* (n 8) 401; G Virgo, 'Restitution and Unjust Enrichment in the Supreme Court: Reflections on *Bank of Cyprus UK Ltd v Menelaou*' University of Cambridge Faculty of Law Research Paper No 10/2016, ssrn.com/abstract=2724024, 16.
[83] *Swynson Ltd v Lowick Rose LLP* [2015] EWCA Civ 629, [2016] 1 WLR 1045 ('*Swynson* (CA)') [47] (Davis LJ).
[84] See s III above.
[85] J Edelman and E Bant, *Unjust Enrichment* (Oxford, Hart Publishing, 2016) 44.
[86] *ITC* (n 13) [41].
[87] *BFC* (n 7).
[88] *Menelaou* (SC) (n 1).
[89] *Swynson* (n 13).

A. *Banque Financière de la Cité SA v Parc (Battersea) Ltd* ('*BFC*')

BFC was the first case in which the House of Lords endorsed the idea that subrogation is a remedy for unjust enrichment.[90] There, D had title to property subject to X's first charge and OOL's second charge. C agreed to make a loan to D to partially pay off X's charge, provided that OOL was bound by a 'postponement letter'. Under that letter, OOL would not demand repayment of its loan until C had been repaid. Purporting to act on behalf of OOL, a Mr Herzig signed the postponement letter and C made its loan, which was used to partially pay off X's charge. It then transpired that Mr Herzig lacked authority to act on behalf of OOL, and so the postponement letter did not bind OOL.

A priority dispute then arose between C and OOL. As the postponement letter did not bind OOL, C could not rely on it to obtain priority. However, a unanimous House of Lords held that OOL had been enriched at C's expense: C's partial discharge of X's first charge had increased the value of OOL's second charge.[91] This enrichment was unjust because C acted in the mistaken belief that Mr Herzig had authority to bind OOL to the postponement letter.[92] To reverse that unjust enrichment, C was subrogated to X's rights, insofar as they were discharged, as against OOL. Accordingly, C could recover its loan from the proceeds of the property ahead of OOL recovering its loan.

This was far from a paradigm example of subrogation.[93] In all other cases, subrogation to extinguished security allowed C to recover ahead of D's unsecured creditors.[94] But in *BFC*, C had only bargained for priority over OOL and not over D's other unsecured creditors, and so C conceded that it was not entitled to recover ahead of the other creditors. Instead, C sought, and the House awarded, subrogation to X's extinguished rights only as against OOL and not as against D's other creditors.[95]

In part because of this unusual effect, the decision has received academic criticism. Some commentators say that there was no justification for subrogation.[96] Others claim that C's subsisting contract with D should have excluded C from

[90] *BFC* (n 7).

[91] ibid 227B–C (Lord Steyn), 234G (Lord Hoffmann), 238B–C (Lord Clyde), 239B–H (Lord Hutton).

[92] ibid 227E (Lord Steyn), 234G–35A (Lord Hoffmann).

[93] P Watts, 'Subrogation – a Step Too Far?' (1998) 114 *LQR* 341, 343; Mitchell and Watterson (n 6) paras 8.58–8.60; Mitchell, Mitchell and Watterson (n 13) paras 39-67–39-69.

[94] Mitchell and Watterson (n 6) paras 8.54–8.55; Mitchell, Mitchell and Watterson (n 13) para 39–64.

[95] *BFC* (n 7) 228B–F (Lord Steyn), 229B–D, 236H–37D (Lord Hoffmann), 237G–38A (Lord Clyde), 242F–H (Lord Hutton).

[96] Watts, 'Subrogation' (n 93); R Stevens, 'The Unjust Enrichment Disaster' (2018) 134 *LQR* 574, 593.

claiming a remedy for unjust enrichment[97] or that C had not bargained for priority over OOL in the event of D's insolvency.[98] Consequently, even in *BFC*, the leading case for the proposition that subrogation is a remedy for unjust enrichment, the award of subrogation is controversial.

B. *Menelaou v Bank of Cyprus UK Ltd*

In *Menelaou*, Mr and Mrs Menelaou had title to Rush Green Hall, which was subject to C's two charges. Mr and Mrs Menelaou decided to sell Rush Green Hall and use the proceeds to buy a new property, Great Oak Court, from X. C released its charges over Rush Green Hall in exchange for a new charge over Great Oak Court. However, Mr and Mrs Menelaou registered Great Oak Court in the name of their daughter, D. D had not consented to C's new charge, which was therefore invalid.

However, a contract for sale of land gives the vendor an 'unpaid vendor's lien', which allows them to retain possession until they receive the purchase price.[99] In *Menelaou*, X's unpaid vendor's lien had been extinguished when they received the purchase price. The Supreme Court unanimously held that C was subrogated to X's extinguished unpaid vendor's lien over Great Oak Court. Nevertheless, the Court was split in its reasoning, and in particular over whether subrogation required C to use the rules of tracing to show that the payment which discharged X's lien represented the proceeds of its charge over Rush Green Hall.

Giving the leading judgment, Lord Clarke said that subrogation is a remedy for unjust enrichment[100] and 'a claim in unjust enrichment does not need to show a property right'.[101] It only required 'a sufficient causal connection … between the loss to [C] and the benefit received by [D]'.[102]

By contrast, Lord Carnwath stated that subrogation required C 'to establish that the money used to pay off [X's rights] was their money. "Tracing" [is] the process by which this [is] done.'[103]

[97] Jaffey (n 1) 309; G McMeel, *The Modern Law of Restitution* (London, Blackstone, 2000) 300–01; S Worthington, 'Subrogation Claims on Insolvency' in F Rose (ed), *Restitution and Insolvency* (Mansfield Press, 2000) 71–73.
[98] MG Bridge, 'Failed Contracts, Subrogation and Unjust Enrichment: *Banque Financière de La Cité v Parc (Battersea) Ltd*' [1998] *JBL* 323, 329–30.
[99] *Barclays Bank Plc v Estates & Commercial Ltd* [1997] 1 WLR 415 (CA) 419H (Millett LJ).
[100] *Menelaou* (SC) (n 1) [37], [49]–[50].
[101] ibid [38].
[102] ibid [27].
[103] ibid [128].

Lord Neuberger agreed with Lord Clarke that subrogation did not require C to trace.[104] However, he also stated that:

> I am also attracted to the view that [C]'s case … could be justified on the alternative basis of an orthodox proprietary claim rather than on unjust enrichment[.] … I am very sympathetic to the notion that [C] had a proprietary interest in the [money] which was [paid to X, discharging X's rights], and if that is right, its subrogation claim becomes relatively uncontroversial.[105]

Lord Kerr and Lord Wilson agreed with both Lord Clarke and Lord Neuberger.[106]

Like *BFC*, *Menelaou* also received sustained criticism, with Virgo describing the case as 'arguably the worst decision in the history of the Supreme Court'.[107] Amongst other things, Virgo criticised the Court's reasoning as to why D's enrichment was unjust, as Chapter 5 will explain.[108] There was also criticism of the majority's suggestion that D's enrichment comes at C's expense if there is a sufficient causal connection … between the loss to [C] and the benefit received by [D]'.[109] Less than 18 months later, a unanimous Supreme Court in *ITC* rejected this expansive test and replaced it with a more restrictive one,[110] which will be examined by Chapter 4.

C. *Swynson Ltd v Lowick Rose LLP*

On the same day as *ITC*, the Supreme Court also gave judgment in *Swynson*.[111] The facts were as follows. X was considering making a loan to EMSL. X contracted D, a firm of accountants, to report on EMSL's finances. D negligently failed to draw X's attention to EMSL's lack of working capital. Had D done so, X would not have gone ahead with the loan. Ignorant of EMSL's financial difficulties, X went ahead with the loan, on which EMSL defaulted.

[104] ibid [85], [92], [96]–[98].
[105] ibid [59], [100].
[106] ibid [141].
[107] Virgo, 'Restitution and Unjust Enrichment in the Supreme Court' (n 14) 1.
[108] See ch 5, s IV below.
[109] *Menelaou* (SC) (n 1) [27] (Lord Clarke) criticised J Leung and SY Wong, 'Subrogation and Unjust Enrichment in the Supreme Court' [2016] *LMCLQ* 337, 339–42; PG Watts, '"Unjust Enrichment" – the Potion That Induces Well-Meaning Sloppiness of Thought' (2016) 69 *CLP* 289, 305–06; Burrows, '"At the Expense of the Claimant"' (n 54) 174, fn 41; Stevens, 'The Unjust Enrichment Disaster' (n 96) 599; R Stevens, *The Laws of Restitution* (Oxford, OUP, 2023) 53–55.
[110] *ITC* (n 13) [37]–[38], [52], [56]–[57], [59]–[60], [72] (Lord Reed).
[111] *Swynson* (n 13).

C then made a new loan to EMSL, which EMSL used to repay X's loan. This meant X suffered no loss as a result of D's negligence so X could not recover damages from D.[112] EMSL then went into liquidation so could not repay C's loan. C therefore sought to be subrogated to X's discharged right to recover damages from D.

Anxious to impose some limits on subrogation after the expansive decision in *Menelaou*, the Supreme Court unanimously denied the subrogation claim in *Swynson*. Lord Sumption said that:

> Failure to recognise these limitations would transform the law of equitable subrogation into a general escape route from any principle of law which the claimant overlooked or misunderstood when he arranged his affairs as he did. ... This result would hardly do credit to the law.[113]

However, the Court was divided over exactly how to understand these limitations. The Court unanimously agreed that subrogation will not give C more than it bargained for and, as C had not bargained for rights against D in this case, his subrogation claim failed. However, Lord Sumption, Lord Mance, and Lord Neuberger each framed this rule differently, as Chapter 5 will explain.

All in all, then, even though the courts have accepted that subrogation is a remedy for unjust enrichment, controversy persists over when subrogation should occur.

VI. What Rights Should Subrogation Create?

In addition to this controversy over when subrogation should occur, there is also controversy over what rights subrogation should create. This is illustrated by the unusual rights created by subrogation in *BFC*, discussed above.[114] Another example is the case where X had legal security. Here there is debate over whether subrogation gives C legal security or only equitable security. To take an example, say D owes a debt to X secured by a legal mortgage. C pays X, discharging D's debt. C is subrogated to X's extinguished mortgage, but the question is whether this gives C a legal mortgage or an equitable mortgage.

[112] ibid [11]–[17] (Lord Sumption), [45]–[54] (Lord Mance), [92]–[108] (Lord Neuberger).
[113] ibid [34]–[35]. See also [120] (Lord Neuberger).
[114] See s V(A) above.

On the one hand, subrogation emerged in the Courts of Equity and is 'an equitable remedy'.[115] Mitchell and Watterson therefore suggest that subrogation only ever gives C equitable rights, even if X's rights were legal,[116] and some cases endorse that position.[117]

On the other hand, some authorities suggest that if X's rights were legal, then subrogation can give C legal rights. Section 5 of the Mercantile Law Amendment Act 1856 provides that if a surety pays a debt, they 'shall be entitled to stand in the place of the creditor, and to use all the remedies … at law or in equity'. Beyond sureties, there are appellate cases in which subrogation entitled C to register a charge by way of legal mortgage over title to land.[118] For instance, in *Cheltenham & Gloucester Plc v Appleyard*, Neuberger LJ explained that 'although [C] would be relying on an equitable principle, namely subrogation, the right they are seeking to obtain by subrogation is a legal right, namely the right of a first legal chargee'.[119] If subrogation is a remedy for unjust enrichment and D has been unjustly enriched by the release of X's legal mortgage at C's expense, then McFarlane argues that in principle subrogation ought to give C a legal mortgage.[120]

VII. What is the Relationship between Subrogation and Marshalling?

A final controversy is the relationship between subrogation and marshalling. Sometimes, marshalling is described as an example of subrogation.[121] Sometimes,

[115] *BFC* (n 7) 231G–H (Lord Hoffmann).

[116] Mitchell and Watterson, (n 6) paras 8.14–8.15, 8.113–8.121; Mitchell, Mitchell and Watterson (n 13) paras 39-48, 39-58, 39-83, 39-93, 39-98; S Watterson, 'Subrogation, Priority Disputes and Rectification: Mapping a Route Through the Thicket' [2016] *RLR* 1, 10, 12–14.

[117] *Boscawen* (n 13) 341A–B, 342D (Millett LJ); *Day* (n 7) [41]–[43] (Gloster LJ).

[118] *Castle Phillips Finance v Piddington* (1995) 70 P & CR 592 (CA) 602 (Peter Gibson LJ); *Cheltenham & Gloucester Plc v Appleyard* [2004] EWCA Civ 291 [23], [69]–[74] (Neuberger LJ); *Primlake Ltd v Matthews Associates (No 2)* [2009] EWHC 2774 (Ch) [17](c), [27] (Jeremy Cousins QC); *Anfield (UK) Ltd v Bank of Scotland Plc* [2010] EWHC 2374 (Ch), [2011] 1 WLR 2414 [6], [40] (Proudman J). See also *Patten* (n 4) 586 (Kay J).

[119] *Appleyard* (n 118) [74].

[120] McFarlane (n 13) 303–05.

[121] *Chase Corporation (Australia) Pty Ltd v North Sydney Brick and Tile Co Ltd* (1994) 35 NSWLR 1 (NSWSC) 25B–C (Cohen J); Mitchell, *The Law of Subrogation* (n 13) 143; C Mitchell, 'Book Review' [2000] *LMCLQ* 589, 590; JD Heydon, MJ Leeming and PG Turner, *Meagher, Gummow and Lehane's Equity: Doctrines and Remedies* (Chatswood NSW, Butterworths, 2015) para 11–020.

marshalling is described as 'akin to subrogation'.[122] At other times, marshalling and subrogation are distinguished.[123]

Chapter 1 argued that marshalling is an example of subrogation.[124] But this leaves unanswered the question of why marshalling and subrogation are routinely analysed separately.[125] For instance, the leading text on subrogation – Mitchell and Watterson's *Subrogation: Law and Practice* – does not address marshalling.[126] Similarly, the leading text on marshalling – Ali's *Marshalling of Securities* – argues that because marshalling is available in different circumstances to the established categories of subrogation, marshalling is not an example of subrogation.[127] It therefore analyses marshalling without further reference to subrogation.

Like subrogation, marshalling is difficult to justify.[128] But while subrogation is said to be a remedy for unjust enrichment, almost[129] nobody says this about marshalling.

The relationship between subrogation and marshalling will therefore be analysed in detail by Chapter 11. It will argue that, even though marshalling is an example of subrogation, marshalling has a different justification compared to other instances of subrogation. Marshalling therefore occurs in different circumstances to other examples of subrogation, and so the availability of subrogation and marshalling are rightly analysed separately in the cases.

VIII. Chapter Summary

To sum up, six controversies surround subrogation:

1. Is subrogation justified?
2. Is subrogation a remedy for unjust enrichment?
3. Is subrogation redundant?

[122] *Highbury Pension Fund Management Co v Zirfin Investments Ltd* [2013] EWHC 238 (Ch), [2014] Ch 359 [15] (Norris J).

[123] *Re Dent Co* [2016] EWHC 2650 (Ch), [2017] Ch 422, [26], [29]–[30] (Norris J); SR Derham, 'Set-Off Against an Assignee' (1991) 107 *LQR* 126, 131–32; C Hare, 'Marshalling Marshalling' in PS Davies, S Douglas and J Goudkamp (eds), *Defences in Equity* (Oxford, Hart Publishing, 2018) 242.

[124] See ch 1, s III(B) above.

[125] *Re Dent* (n 123) [26], [29]–[30] (Norris J); Hare (n 123) 242.

[126] Mitchell and Watterson (n 6).

[127] PAU Ali, *Marshalling of Securities* (Oxford, OUP, 1999) ch 4.

[128] See ch 11, s II below.

[129] M Evans, *Equity and Trusts* (Chatswood, NSW, LexisNexis Butterworths, 2003) para 11.9.

4. When should subrogation occur?
5. What rights should subrogation create?
6. What is the relationship between subrogation and marshalling?

This book seeks to resolve these six controversies. Part II considers whether subrogation is redundant according to the law as it stands. Part III then turns to consider what the law ought to be as a matter of principle, addressing the controversies over whether subrogation is justified, when it should occur, what rights it should create, and its relationship with marshalling. The controversy over whether subrogation is a remedy for unjust enrichment cuts across the division between what the law is and what the law ought to be, and so it addressed by both Parts II and III.

PART II

Is Subrogation Redundant?

3

Enrichment

I. Introduction

The previous chapter identified six controversies surrounding subrogation. Part II of this book addresses one of those controversies: whether subrogation is redundant. It argues that subrogation is governed by different rules compared to a 'direct' unjust enrichment claim. Accordingly, subrogation does not duplicate a direct claim and so subrogation is not redundant. This chapter begins by arguing that subrogation is not governed by the rules which determine whether there was an enrichment in direct claims.

In his monograph on enrichment, Lodder argues that 'there are two concepts of enrichment in the law of unjust enrichment: (i) factual enrichment, that is the receipt of value by the defendant at the claimant's expense; and (ii) legal enrichment, that is the acquisition of a right, or the release of an obligation, at the claimant's expense.'[1] He argues that, as a consequence:

> it is necessary to ascertain whether the claimant is asserting: (i) that the defendant is enriched by the value of the benefit received and seeks monetary restitution of that value; or (ii) that the defendant is enriched by the acquisition of a right (or release of an obligation) at the claimant's expense and seeks specific restitution of that right (or reinstatement of that obligation) in law.[2]

Direct claims are of the first variety. The 'starting point in valuing the enrichment is the objective market value, or market price'[3] and so direct claims reverse D's enrichment conceptualised 'factually, in terms of economic value'.[4]

[1] AVM Lodder, *Enrichment in the Law of Unjust Enrichment and Restitution* (Oxford, Hart Publishing, 2012) 37. See also R Chambers, 'Two Kinds of Enrichment' in R Chambers, C Mitchell and J Penner (eds), *Philosophical Foundations of the Law of Unjust Enrichment* (Oxford, OUP, 2009).

[2] Lodder (n 1) 2.

[3] *Benedetti v Sawiris* [2013] UKSC 50, [2014] AC 938 [15] (Lord Clarke).

[4] Lodder (n 1) 1; S Watterson, 'Modelling Subrogation as an "Equitable Remedy"' (2016) 2 *CJCCL* 609, 615; S Watterson, 'Subrogation' in G Virgo and S Worthington (eds), *Commercial Remedies: Resolving Controversies* (Cambridge, CUP, 2017) 440.

Meanwhile, in subrogation cases, Mitchell, Mitchell, and Watterson identify two enrichments:

> The primary enrichment accrues to [D], who is released from liability to [X], and whose asset is released from [X]'s security interest. However, there are also secondary enrichments that may immediately accrue to other parties, whose position is materially improved when [X]'s rights are extinguished. Such secondary enrichments may accrue to a junior secured creditor, who held a security interest over the same asset which was subordinate to [X]'s security interest, and whose subordinate security interest was strengthened to the extent that the debt secured by the prior-ranking security interest is discharged.[5]

These secondary enrichments are increases in the value of pre-existing rights. Thus, like enrichments in direct claims, secondary enrichments are in the form of value.[6]

The primary enrichment – the discharge of D's debt – also leaves D factually better off. However, there are two problems with treating subrogation as reversing D's factual enrichment. First, in cases where D's gain exceeds C's loss, subrogation gives C a right to compensation for their loss, and not to restitution of D's gain. Second, treating subrogation as reversing D's factual enrichment cannot justify the form of rights created by subrogation. It follows that, while direct claims reverse D's factual enrichment, subrogation does not. Each problem will now be explained in turn.

II. Gains or Losses?

The first of these problems is illustrated by *Reed v Norris*.[7] The facts were complex, but at their simplest they were as follows. In 1801, Richard Bevan the elder (D) owed Lord Vernon (X) £500. Bevan's son, Richard Bevan the younger (C), agreed to stand as surety for his father's debt. By 1835, interest had swelled the debt to

[5] C Mitchell, P Mitchell and S Watterson, *Goff and Jones: The Law of Unjust Enrichment* (London, Sweet & Maxwell, 2022) para 39-27 (footnotes omitted). See also eg *National Westminster Bank Plc v Mayfair Estates Property Investments Ltd* [2007] EWHC 287 (Ch) [24] (Sir Donald Rattee); *Anfield (UK) Ltd v Bank of Scotland Plc* [2010] EWHC 2374 (Ch), [2011] 1 WLR 2414 [11] (Proudman J); *Swynson Ltd v Lowick Rose LLP* [2017] UKSC 32, [2018] AC 313 [57] (Lord Mance); C Mitchell and S Watterson, *Subrogation: Law and Practice* (Oxford, OUP, 2007), ch 4 esp para 4.08; A Burrows, *A Restatement of the English Law of Unjust Enrichment* (Oxford, OUP, 2012) 174–75.

[6] Chambers (n 1) 269–71.

[7] *Reed v Norris* (1837) 2 My & Cr 361, 40 ER 678.

almost £950. Lord Vernon agreed to accept £600 from the son to discharge the debt.[8] The son was therefore entitled to be subrogated to Lord Vernon's extinguished rights against the father.

One question for the court was whether the son was subrogated to Lord Vernon's extinguished right to the full £950, or only subrogated to the extent necessary to recover the £600 paid. Lord Cottenham LC cited Lord Eldon LC's decisions in *Ex parte Rushforth*[9] and *Butcher v Churchill*[10] for the proposition that:

> where a surety gets rid of and discharges an obligation at a less sum than its full amount, he cannot, as against his principal, make himself a creditor for the whole amount; but can only claim, as against his principal, what he has actually paid in discharge of the common obligation.[11]

In effect, then, the son's payment of £600 discharged the father's debt of £950. The father was enriched by the discharge of £950 debt. Yet the son was only subrogated to a right to £600. On the face of it, subrogation seemed to reverse the son's loss, and not the father's enrichment. There are dicta to the same effect in more modern cases.[12]

Mitchell and Watterson suggest a number of ways of reconciling these cases with the idea that subrogation is a remedy for unjust enrichment. First, they suggest that £600 'could be justified as the proper measure of the debtor's enrichment, where the creditor would have accepted a similarly reduced sum from the debtor'.[13] However, in *Reed v Norris* the court did not find as a fact that Lord Vernon would have accepted £600 from the father to discharge the £950 debt.

Second, they suggest that in 'some cases it may also be incompatible with the relationship from which [C]'s right to restitution arose for him to recover more than the amount of his loss'.[14] This concedes that, at least in some cases, subrogation seeks to indemnify loss rather than reverse enrichment. In *Reed*, for instance, the son was his father's surety, and Lord Cottenham LC said that the 'contract

[8] In fact, by 1835 all three original parties had died, and so it was the son's representatives who paid £600 to Lord Vernon's executors to discharge the debt of the father's estate. For ease of comprehension, the main text continues to refer to the father, son, and Lord Vernon.

[9] *Ex p Rushforth* (1805) 10 Ves Jun 409, 32 ER 903.

[10] *Butcher v Churchill* (1808) 14 Ves Jun 567, 33 ER 638.

[11] *Reed v Norris* (1837) 2 My & Cr 361, 375–76, 40 ER 678, 683.

[12] *Jamieson v Hotel Renfrew Ltd* [1941] 4 DLR 470 (Ontario SC) [57] (Roach J); *Trades House of Glasgow v Ferguson* [1979] SLT 187 (IH) 192 (Lord Wilson); *Gnitrow Ltd v Cape Plc* [2000] 1 WLR 2327 (CA) 2331E–F (Pill LJ).

[13] Mitchell, Mitchell and Watterson (n 5) para 39-108. See also Mitchell and Watterson (n 5) para 5.12.

[14] Mitchell and Watterson (n 5) para 5.13.

between [a surety] and his principal is that the principal shall indemnify him from whatever loss he may sustain by reason of incurring an obligation together with the principal'.[15]

III. Form

A second problem with treating subrogation as reversing D's factual enrichment is that this does not explain the form of the rights created by subrogation.[16] Watterson explains that the 'natural restitutionary response'[17] to enrichments in the form of value is 'an order to pay a money sum reflecting the monetary value of [D]'s enrichment'.[18] So if enrichment is assessed factually, it is difficult to explain why subrogation can give C proprietary rights.

One might say that subrogation can give C proprietary rights to 'reinforc[e] C's monetary claim against D, by imposing a new equitable lien/charge as security for its satisfaction'.[19] But Watterson explains that if the purpose of C's new security is simply to reinforce a monetary claim, then there is no reason why it should have prima facie the same content as X's extinguished security.[20] Accordingly, a focus on factual enrichment cannot explain why subrogation gives C rights with prima facie the same content as X's extinguished rights. Watterson argues that this can only be explained by recognising that subrogation 'operates as a specific restitutionary mechanism, addressed to the release of D's liabilities, conceived as a "legal" enrichment'.[21]

This concedes that subrogation is governed by different rules to direct claims. The enrichment in direct claims is being factually better off, whereas the primary enrichment in subrogation cases is the discharge of a legal liability. Subrogation

[15] *Reed v Norris* (1837) 2 My & Cr 361, 375, 40 ER 678, 683.

[16] JA Dieckmann, 'The Province of Subrogation Determined: Some Corrections – a Functional Analysis of the Guarantor's Right to Derivative Recourse, Comprising a Critique of the Restitutionary Thesis' (2012) 20 *ERPL* 989, 1026; Lodder (n 1) 141–47; Watterson, 'Subrogation' (n 4) 439–48; Watterson, 'Modelling Subrogation as an "Equitable Remedy"' (n 4) 615–17; W Swadling, 'In Defence of Formalism' in A Robertson and J Goudkamp (eds), *Form and Substance in the Law of Obligations* (Oxford, Hart Publishing, 2019) 114–15.

[17] Watterson, 'Subrogation' (n 4) 440.

[18] ibid 438.

[19] ibid 439 (emphasis omitted).

[20] ibid 439–40.

[21] ibid 441 (emphasis omitted).

therefore 'responds to a distinctive form of "enrichment"'[22] compared to direct claims, so subrogation is not 'needlessly duplicative' or 'invariably redundant for C'.[23]

IV. Chapter Summary

Unlike direct claims, subrogation does not reverse D's factual enrichment. In cases where D's gain exceeds C's loss, subrogation compensates C's loss rather than reversing D's gain. And in order for an unjust enrichment approach to explain why subrogation gives C rights with prima facie the same content as X's extinguished rights, it is necessary to say that subrogation responds to a different type of enrichment. Consequently, subrogation and direct claims are governed by different rules. Subrogation does not merely duplicate a direct claim.

[22] Mitchell, Mitchell and Watterson (n 5) para 39-19.
[23] Watterson, 'Subrogation' (n 4) 446–48.

4

At the Claimant's Expense

I. Introduction

This chapter[1] turns to the question of whether an enrichment came at C's expense. Section II identifies the rules which govern the answer to that question for direct claims. Section III then shows that these rules do not govern subrogation.

II. Direct Claims

A. Sufficient Causal Connection

Until recently, the test in direct claims was one of 'economic reality'[2] or whether there was a 'sufficient causal connection' between C's loss and D's gain.[3] It was easy to say that subrogation was governed by these tests. For example, in *Menelaou*, a majority of the Supreme Court used both tests to show that D's enrichment came at C's expense.[4] Similarly, Mitchell and Watterson treated both primary

[1] Elements of this chapter were published as R Gregson, 'Is Subrogation a Remedy for Unjust Enrichment?' (2020) 136 *LQR* 481.

[2] *Investment Trust Companies v Revenue and Customs Commissioners* [2012] EWHC 458 (Ch) ('*ITC* (Ch)') [72] (Henderson J); *Menelaou v Bank of Cyprus Plc* [2013] EWCA Civ 1960, [2014] 1 WLR 854 ('*Menelaou* (CA)') [48] (Floyd LJ); *Relfo Ltd v Varsani* [2014] EWCA Civ 360 [92], [96]–[97] (Arden LJ), [103] (Gloster LJ), [115] (Floyd LJ); *Investment Trust Companies v Revenue and Customs Commissioners* [2015] EWCA Civ 82 ('*ITC* (CA)') [67], [69] (Patten LJ); *Menelaou v Bank of Cyprus UK Ltd* [2015] UKSC 66, [2016] AC 176 ('*Menelaou* (SC)') [31] (Lord Clarke), [73] (Lord Neuberger).

[3] *ITC* (Ch) (n 2) [68] (Henderson J); *Menelaou* (CA) (n 2) [42] (Floyd LJ); *TFL Management Ltd v Lloyds TSB Bank Plc* [2013] EWCA Civ 1415, [2014] 1 WLR 2006 [57] (Floyd LJ), [61] (Moses LJ); *Relfo* (n 2) [83], [95]–[96] (Arden LJ), [103]–[104] (Gloster LJ), [115], [122] (Floyd LJ); *ITC* (CA) (n 2) [67], [69] (Patten LJ); *Menelaou* (SC) (n 2) [27] (Lord Clarke).

[4] *Menelaou* (SC) (n 2) [24]–[35] (Lord Clarke), [66], [77] (Lord Neuberger), [141] (Lord Kerr and Lord Wilson). See also *Banque Financière de La Cité SA v Parc (Battersea) Ltd* [1999] 1 AC 221 (HL) ('*BFC*') 227C (Lord Steyn), 238B (Lord Clyde), 239G (Lord Hutton); *Filby v Mortgage Express (No 2) Ltd* [2004] EWCA Civ 759 [50], [62] (May LJ).

and secondary enrichments as accruing at C's expense because C could 'establish a causal connection between his loss and the[se] gains'.[5]

B. *ITC*

However, these expansive tests were rejected in *ITC*.[6] There, the customer bought services from the managers. As part of the price, the customer paid Value Added Tax ('VAT') to the managers. The managers accounted to the Revenue for the VAT. It then transpired that the services ought to have been exempt from VAT. The customer sought to recover the VAT from the Revenue.

The Supreme Court denied the customer's claim. Giving the only judgment, Lord Reed held that an enrichment is only at C's expense if 'there has been a transfer of value'.[7] He continued:

> The expression 'transfer of value' is, however, also too general to serve as a legal test. More precisely, it means … that [D] has received a benefit from [C] … [and C] suffered a loss through his provision of the benefit.[8]

This test is 'usually'[9] – or possibly only[10] – satisfied 'where the parties have dealt directly with one another, or with one another's property', such as where C pays D.[11] There are 'a number of situations' in which there is no 'direct transfer', but 'which, for the purposes of the rule, the law treats as equivalent to a direct transfer'.[12] These include:

- 'where the agent of one of the parties is interposed between them';[13]
- 'cases … in which a set of co-ordinated transactions has been treated as forming a single scheme or transaction for the purpose of the "at the expense of"

[5] C Mitchell and S Watterson, *Subrogation: Law and Practice* (Oxford, OUP, 2007) paras 5.15–5.20, 5.48–5.50. See also P Birks, *Unjust Enrichment* (Oxford, OUP, 2005) 96–98; S Watterson, '"Direct Transfers" in the Law of Unjust Enrichment' (2011) 64 *CLP* 435, 458–59, 464–66.
[6] *Investment Trust Companies v Revenue and Customs Commissioners* [2017] UKSC 29, [2018] AC 275 ('*ITC* (SC)') [37]–[38], [52], [56]–[57], [59]–[60], [72] (Lord Reed).
[7] ibid [42]–[43].
[8] ibid [43].
[9] ibid [46].
[10] ibid [50].
[11] ibid [46].
[12] ibid [50].
[13] ibid [48].

inquiry, on the basis that to consider each individual transaction separately would be unrealistic';[14]

- 'situations where [D] receives property from a third party into which [C] can trace an interest';[15] and
- cases 'where [C] discharges a debt owed by [D] to a third party'.[16]

Furthermore, the requirement that C 'must … incur a loss through the provision of the benefit … will not normally be satisfied where the provision of the benefit was merely an incidental or collateral result of his expenditure'.[17] These rules were affirmed in *Swynson* and *Prudential*.[18]

On the facts of *ITC*, Lord Reed held that there was a transfer of value from the customer to the managers, and from the managers to the Revenue. However, '[t]hese two transfers [could not] be collapsed into a single transfer of value' from the customer to the Revenue.[19] The customer could not rely on any of the equivalents to a direct transfer:

> since the payments made by [the customer] formed part of the managers' general assets, to do with as they pleased, it is impossible to trace those payments into the payments subsequently made by the managers to the [Revenue. In addition,] there is no question of the transactions … comprising a single scheme.[20]

Therefore, the Revenue's enrichment was not at the customer's expense, so the customer had no claim against the Revenue.[21]

III. Subrogation

However, subrogation is not governed by the *ITC* rules. To demonstrate this, subsection A shows that *ITC*'s requirement of a transfer of value does not apply

[14] ibid.
[15] ibid.
[16] ibid [49].
[17] ibid [52].
[18] *Swynson Ltd v Lowick Rose LLP* [2017] UKSC 32, [2018] AC 313 [56], [58], [67], [89] (Lord Mance), [114]–[115], [117], [120] (Lord Neuberger); *Prudential Assurance Co Ltd v Revenue and Customs Commissioners* [2018] UKSC 39, [2018] 3 WLR 652 [68], [102] (Lord Mance, Lord Reed, and Lord Hodge). For criticism, see C Mitchell, 'End of the Road for the Overpaid Tax Litigation?' (2017–18) 9 *UKSCYB* 225, 236–42.
[19] *ITC* (SC) (n 6) [71].
[20] ibid [72].
[21] ibid [73]–[74].

to subrogation. Subsection B then shows that *ITC*'s directness rule does not apply to subrogation. Subsections C and D then show that Lord Reed's equivalents to a direct transfer cannot reconcile subrogation cases with these rules. Subsection E shows that *ITC*'s incidental benefits rule does not apply to subrogation. Finally, subsection F shows that secondary enrichments in subrogation cases do not come at C's expense according to the *ITC* rules.

A. Transfer of Value

In Chapter 1, a division was introduced between common liability cases, misappropriation cases, and lending cases. A different way of dividing subrogation cases is according to how D's debt was discharged. This reveals four different types of case:[22]

- In type 1 cases, C pays X, discharging D's debt to X.[23]
- In type 2 cases, C pays D, then D pays X, discharging D's debt to X.[24]
- In type 3 cases, C pays a fourth party, who then pays X, discharging D's debt to X.[25]
- In type 4 cases, C releases a fourth party's property from a charge. The property is sold and X is paid from the proceeds, discharging D's debt to X. *Menelaou* seems to be the only example.[26]

In *ITC*, the Supreme Court held that there were 'two separate transactions – first, between [the customer] and the managers, and secondly between the managers and'[27] the Revenue – which 'cannot be collapsed into a single transfer of value' from the customer to the Revenue.[28] This reasoning suggests that there is no

[22] Types 1–3 were distinguished in P Birks, *An Introduction to the Law of Restitution* (Oxford, Clarendon Press, 1989) 94; C Mitchell, 'The Law of Subrogation' [1992] *LMCLQ* 483, 493–94; C Mitchell, *The Law of Subrogation* (Oxford, Clarendon Press, 1994) 113–14; Mitchell and Watterson (n 5) paras 5.18, 5.20, 5.23.
[23] *Ghana Commercial Bank v Chandiram* [1960] AC 732 (PC) 737.
[24] *Baroness Wenlock v River Dee Co (No 2)* (1887) 19 QBD 155 (CA) 166 (Fry LJ); *Chetwynd v Allen* [1899] 1 Ch 353 (Ch) 354; *Halifax Plc v Omar* [2002] EWCA Civ 121, [2002] 2 P&CR 26 [4]–[5] (Jonathan Parker LJ); *Anfield (UK) Ltd v Bank of Scotland Plc* [2010] EWHC 2374 (Ch), [2011] 1 WLR 2414 [3]–[4] (Proudman J); *Day v Tiuta International Ltd* [2014] EWCA Civ 1246 [4] (Gloster LJ).
[25] eg *Lehman Commercial Mortgage Conduit Ltd v Gatedale Ltd* [2012] EWHC 848 (Ch) [7] (Vos J).
[26] *Menelaou* (SC) (n 2). For the facts, see ch 2, s V(B) above.
[27] *ITC* (SC) (n 6) [72] (Lord Reed).
[28] ibid [71] (Lord Reed).

transfer of value in some subrogation cases.[29] To demonstrate this, each of the four types of subrogation case will be considered in turn.

In type 1 cases, C pays X, discharging D's debt to X. Is this one transaction (a payment which discharges) or two (a payment, then a discharge)? It is difficult to find authority which directly addresses this technical point. The closest seems to be *Hirachand Punamchand v Temple*.[30] There, Lieutenant Temple owed 1,953 Rupees to a creditor. His father, Sir Richard Temple, paid the creditor 650 Rupees in order to settle his son's debt. The creditor then sued Lieutenant Temple for the balance of 1,303 Rupees.

The Court of Appeal held that Lieutenant Temple was not liable as Sir Richard had discharged his debt. The creditor knew that Sir Richard paid in order to discharge the whole debt, so the creditor could not treat the payment as only a partial discharge: the creditor 'could only accept [Sir Richard's] money on the terms upon which it was offered'.[31]

This suggests that, once X accepts C's payment, X cannot choose whether or not it discharges D's debt.[32] As a result, it would be artificial to treat the payment and the discharge as separate transactions. There is only one transaction: a payment which discharges.

Thus, while in *ITC* there was no transfer of value because there were two separate transactions, this problem does not affect type 1 subrogation cases. This accords with Lord Reed's treatment of 'the case where [C] discharges a debt owed by [D] to [X]' as a 'transfer of value' from C and D.[33]

In type 2 cases, C pays D, then D pays X, discharging D's debt to X. When C pays D, there is a transfer of value from C to D.[34] For subrogation, however, the relevant enrichment is not D's receipt of the money. Rather, it is said to be the discharge of D's debt to X.[35] C is only linked to this discharge via two transactions: the transaction between C and D (when C pays D), and the transaction between D and X (when D pays X, discharging D's debt). Thus, analogously to *ITC*, there

[29] F Wilmot-Smith, 'A Prudent Decision' (2019) 135 LQR 195, 198.

[30] *Hirachand Punamchand v Temple* [1911] 2 KB 330 (CA).

[31] ibid 342 (Farwell LJ). See also 336 (Vaughan Williams LJ), 338–39 (Fletcher Moulton LJ).

[32] P Birks and J Beatson, 'Unrequested Payment of Another's Debt' (1976) 92 *LQR* 188, 194, 197; D Friedmann, 'Payment of Another's Debt' (1983) 99 *LQR* 534, 539, 542. cf *Absa Bank Ltd v Moore* [2016] ZACC 34 [32] (Cameron J); A Burrows, *The Law of Restitution* (Oxford, OUP, 2011) 463.

[33] *ITC* (SC) (n 6) [49].

[34] ibid [46] (Lord Reed).

[35] *Swynson* (n 18) [57] (Lord Mance); Mitchell and Watterson (n 5) ch 4; C Mitchell, P Mitchell and S Watterson, *Goff and Jones: The Law of Unjust Enrichment* (London, Sweet & Maxwell, 2022) para 39-27.

are two transactions interposed between C and D's enrichment. Consequently, applying *ITC*, there appears to be no transfer of value from C to D in respect of the discharge of D's debt. Subrogation does not share *ITC*'s requirement of a transfer of value.

In type 3 cases, C pays a fourth party, who then pays X, discharging D's debt to X. Again, like *ITC*, there are two separate transactions: first, between C and the fourth party; and second, between the fourth party and X. Applying *ITC*, there is no transfer of value from C to X. C is only connected to D's enrichment via the payment to X. Thus, if there is no transfer of value from C to X, then it follows a fortiori that there is no transfer of value from C to D.

In type 4 cases, C releases a fourth party's property from a charge, the property is sold, and X is paid from the proceeds, discharging D's debt to X. Here, there are three transactions interposed between C and D's enrichment: first, the release of C's charge; second, the sale of the property; and third, the payment to X which discharges D's debt to X. Again, the result in *ITC* suggests there is no transfer of value from C to D here.[36]

On the face of it, then, there is no transfer of value in type 2, 3, and 4 cases. Consequently, it seems that direct claims require a transfer of value whereas subrogation does not. This conclusion might be rebutted if subrogation cases fitted into one of Lord Reed's 'equivalents' to a transfer of value.[37] However, this possibility will be rejected in subsections C and D.

B. Directness

In addition to requiring a transfer of value, the Supreme Court in *ITC* stated that the transfer 'usually' – perhaps always – must be 'direct'.[38] Lord Reed gave examples, but did not define 'direct'.[39] In this context, the word 'direct' has a different meaning compared to when 'direct unjust enrichment claims' are contrasted with subrogation. A 'direct unjust enrichment claim' is one in which C's rights are defined without reference to X's extinguished rights.[40] By contrast, the need

[36] E Ball, 'At the Claimant's Expense' (2014) 130 *LQR* 13, 16; TRS Cutts, 'Modern Money Had and Received' (2018) 38 *OJLS* 1, 23.

[37] *ITC* (SC) (n 6) [50].

[38] ibid [46], [50] (Lord Reed). cf *Swynson* (n 18) [114]–[116] (Lord Neuberger).

[39] *ITC* (SC) (n 6) [46]–[51].

[40] Birks, *Introduction* (n 22) 191–92; S Hedley, *Restitution: Its Division and Ordering* (London, Sweet & Maxwell, 2001) 142; Burrows, *Restitution* (n 32) 147.

for a 'direct' transfer of value is generally understood to mean that D must be enriched by C and not by a third party.[41]

In all four types of subrogation case, a payment to X discharges D's debt to X. This requires X to accept the payment.[42] One view is that subrogation offends the directness rule, presumably on the grounds that D is enriched by the action of X, a third party, accepting the payment. For example, in *Prudential*, the Supreme Court stated that:

> as a general rule, a cause of action based on unjust enrichment is only available in respect of a benefit which [C] has provided directly to [D] (the only true exception identified being subrogation following the discharge of a debt, which is arguably based on a different principle).[43]

On this strict view, no subrogation case complies with *ITC*'s directness rule.

However, there is a more generous view which was endorsed by Lord Reed in *ITC*:

> Although it is [X] who receives the payment from [C], [D] is directly enriched, since the payment discharges his debt: the enrichment is not the payment which [X] receives, but the discharge which [D] receives.[44]

On this more generous view, C directly enriches D despite X's involvement. Accordingly, type 1 – and presumably type 2 – subrogation cases fit *ITC*'s directness rule.

But even if this more generous view is correct, type 3 and 4 cases still do not fit the directness rule. In those cases, a fourth party pays X, discharging D's debt to X. The more generous view allows X to drop out. But even then the fourth

[41] A Tettenborn, 'Lawful Receipt – a Justifying Factor?' [1997] *RLR* 1, 1; L Smith, 'Restitution: The Heart of Corrective Justice' (2001) 79 *Texas LR* 2115, 2155; B McFarlane, 'Unjust Enrichment, Property Rights and Indirect Recipients' [2009] *RLR* 37, 38; Burrows, *Restitution* (n 32) 69–70; Watterson, 'Direct Transfers' (n 5) 439; A Burrows, *A Restatement of the English Law of Unjust Enrichment* (Oxford, OUP, 2012) 48; G Virgo, *The Principles of the Law of Restitution* (Oxford, OUP, 2015) 105–06; A Burrows, '"At the Expense of the Claimant": A Fresh Look' [2017] *RLR* 167, 174.

[42] *Hirachand* (n 30) 336 (Vaughan Williams LJ) 338–39 (Fletcher Moulton LJ), 342 (Farwell LJ); *Barclays Bank Ltd v WJ Simms Son & Cooke (Southern) Ltd* [1980] QB 677 (QB) 695G (Robert Goff J); R Stevens, 'The Unjust Enrichment Disaster' (2018) 134 *LQR* 574, 582; R Stevens, *The Laws of Restitution* (Oxford, OUP, 2023) 49–50.

[43] *Prudential* (n 18) [68] (Lord Mance, Lord Reed, and Lord Hodge). See also *Menelaou* (CA) (n 2) [60] (Moses LJ); L Smith, 'Restitution: A New Start?' in P Devonshire and R Havelock (eds), *The Impact of Equity and Restitution in Commerce* (Oxford, Hart Publishing, 2019) 99.

[44] *ITC* (SC) (n 6) [49]. See also McFarlane (n 41) 49; Burrows, *Restatement* (n 41) 49; Virgo (n 41) 106.

party, 'not C, is the direct provider of D's enrichment', as Burrows observes.[45] He therefore accepts that 'some examples of subrogation are exceptions to the "direct providers" rule'.[46]

In sum, on either the strict or generous view, subrogation does not seem to be governed by *ITC*'s directness rule. Again, subrogation and direct unjust enrichment claims seem to be governed by different rules.

C. Co-ordinated Transactions

On the face of it, then, subrogation is not governed by *ITC*'s requirement of a direct transfer of value. In *ITC*, however, Lord Reed explained the subrogation cases of *BFC* and *Menelaou* as exemplifying facts 'equivalent to a direct transfer':[47]

> These are cases in which, for the purpose of answering the 'at the expense of' question, the court has treated a set of related transactions, operating in a co-ordinated way, as forming a single scheme or transaction, on the basis that to answer the question by considering each of the individual transactions separately would be unrealistic.[48]

Lord Reed therefore endorsed Lord Clarke's reasoning in *Menelaou* that 'the two arrangements, namely the sale of Rush Green Hall and the purchase of Great Oak Court, were not separate but part of one scheme', and so there was a transfer of value from C to D.[49]

However, this 'co-ordinated transactions' reasoning is problematic for at least three reasons: it is over-inclusive, uncertain, and only applied to subrogation cases.[50] Each problem will be explained in turn.

i. Problem 1: Over-Inclusive

First, if the transactions could be collapsed into a single scheme in *Menelaou*, then the same could be said of the transactions from C to the managers and

[45] Burrows, *Restatement* (n 41) 51. See also *Menelaou* (CA) (n 2) [60] (Moses LJ); McFarlane (n 41) 49; Burrows, *Restitution* (n 32) 78–79.

[46] Burrows, *Restatement* (n 41) 51. See also Burrows, *Restitution* (n 32) 78.

[47] *ITC* (SC) (n 6) [50].

[48] ibid [61].

[49] *Menelaou* (SC) (n 2) [25] approved in *ITC* (SC) (n 6) [65]–[66] (Lord Reed).

[50] W Day, '"At the Expense of" in Unjust Enrichment: Causal, Direct or Intentional Transfers of Value?' [2017] *LMCLQ* 588, 599–600.

from the managers to D in *ITC*.[51] The Supreme Court, however, expressly rejected this.[52] Co-ordinated transactions reasoning therefore appears over-inclusive, catching *ITC* when it should not.

There are at least four potential solutions to this problem. Each will be rejected in turn. First, Burrows suggests *Menelaou*

> can perhaps be justified as turning on the close family relationship involved (parents and daughter) so that [C] regarded there as being a single scheme involving the conferral of a benefit by them in return for real security. It was, arguably, a pure matter of form not substance that the conferral of the benefit and the provision of the security were in two transactions involving different parties rather than one transaction involving the same parties.[53]

This reasoning could be used to distinguish *ITC* – where there was no 'family relationship' – explaining why the transactions were co-ordinated in *Menelaou* and not *ITC*.

Burrows' argument, however, seems to contradict *Swynson*, in which the Supreme Court held that a company and its controlling shareholder were distinct legal persons[54] so loss to the latter could not be treated as loss to the former.[55] By analogy, in *Menelaou*, D and her parents were – however 'close' their relationship – distinct legal persons, so the conferral of a benefit on the former cannot, without more, be treated as the conferral of a benefit on the latter. Indeed, while a controlling shareholder owns and controls their company, parents do not own and control their (adult) children, so if anything *Menelaou* was a less deserving case. A 'close family relationship' is therefore not enough to explain why the transactions were co-ordinated in *Menelaou*. The distinction between *Menelaou* and *ITC* must be something else.

Second, in *Swynson* itself, Mr Hunt made a loan to EMSL, which EMSL used to repay a loan from Swynson.[56] Lord Neuberger stated that:

> I consider that in this case, as in [*BFC*] and in *Menelaou*, the fact that the money passed from Mr Hunt to EMSL and then from EMSL to Swynson does not present a problem for an unjust enrichment claim. The new loan was advanced not merely on

[51] Mitchell, 'End of the Road for the Overpaid Tax Litigation?' (n 18) 238.
[52] *ITC* (SC) (n 6) [71]–[72] (Lord Reed).
[53] Burrows, '"At the Expense of the Claimant"' (n 41) 174.
[54] *Swynson* (n 18) [1] (Lord Sumption).
[55] ibid [12]–[13], [17] (Lord Sumption), [46]–[50], [54] (Lord Mance), [99], [107]–[108] (Lord Neuberger).
[56] *Swynson* (n 18). For the full facts, see ch 2, s V(C) above.

> the basis that it was expected to be used to pay off the original loan: it was required to be used for that purpose.[57]

This suggests that two payments are co-ordinated when the first must be used to make the second. In these circumstances, however, the first payment is subject to a *Quistclose* trust, enabling C to trace through the second payment and thereby establish D's enrichment at C's expense.[58] This collapses co-ordinated transactions reasoning into a tracing exercise. Given that Lord Reed listed tracing and co-ordinated transactions as two different equivalents to a direct transfer, this is unlikely to be what the Supreme Court in *ITC* intended.[59]

Third, Leung and Wong suggest that two transactions are co-ordinated when the second would not have occurred but for the first.[60] For instance, in *Menelaou*, D would not have acquired Great Oak Court but for C releasing its charge over Rush Green Hall, so the two transactions were co-ordinated.[61] By contrast, in *ITC*, Lord Reed held that 'there is no question of the transactions … comprising a single scheme. The first transfer did not even bring about the second transfer as a matter of causation:'[62] the managers were liable to the Revenue even before the customer paid the managers.[63] Causation therefore seems to explain why the transactions were co-ordinated in *Menelaou* but not *ITC*.

However, co-ordinated transactions reasoning must demand something more than causation, otherwise it would introduce a causal test for whether D was enriched at C's expense,[64] which was what *ITC* explicitly rejected.[65] Consequently, the reason why the transactions were co-ordinated in *Menelaou* but not in *ITC* must be something else.

Finally, Mitchell, Mitchell, and Watterson suggest that transactions are co-ordinated if they 'implemented an overarching intent to confer a benefit

[57] ibid [114] (citations omitted).

[58] *Orakpo v Manson Investments Ltd* [1978] AC 95 (HL) 119C–D (Lord Keith); *Menelaou* (SC) (n 2) [100]–[103] (Lord Neuberger), [133]–[140] (Lord Carnwath); Birks, *Introduction* (n 22) 390–91; McFarlane (n 41) 49–50; S Watterson, 'Subrogation' in G Virgo and S Worthington (eds), *Commercial Remedies: Resolving Controversies* (Cambridge, CUP, 2017) 456; NJ McBride, *The Humanity of Private Law: Part I: Explanation* (Oxford, Hart Publishing, 2019) 218–19.

[59] *ITC* (SC) (n 6) [48], [72].

[60] J Leung and SY Wong, 'Subrogation and Unjust Enrichment in the Supreme Court' [2016] *LMCLQ* 337, 340.

[61] *Menelaou* (SC) (n 2) [24], [27] (Lord Clarke), [66] (Lord Neuberger); Leung and Wong (n 60) 340.

[62] *ITC* (SC) (n 6) [72].

[63] ibid [33] (Lord Reed).

[64] R Shah, 'Indirect Enrichment in the Supreme Court' (2017) 76 *CLJ* 490, 491–92.

[65] *ITC* (SC) (n 6) [37]–[38], [52], [56]–[57], [72].

on [D]'.[66] For instance, in *Menelaou*, the transactions were co-ordinated because of 'the mutual understanding of [C and D's] parents that [C] would release its charge, to enable the sale of Rush Green Hall and the purchase of Great Oak Court in the name of [D], over which [C] would obtain a new charge'.[67] This, however, does not seem to distinguish *ITC*. When the customer paid tax on the managers' services, the customer intended this tax to ultimately reach the Revenue.[68]

In sum, however it is understood, co-ordinated transactions reasoning catches *ITC* and so proves too much.

ii. Problem 2: Uncertain

This also reveals a second problem with co-ordinated transactions reasoning. Lord Reed gave little guidance as to when it applies and, as this discussion has shown, it can be interpreted in different ways. As Leung and Wong put it, 'the "single composite transaction" language seems at times more conclusionary than it is explanatory'.[69]

iii. Problem 3: Subrogation Provides the Only Examples

A final problem is that the subrogation cases of *BFC* and *Menelaou* were Lord Reed's only examples of co-ordinated transactions reasoning.[70] This reasoning only seems to apply to subrogation and has not been applied to direct claims.[71] Accordingly, even if co-ordinated transactions reasoning can explain subrogation cases, this does not show that subrogation and direct claims are governed by the same rules.

[66] Mitchell, Mitchell and Watterson (n 35) para 6-59. See also *Boscawen v Bajwa* [1996] 1 WLR 328 (CA) 338B–39H (Millett LJ); *Relfo* (n 2) [121] (Floyd LJ); *Brazil v Durant International Corp* [2015] UKPC 35, [2016] AC 297 [38] (Lord Toulson); *CMOC Sales and Marketing Ltd v Persons Unknown* [2018] EWHC 2230 (Comm) [148] (Judge Waksman QC); Day, '"At the Expense of" in Unjust Enrichment' (n 50) 598.

[67] Mitchell, Mitchell and Watterson (n 35) para 6-62.

[68] *ITC* (Ch) (n 6) [70] (Henderson J); F Wilmot-Smith, 'Taxing Questions' (2015) 131 *LQR* 531, 535.

[69] Leung and Wong (n 60) 340.

[70] *ITC* (SC) (n 6) [61]–[66].

[71] *CMOC* (n 66) [155]([3]) (Judge Waksman QC); *Begum v Maran (UK) Ltd* [2020] EWHC 1846 (QB) [66]–[74] (Jay J).

iv. Summary

To sum up, co-ordinated transactions reasoning is over-inclusive and uncertain. It is therefore an ineffective and unsatisfactory way of reconciling the subrogation cases with *ITC*'s requirement of a direct transfer of value. Yet co-ordinated transactions reasoning exists solely for this purpose, as it is only used to explain subrogation cases. As a result, it still seems that subrogation cases are not governed by the *ITC* rules and so subrogation is governed by different rules to direct claims.

D. Tracing

If co-ordinated transactions reasoning cannot establish a direct transfer of value in subrogation cases, perhaps tracing can. Tracing is:

> the process by which [C] demonstrates what has happened to his property, identifies its proceeds and the persons who have handled or received them, and justifies his claim that the proceeds can properly be regarded as representing his property.[72]

In *ITC*, Lord Reed stated that 'situations where [D] receives property from a third party into which [C] can trace an interest' are 'equivalent' to direct transfers of value.[73] By analogy,[74] situations where D's debt is discharged using property into which C can trace an interest could be considered 'equivalent' to direct transfers of value. If so, tracing could establish the equivalent of a direct transfer of value in subrogation cases, satisfying the *ITC* rules.

Tracing does feature in the reasoning of some subrogation cases. One prominent example is *Boscawen v Bajwa*.[75] There, D owned a house subject to X's charge. D agreed to sell the property to purchasers. C agreed to loan the purchasers funds for the purchase, in exchange for a charge over the property. C paid the loan to the purchasers' solicitors, who paid it to D's solicitors. D's solicitors were authorised to pay the monies to X on completion of the sale of the property.

[72] *Foskett v McKeown* [2001] 1 AC 102 (HL) 128D (Lord Millett).
[73] *ITC* (SC) (n 6) [48], [50]. See also *BFC* (n 4) 235C–D (Lord Hoffmann); *Swynson* (n 18) [60] (Lord Mance).
[74] *Boscawen* (n 66) 334B–35F (Millett LJ); Birks, *Introduction* (n 22) 84, 96, 390; Birks, *Unjust Enrichment* (n 5) 298–99; McBride (n 58) 218.
[75] *Boscawen* (n 66). See also *Filby* (n 4) [28]–[31] (May LJ); *Swynson* (n 18) [58]–[61] (Lord Mance).

However, D's solicitors acted too soon, and paid the monies to X before completion, partially discharging X's charge.

The sale then fell through and completion never took place. This left D with unencumbered title to the house. Meanwhile, C had paid out the loan monies but had not received any security.

To remedy this, Millett LJ held that C was subrogated to X's extinguished charge. He explained that the Buyers' solicitors had held the loan monies on trust for C.[76] C could then trace the monies from the purchasers' solicitors, through D's solicitors, and into the payment to X which discharged X's charge.[77] This enabled C to show that X's charge had been discharged at his expense and so '[D]'s unjust enrichment was at his expense'.[78]

But even though tracing features in some subrogation cases like *Boscawen*, tracing fails for two reasons to explain how the subrogation cases satisfy the *ITC* rules. First, tracing is not possible in some subrogation cases. Second, even where tracing is possible, it cannot establish a transfer of value. Each problem will be explained in turn.

i. Problem 1: Tracing not Possible

To begin with, tracing is not possible in some cases in which subrogation was awarded.[79] *Anfield (UK) Ltd v Bank of Scotland Plc* is a good example.[80] There, D owned property, subject to X's first legal charge. C made a loan to D, who used it to redeem X's charge. In return, C acquired a new charge ('the 2006 charge') but failed to register it. Subsequently, Anfield obtained a charging order over the property and registered it, gaining priority over C's 2006 charge. However, Proudman J held that C was entitled to be subrogated to X's extinguished charge, which had priority over Anfield's charge.

Anfield was a type 2 case and so subrogation succeeded even though there was no relevant transfer of value from C to D. One might try to use tracing to establish the equivalent of a direct transfer of value. However, when C paid the loan monies to D, C lost any entitlement to them, and D acquired title to

[76] *Boscawen* (n 66) 332F.
[77] ibid 335F–338A.
[78] ibid 334E–F.
[79] Hedley (n 40) 144–146; Watterson, 'Subrogation' (n 58) 454–61.
[80] *Anfield* (n 24). See also *Lehman* (n 25).

the loan monies free from any trust or mere equity.[81] This prevented C from tracing the money any further.[82] As a result, C could not use tracing to establish the equivalent of a direct transfer of value.

To avoid this conclusion, one might argue that D held the loan monies on trust for C until they were paid to X. This '*Quistclose*' trust[83] would enable C to trace into the payment which discharged X's charge.[84] However, it is not clear whether a *Quistclose* trust existed in *Anfield*, especially as the court did not specify whether the loan monies were segregated from D's other assets. While segregation is not necessary for a *Quistclose* trust,[85] it is good evidence of one.[86]

In *Anfield*, then, tracing may not be possible, and so may not be able to establish a direct transfer of value. Yet subrogation succeeded despite this. Cases like *Anfield*, therefore, does not to fit *ITC*'s requirement of a direct transfer of value, and so subrogation is governed by different rules to direct claims.

ii. Problem 2: No Transfer of Value

Furthermore, even in cases like *Boscawen* where C can trace into the payment which discharged X's rights against D, this cannot establish a transfer of value from C to D,[87] so cannot satisfy the *ITC* rules.

In *ITC*, Lord Reed stated that tracing could establish the 'equivalent' of a direct transfer of value.[88] His reasoning was that since 'the property [traced into] is, in law, the equivalent of [C]'s property, [D] is therefore treated as if he had received

[81] *Re Goldcorp Exchange Ltd* [1995] 1 AC 74 (PC) 100D–01E, 102H (Lord Mustill); *Westdeutsche Landesbank Girozentrale v Islington LBC* [1996] AC 669 (HL) 689G–90A (Lord Browne-Wilkinson); *ITC* (SC) (n 6) [70], [72] (Lord Reed); Hedley (n 40) 144–45; Watterson, 'Subrogation' (n 58) 456.

[82] *Re Goldcorp* (n 81) 104G–H (Lord Mustill); *Boscawen* (n 66) 334E (Millett LJ); *Filby* (n 4) [16]–[19], [28]–[30] (May LJ); *ITC* (SC) (n 6) [70], [72] (Lord Reed).

[83] *Barclays Bank Ltd v Quistclose Investments Ltd* [1970] AC 567 (HL).

[84] *Orakpo* (n 58) 119C–D (Lord Keith); *Menelaou* (SC) (n 2) [100]–[103] (Lord Neuberger), [133]–[140] (Lord Carnwath); Birks, *Introduction* (n 22) 390–91; McFarlane (n 41) 49–50; Watterson, 'Subrogation' (n 58) 456; McBride (n 58) 218–19.

[85] *Re Kayford Ltd* [1975] 1 WLR 279 (Ch) 282 (Megarry J); *Re Farepak Food and Gifts Ltd* [2006] EWHC 3272 (Ch), [2008] BCC 22 [34] (Mann J).

[86] *Quistclose* (n 83) 579E (Lord Wilberforce); *Re Kayford* (n 85) 282 (Megarry J); *Re Farepak* (n 85) [34] (Mann J); *Patel v Mirza* [2014] EWCA Civ 1047, [2015] Ch 271, [18] (Rimer LJ), [91] (Gloster LJ); *ITC* (SC) (n 6) [70] (Lord Reed); *First City Monument Bank Plc v Zumax Nigeria Ltd* [2019] EWCA Civ 294 [35] (Newey LJ).

[87] L Smith, 'Unjust Enrichment, Property and the Structure of Trusts' (2000) 116 *LQR* 412, 420; A Burrows, 'Proprietary Restitution: Unmasking Unjust Enrichment' (2001) 117 *LQR* 412, 417 (text to fn 29); Burrows, *Restitution* (n 32) 76; Burrows, *Restatement* (n 41) 7–9 (separating transfers of value from tracing); Burrows, '"At the Expense of the Claimant"' (n 41) 168 fn 10, 170–71, 174 fn 41; Day, '"At the Expense of" in Unjust Enrichment' (n 50) 601.

[88] *ITC* (SC) (n 6) [48], [50].

[C]'s property'.[89] However, even if D received C's property, this does not establish a transfer of value from C to D or its 'equivalent'. As Smith explains:

> if you possess something I own (call it A), and you transfer it away in exchange for something else (call it B), then I can claim ownership of B. … Although there was a transfer of wealth from [me] to [you] when [you] acquired asset A, there is not another transfer when the substitution is made. [You do] not get asset B as a transfer from [me], the owner of A; rather, [you get] B from (at the expense of) some third party.[90]

In other words, there are two separate transactions which, analogously to *ITC*,[91] cannot be collapsed into single transfer of value.[92]

There are further differences between tracing and a transfer of value. A transfer of value measures value abstracted from any particular asset, whereas tracing identifies specific assets.[93] Tracing operates independently of whether an asset was valuable, or whether D was enriched, in direct contrast to a transfer of value.[94] As Burrows observes, this means that tracing 'may give [C] a higher value claim against [D]' than a transfer of value.[95]

Thus, transfers of value and tracing are different, not 'equivalent' as Lord Reed suggested in *ITC*.[96] Invoking tracing, therefore, cannot disturb the conclusion that direct claims require a transfer of value whereas subrogation does not.

To sum up, subsection A showed that subrogation is not governed by *ITC*'s requirement of a transfer of value, and subsection B showed that subrogation is

[89] ibid [48].

[90] Smith, 'Restitution: The Heart of Corrective Justice' (n 41) 2157–58. See also Smith, 'Unjust Enrichment, Property and the Structure of Trusts' (n 87) 424–25.

[91] *ITC* (SC) (n 6) [71] (Lord Reed).

[92] Smith, 'Unjust Enrichment, Property and the Structure of Trusts' (n 87) 420.

[93] *Foskett* (n 72) 128D, 129E–G (Lord Millett); Smith, 'Unjust Enrichment, Property and the Structure of Trusts' (n 87) 419–20; Smith, 'Restitution: The Heart of Corrective Justice' (n 41) 2159; L Smith, 'Tracing' in A Burrows and Lord Rodger of Earlsferry (eds), *Mapping the Law: Essays in Memory of Peter Birks* (Oxford, OUP, 2006) 126–29, 135–37; R Chambers, 'Two Kinds of Enrichment' in R Chambers, C Mitchell and J Penner (eds), *Philosophical Foundations of the Law of Unjust Enrichment* (Oxford, OUP, 2009) 246–47, 260; L Smith, 'Philosophical Foundations of Proprietary Remedies' in R Chambers, C Mitchell and J Penner (eds), *Philosophical Foundations of the Law of Unjust Enrichment* (Oxford, OUP, 2009) 298–99, 303–04; R Nolan, 'Civil Recovery After Fraud' (2015) 131 *LQR* 8, 12; T Cutts, 'Tracing, Value and Transactions' (2016) 79 *MLR* 381, 394–95; Mitchell, Mitchell and Watterson (n 35) paras 7-28–7-30, 7-63–7-66; Day, '"At the Expense of" in Unjust Enrichment' (n 50) 601; W Day, 'Further Narrowing the Scope of Unjust Enrichment' (2019) 78 *CLJ* 24, 27.

[94] *Foskett* (n 72) 129E–G (Lord Millett); Smith, 'Tracing' (n 93) 126–29, 135–37; Chambers (n 93) 259–60; Watterson, 'Direct Transfers' (n 5) 465; Cutts, 'Tracing, Value and Transactions' (n 93) 392–96; Mitchell, Mitchell and Watterson (n 35) paras 7-28–7-29; P Sales, 'The Future of Tracing: Practical and Conceptual Issues' [2017] *RLR* 183, 186.

[95] Burrows, *Restatement* (n 41) 58.

[96] *ITC* (SC) (n 6) [48], [50].

not governed by *ITC*'s directness rule. Subsections C and D then showed that these conclusions cannot be escaped using co-ordinated transactions reasoning or tracing. In short, subrogation is not governed by *ITC*'s requirement of a direct transfer of value, and therefore subrogation is governed by different rules to direct unjust enrichment claims.

E. Incidental Benefits

Furthermore, subrogation is not governed by *ITC*'s incidental benefits rule. Lord Reed formulated this rule as follows:

> [C] must … incur a loss through the provision of the benefit. … That requirement will not normally be satisfied where the provision of the benefit was merely an incidental or collateral result of … the reason why the expenditure was incurred.[97]

However, this rule does not apply to common liability or misappropriation cases.

First, in common liability cases, C and D owe a common debt to X. If C pays X, discharging the common debt, it is generally because C is legally obliged to.[98] It is seldom because C wants to benefit D. For example, a commercial guarantor honours its guarantee because it has to, not because it wants to improve the position of the principal debtor.[99] Indeed, by bringing subrogation proceedings against D, C shows that it has no intention of benefiting D. Accordingly, D's benefit is 'incidental or collateral to the reason why the expenditure was incurred'. Therefore, according to *ITC*'s incidental benefits rule, C's claim should fail. Yet subrogation succeeds despite this, so subrogation is not governed by *ITC*'s incidental benefits rule.[100] Burrows and Mitchell acknowledge this by treating common liability cases as justified exceptions to the incidental benefits rule.[101]

[97] ibid [52]. cf Mitchell and Watterson (n 5) para 4.13.

[98] J Hilliard, 'A Case for the Abolition of Legal Compulsion as a Ground of Restitution' (2002) 61 *CLJ* 551, 551; Burrows, *Restatement* (n 41) 55; Day, '"At the Expense of" in Unjust Enrichment' (n 50) 594; Smith, 'Restitution: A New Start?' (n 43) 99.

[99] Day, '"At the Expense of" in Unjust Enrichment' (n 50) 594.

[100] Day, '"At the Expense of" in Unjust Enrichment' (n 50); Shah (n 64) 492; Burrows, '"At the Expense of the Claimant"' (n 41) 176–77; Stevens, 'The Unjust Enrichment Disaster' (n 42) 579, fn 24; Smith, 'Restitution: A New Start?' (n 43) 98–99; Stevens, *The Laws of Restitution* (n 42) 35 fn 34. cf *Croxen v Gas and Electricity Markets Authority* [2022] EWHC 2826 (Ch) [208]–[209] (Zacaroli J); Burrows, *Restatement* (n 41) 55.

[101] C Mitchell, *The Law of Contribution and Reimbursement* (Oxford, OUP, 2003) para 3.31; Burrows, '"At the Expense of the Claimant"' (n 41) 177; A Burrows, 'In Defence of Unjust Enrichment' (2019) 78 *CLJ* 521, 542.

Second, the incidental benefits rule does not apply to misappropriation cases, in which money held on trust for C is paid to X without C's consent, discharging D's debt to X. C had no reason to incur the expenditure, so D's benefit is 'incidental or collateral to the reason why the expenditure was incurred'. Again, according to *ITC*'s incidental benefits rule, C's claim should fail. Yet subrogation succeeds. *ITC*'s incidental benefits rule is therefore another rule which applies to direct claims but not subrogation.

F. Secondary Enrichments

Mitchell, Mitchell, and Watterson suggest that subrogation does not only reverse D's primary enrichment, but also the secondary enrichment of junior secured creditors, whose security is worth more when X's prior-ranking security is extinguished.[102] However, it is even more difficult to show that these secondary enrichments come at C's expense according to the *ITC* rules.

This is illustrated by *BFC*.[103] To recap the facts, D owned property subject to X's first charge and OOL's second charge. C agreed to loan money to D – via an intermediary – to partially pay off X's charge, provided that OOL was bound by a 'postponement letter'. Under that letter, OOL would not demand repayment of its loan until C had been repaid. C performed its side of the bargain before discovering that the postponement letter did not bind OOL.

A priority dispute then arose between C and OOL. As the postponement letter did not bind OOL, C could not rely on it to obtain priority. However, a unanimous House of Lords held that the partial discharge of X's first charge left OOL unjustly enriched by the increase in value of its second charge. To reverse that unjust enrichment, C was subrogated to X's rights, insofar as they were discharged, as against OOL.

One difficulty with reconciling this result with *ITC* is that there was no transfer of value in respect of OOL's secondary enrichment. Cutts observes that there was no 'transactional nexus between [C] and [OOL]' and so no transfer of value from C to OOL.[104] As Watterson says, it 'seems impossible to explain why such secondary enrichments are "at the expense of" [C], except by a causal test',[105]

[102] See ch 3, s I above.
[103] *BFC* (n 4).
[104] Cutts, 'Modern Money Had and Received' (n 36) 22.
[105] Watterson, 'Direct Transfers' (n 5) 459.

which *ITC* rejected.[106] Furthermore, Burrows suggests that OOL was 'directly benefited by D not C', so the case is also an exception to the directness rule.[107]

Lord Reed suggested that the payments from C to the intermediary and from the intermediary to D were co-ordinated transactions,[108] establishing the equivalent of a direct transfer of value from C to D.[109] However, this reasoning overlooks the fact that C's claim was not against D but OOL. OOL was not party to any transaction, so co-ordinated transactions reasoning cannot establish a transfer of value from C to OOL,[110] even if the other problems with that reasoning are ignored.

For the same reason, tracing cannot explain why secondary enrichments come at C's expense. Lord Hoffmann said that C could trace the loan monies from C to the intermediary, from the intermediary to D, and into D's payment to X which partially discharged X's first charge.[111] Again, however, this reasoning overlooks the fact that C's claim was against OOL. OOL never received any rights, nor was one of its debts discharged.[112] As a result, OOL had nothing that C could identify as the traceable proceeds of its rights. Instead, the discharge of D's debt to X caused OOL's pre-existing second charge to increase in value. But this causal link is insufficient for tracing; tracing requires transactional links,[113] and there were no transactional links between C's loan and OOL's second charge. Consequently, tracing cannot establish the equivalent of a direct transfer of value from C to OOL.

As such, there was no way of establishing a direct transfer of value from C to OOL in *BFC*. Yet C's subrogation claim against OOL succeeded, showing that subrogation does not require a direct transfer of value, and so subrogation is governed by different rules to a direct unjust enrichment claim.

Furthermore, practically all secondary enrichments fall foul of *ITC*'s incidental benefits rule, as C seldom discharges D's debt in order to benefit secondary

[106] *ITC* (SC) (n 6) [37]–[38], [52], [56]–[57], [72] (Lord Reed).

[107] Burrows, *Restitution* (n 32) 79. See also N Tamblyn, 'Separating Unjust Enrichment and Subrogation' (2017) 44 *Exeter LR* 1, 7; T Liau and R Leow, 'Proprietary Restitution' in E Bant, K Barker and S Degeling (eds), *Research Handbook on Unjust Enrichment and Restitution* (Cheltenham, Edward Elgar Publishing, 2020) 497.

[108] *ITC* (SC) (n 6) [61]–[62]. See also *BFC* (n 4) 227C (Lord Steyn), 238B (Lord Clyde), 238G (Lord Hutton). Criticised by Day, '"At the Expense of" in Unjust Enrichment' (n 50) 599–600.

[109] *ITC* (SC) (n 6) [48], [50].

[110] Cutts, 'Modern Money Had and Received' (n 36) 23.

[111] *BFC* (n 4) 235C.

[112] *Swynson* (n 18) [62] (Lord Mance); Liau and Leow (n 107) 497.

[113] *Foskett* (n 72) 128 (Lord Millett); *Menelaou* (SC) (n 2) [128] (Lord Carnwath).

enrichees.[114] In *BFC*, C did not partially pay off X's first charge in order to increase the value of OOL's second charge. In fact, the ineffective postponement letter showed that C did not intend to improve OOL's position at all. Thus, the benefit received by OOL was 'incidental or collateral to the reason why the expenditure was incurred'.[115] Therefore, according to *ITC*'s incidental benefits rule, C's claim in *BFC* should have failed. But C's claim succeeded, showing that the incidental benefits rule does not apply to subrogation.

IV. Chapter Summary

Before *ITC*, subrogation could be said to share the same broad 'at the expense of' rules as direct unjust enrichment claims. However, in *ITC*, the Supreme Court rejected these expansive rules and laid down narrower ones. This chapter asked whether subrogation is governed by the *ITC* rules.

The table overleaf summarises the results. It shows that, at best, only type 1 lending cases can be reconciled with the *ITC* rules. Even in these cases, it is only the primary enrichment which comes at C's expense according to the *ITC* rules. Secondary enrichments, common liability cases, misappropriation cases, and type 2, 3, and 4 lending cases are not governed by the *ITC* rules. In *Anfield*, *BFC*, and *Menelaou* subrogation succeeded, whereas the *ITC* rules would now bar a direct claim.

It follows that subrogation is not governed by these rules. Subrogation does not share *ITC*'s requirement of a transfer of value from C to D. Subrogation is not governed by *ITC*'s directness rule, or its incidental benefits rule. Co-ordinated transactions reasoning and tracing fail to overcome these difficulties. In short, the *ITC* rules apply to direct unjust enrichment claims but not subrogation; direct claims are governed by different rules to subrogation.

[114] Mitchell and Watterson (n 5) para 4.11 cf para 4.13; Day, '"At the Expense of" in Unjust Enrichment' (n 50) 600; S Meier, 'Enrichment "at the Expense of Another" and Incidental Benefits in German Law' [2019] *Acta Juridica* 453, 462.

[115] *ITC* (SC) (n 6) [52] (Lord Reed).

	Primary enrichment				Secondary enrichments
	Type 1	**Type 2**	**Type 3**	**Type 4**	
Prima facie, is there a transfer of value from C to D?	Yes pages 45 to 46	No pages 46 to 47	No page 47	No page 47	No page 58
Prima facie, does the directness rule apply?	Yes? pages 47 to 48		No pages 48 to 49		No page 59
Can co-ordination transactions reasoning nevertheless establish a direct transfer?	N/A	No pages 49 to 53			No page 59
Can tracing nevertheless establish a direct transfer?	N/A	No pages 54 to 56		No pages 55 to 56	No page 59
Does the incidental benefits rule apply?	Not to misappropriation and common liability cases pages 57 to 58				No pages 59 to 60
Overall, do the *ITC* rules apply?	Yes? But only in lending cases	No	No	No	No

5

Unjust

I. Introduction

This chapter shows that direct unjust enrichment claims and subrogation are governed by different rules for determining whether D's enrichment was unjust. In direct claims, to prove that D's enrichment was unjust, C must prove one of a list of 'unjust factors' or 'grounds for restitution'.[1] In their monograph on subrogation, Mitchell and Watterson wrote that:

> secondary liability, ignorance, mistake and failure of consideration … are the grounds which can most commonly support a subrogation claim in practice. In principle, however, any recognized ground of restitution should be capable of justifying subrogation in appropriate circumstances. But, equally clearly, *only* a recognized ground of restitution should be capable of supporting the remedy of subrogation: in this respect it is no different from any other remedy for unjust enrichment.[2]

In their most recent work, however, the authors have retreated from this position. They write that it 'cannot be said with confidence that the remedy will be available wherever another's secured debt is discharged in circumstances that might reveal a ground for restitution sufficient to support a personal restitutionary remedy'.[3]

[1] *Deutsche Morgan Grenfell Group Plc v Inland Revenue Commissioners* [2006] UKHL 49, [2007] 1 AC 558 [21] (Lord Hoffmann); *Test Claimants in the FII Group Litigation v Revenue and Customs Commissioners* [2012] UKSC 19, [2012] 2 AC 337 [162] (Lord Sumption); *Swynson Ltd v Lowick Rose LLP* [2017] UKSC 32, [2018] AC 313 [22] (Lord Sumption).

[2] C Mitchell and S Watterson, *Subrogation: Law and Practice* (Oxford, OUP, 2007) para 6.02 (original emphasis). See also A Burrows, *The Law of Restitution* (Oxford, OUP, 2011) 147, 148, 167; A Burrows, *A Restatement of the English Law of Unjust Enrichment* (Oxford, OUP, 2012) 173; S Watterson, 'Modelling Subrogation as an "Equitable Remedy"' (2016) 2 *CJCCL* 609, 619.

[3] C Mitchell, P Mitchell and S Watterson, *Goff and Jones: The Law of Unjust Enrichment* (London, Sweet & Maxwell, 2022) para 39-29.

This chapter argues that this caution is justified. In particular, a defeated unilateral expectation about the future can render D's enrichment unjust in subrogation cases, whereas this is not so in direct claims. Again, subrogation and direct claims are governed by different rules; subrogation succeeds where a direct claims fails and so subrogation is not redundant.

To substantiate this argument, section II begins by showing that some subrogation cases rely on, and are consistent with, the unjust factors of mistake and failure of basis. Section III then introduces Lord Sumption's suggestion in *Swynson* that subrogation is not restricted by the rules governing the unjust factors of mistake and failure of basis, and that subrogation instead has a unique and broader unjust factor: 'defeat of an expectation of benefit'.[4] Sections IV and V show that Lord Sumption's approach finds support in the reasoning and results of previous cases.

II. Mistake and Failure of Basis

In brief, the unjust factor of mistake requires that D would not have been enriched but for C's mistaken conscious belief, or mistaken tacit assumption, about the past or present.[5] *BFC* is an example of a subrogation case where the court relied on this unjust factor.[6] But for its mistaken belief that Mr Herzig had authority to bind OOL to the postponement letter, C would not have loaned money to D to partially pay off X's charge.[7]

Failure of basis requires that C's enrichment of D was subject to a condition which failed.[8] *Lehman* is an example of a subrogation case which relies on this unjust factor.[9] There, one company, Brookdane, owned another, D. C loaned money to Brookdane. Brookdane used the loan to pay off X's charge over D's property.

[4] *Swynson* (n 1) [30].

[5] *Barclays Bank Ltd v WJ Simms Son & Cooke (Southern) Ltd* [1980] QB 677 (QB) 695C (Robert Goff J); *Dextra Bank & Trust Co Ltd v Bank of Jamaica* [2001] UKPC 50, [2002] 1 All ER (Comm) 193 [28] (Lord Bingham and Lord Goff); *Deutsche Morgan Grenfell* (n 1) [59]–[60] (Lord Hope), [84] (Lord Scott), [143] (Lord Walker); *Pitt v Holt* [2013] UKSC 26, [2013] 2 AC 108 [108] (Lord Walker).

[6] *Banque Financière de La Cité SA v Parc (Battersea) Ltd* [1999] 1 AC 221 (HL) ('*BFC*'). For the facts, see ch 2, s V(A) above.

[7] ibid 227E (Lord Steyn), 234G–35A (Lord Hoffmann).

[8] *Fibrosa Spolka Akcyjna v Fairbairn Lawson Combe Barbour Ltd* [1943] AC 32 (HL) 48 (Viscount Simon LC); *Barnes v Eastenders Cash & Carry Plc* [2014] UKSC 26, [2015] AC 1 [103]–[116] (Lord Toulson).

[9] *Lehman Commercial Mortgage Conduit Ltd v Gatedale Ltd* [2012] EWHC 848 (Ch).

C had contracted with Brookdane for a charge over D's property, and D executed a third party charge in favour of C. But legislation rendered this charge void. Prima facie, then, C was unsecured.

However, Vos J held that D was unjustly enriched at C's expense, and so C was subrogated to X's extinguished charge over D's property. Vos J held that the unjust factor was that C 'bargained for the charge over the property but did not get it … [and] had made [the charge] a condition of the transaction'.[10] In other words, the basis upon which C enriched D had failed.

Many other subrogation cases are consistent with the unjust factors of mistake and failure of basis.[11]

III. *Swynson Ltd v Lowick Rose LLP*

However, in *Swynson*, a majority of the Supreme Court suggested that subrogation is governed by a different unjust factor, compared to direct claims.[12] To recap the facts, X was considering making a loan to EMSL. X contracted D, a firm of accountants, to report on EMSL's finances. D negligently failed to draw X's attention to EMSL's lack of working capital. Had D done so, X would not have gone ahead with the loan. Ignorant of EMSL's financial difficulties, X went ahead with the loan, on which EMSL defaulted.

C then made a new loan to EMSL, which EMSL used to repay X's loan. This meant X suffered no loss as a result of D's negligence so X could not recover damages from D.[13] EMSL then went into liquidation so could not repay C's loan. C therefore sought to be subrogated to X's discharged right to recover damages from D.

The Court unanimously denied C's claim because C had not bargained for rights against D and subrogation does not give C more than he bargained for. Lord Sumption, Lord Mance, and Lord Neuberger each gave a substantive judgment. Each framed their reasoning slightly differently, and these differences have implications for the relationship between subrogation and direct claims, and whether subrogation is redundant.

[10] ibid [28].
[11] Mitchell and Watterson (n 2) paras 6.51–6.97; Burrows, *Restitution* (n 2) 151; Burrows, *Restatement* (n 2) 173; Mitchell, Mitchell and Watterson (n 3) para 39-32.
[12] *Swynson* (n 1).
[13] ibid [11]–[17] (Lord Sumption), [45]–[54] (Lord Mance), [92]–[108] (Lord Neuberger).

A. Lord Sumption

Lord Sumption gave the leading judgment, with whom Lord Neuberger, Lord Clarke, and Lord Hodge agreed. Lord Sumption stated that:

> it would be unwise to draw too close an analogy with the role of mistake in other legal contexts or to try to fit the subrogation cases into any broader category of unjust enrichment. It is in many ways sui generis. … [Subrogation] may be equally capable of analysis in terms of failure of basis for the transfer. Restitution on that ground ordinarily requires that the expectation should be mutual, whereas this is not a requirement for equitable subrogation. … What this suggests is that the real basis of [subrogation] is the defeat of an expectation of benefit which was the basis of [C]'s consent to the payment of the money for the relevant purpose. Mistake is not the critical element. It is only one, admittedly common, explanation of how that expectation came to be disappointed.[14]

On the facts, C was not entitled to subrogation because:

> [C] did not in any sense bargain for a right to recover substantial damages from [D]. … [C made] an error, but it does not follow that its consequences constitute an injustice which falls to be corrected by the law of equitable subrogation. Unless [C] has been defeated in his expectation of some feature of the transaction for which he may be said to have bargained, he does not suffer an injustice recognised by law ….[15]

Here, then, Lord Sumption suggested that rules governing the unjust factors of failure of basis and mistake do not apply to subrogation. He stated that 'failure of basis … ordinarily requires that the expectation should be mutual, whereas this is not a requirement for equitable subrogation'.[16] Furthermore, in direct claims the unjust factor of mistake requires an incorrect conscious belief or tacit assumption about the past or present; mispredictions about the future are not actionable.[17] But Lord Sumption suggested that 'the real basis of [subrogation] is the defeat of an expectation of benefit'.[18] This 'expectation' is a misprediction about the future and so would not operate as an unjust factor in a direct claim. Consequently, a defeated unilateral expectation about the future can render D's enrichment unjust in subrogation cases, whereas this is not so in direct claims.

[14] ibid [30].
[15] ibid [33]–[34].
[16] ibid [30]. See also *Cheltenham & Gloucester Plc v Appleyard* [2004] EWCA Civ 291 [40] (Neuberger LJ).
[17] *Dextra Bank* (n 5) [29] (Lord Bingham and Lord Goff); *Pitt* (n 5) [104] (Lord Walker).
[18] *Swynson* (n 1) [30] (Lord Sumption).

Lord Sumption cannot be right that C's defeated expectation is the unjust factor in 'all cases'[19] of subrogation.[20] In common liability cases, C may be subrogated to X's extinguished security even if C was unaware of that security, and so subrogation can give C more than it expected.[21] In misappropriation cases, C has no 'expectation of benefit which was the basis of [C]'s consent to the payment',[22] because C did not consent to the misappropriated payment.[23] However, it is plausible that *in lending cases* the unjust factor is C's defeated expectation.

B. Lord Mance

By contrast, Lord Mance applied the rules which govern the unjust factor of mistake in direct claims. He found that C had 'a mistaken conscious belief or mistaken tacit assumption', that he 'did not intend to run' the 'risk of being wrong', and that his mistake was 'causative'.[24] Ordinarily, this would be enough for the unjust factor of mistake to render D's enrichment unjust.[25] However, Lord Mance explained that:

> [C's] mistake [was not] one in respect of which equity should grant relief, by way of subrogation[.] [S]ubrogation cannot improve a lender's position, by giving him more than he expected to get. … [Here, C]'s loan to EMSL and EMSL's consequent discharge of [X]'s loan were exactly as [C] specified and intended. … [Thus, C] was not mistaken in any way which … could give him any arguable claim to be subrogated to a claim by [X] against [D]. … This conclusion can be explained … either on the basis that there was no sufficiently direct transfer of value from [C] to [D], or on the basis that there is no relevant unjust factor, or both.[26]

In short, Lord Mance found that the requirements of the unjust factor of mistake were satisfied but denied C's claim because of a rule specific to subrogation. On this view, subrogation to personal rights is redundant because it is available in a narrower range of cases than direct claims.

[19] ibid.

[20] Mitchell, Mitchell and Watterson (n 3) paras 39-35–39-36.

[21] *Mayhew v Crickett* (1818) 2 Swans 185, 191, 36 ER 585, 587 (Lord Eldon LC).

[22] *Swynson* (n 1) [30] (Lord Sumption).

[23] M Cleaver, 'Equitable Subrogation in Australia and England' (2018) 29 *Journal of Banking and Finance Law and Practice* 34, 54.

[24] *Swynson* (n 1) [78]–[82].

[25] N Tamblyn, 'Separating Unjust Enrichment and Subrogation' (2017) 44 *Exeter LR* 1, 22.

[26] *Swynson* (n 1) [83], [86]–[89].

C. Lord Neuberger

Lord Neuberger also found that C 'made a mistake' but that it was 'not the sort of mistake which renders [D's enrichment] "unjust"'.[27] This was because:

> in the context of an unjust enrichment claim arising out of a transaction, there must, in my view, at least normally (and quite possibly always), be some defect in the transaction itself for the doctrine of unjust enrichment to come into play. In other words, for some reason, including but not limited to a mistake on his part, [C] must be able to show that he did not get all that he expected or thought that he had bargained for. …
>
> In this case, [C] got precisely what he thought he was getting from the transaction in question, namely repayment [by EMSL] to [X] of the original loan, and a right to recover the new loan from EMSL.[28]

At first glance, this supports the view that subrogation and direct claims are governed by the same rules. Lord Neuberger stated a rule which applies 'in the context of an unjust enrichment claim arising out of a transaction' and applied that rule to subrogation.

Nevertheless, Lord Neuberger was unorthodox in stating this particular rule. In lending cases like *Swynson*, it is well established that subrogation cannot give C more than it bargained for.[29] But it was novel to apply this rule beyond lending cases, beyond subrogation, to all or most 'unjust enrichment claim[s] arising out of a transaction'.[30]

Lord Neuberger's radical expansion of this rule deserves to be met with caution. As Lord Sumption and Lord Mance suggest, the rule is usually treated as unique to subrogation. In fact, the rule is unique to subrogation in lending cases, as it does not apply in common liability[31] and misappropriation[32] cases, where C may be subrogated to X's extinguished security even if C did not bargain for any security.

To take another example, Lord Neuberger's rule does not seem to apply to undue influence cases, as is illustrated by the seminal case of *Allcard v Skinner*.[33]

[27] ibid [117].
[28] ibid [118]–[119].
[29] *Paul v Speirway* [1976] Ch 220 (Ch) 233B (Oliver J); *BFC* (n 6) 235D (Lord Hoffmann), 237H (Lord Clyde), 242F–G (Lord Hutton); *Appleyard* (n 16) [38], [41] (Neuberger LJ); *Swynson* (n 1) [31]–[34] (Lord Sumption), [86] (Lord Mance); Mitchell and Watterson (n 2) para 7.26.
[30] *Swynson* (n 1) [118] (Lord Neuberger).
[31] *Mayhew v Crickett* (1818) 2 Swans 185, 191, 36 ER 585, 587 (Lord Eldon LC); *Duncan Fox & Co v North & South Wales Bank* (1880) 6 App Cas 1 (HL); *Forbes v Jackson* (1882) 19 ChD 615 (Ch) 621 (Hall VC); *Insol Funding Co Ltd v Cowlam* [2017] EWHC 1822 (Ch) [120] (Master Bowles).
[32] *Patten v Bond* (1889) 60 LT 583 (Ch); *Boscawen v Bajwa* [1996] 1 WLR 328 (CA) 338B–340A (Millett LJ).
[33] *Allcard v Skinner* (1887) 36 ChD 145 (CA).

C became a nun, and gave all her property to her lady superior. C later left the sisterhood, and sought to recover the property. The Court of Appeal held that C made the gift under the undue influence of her confessor and spiritual advisor, as well as the lady superior. In principle, therefore, C was entitled to rescind the gift. However, her claim was barred by her laches and acquiescence.

C's claim was 'an unjust enrichment claim arising out of a transaction'[34] – the transaction was C's gift – thus engaging Lord Neuberger's rule. C made the gift under undue influence, so there was a 'defect in the transaction', apparently satisfying the first sentence of Lord Neuberger's rule.[35] But Lord Neuberger added a second sentence: C 'must be able to show that he did not get all that he expected or thought that he had bargained for'.[36] Yet in *Allcard*, C had a claim in principle, even though she could not show this: she did not expect or think that she had bargained for anything. Consequently, the second sentence of Lord Neuberger's rule does not seem to be satisfied.

D. Summary

In *Swynson*, the Supreme Court unanimously held that C's subrogation claim failed for want of an unjust factor because subrogation would give C more than he expected to get. Nevertheless, each judge framed this conclusion slightly differently and this has implications for whether subrogation is redundant.

For Lord Sumption, subrogation and direct claims are governed by different rules. Subrogation has its own unique unjust factor – 'defeat of an expectation of benefit'[37] – which was not made out on the facts. On this view, subrogation and direct claims are available in different circumstances and so subrogation is not redundant.

For Lord Mance, subrogation is governed by the same rules as direct claims and is also governed by an additional rule – unique to subrogation – which barred C's claim. On this view, subrogation is redundant because it is available in a narrower range of cases than direct claims.

[34] *Benedetti v Sawiris* [2013] UKSC 50, [2014] AC 938 [175] (Lord Neuberger); *Hart v Burbidge* [2014] EWCA Civ 992 [43] (Vos LJ); Burrows, *Restitution* (n 2) ch 11; Burrows, *Restatement* (n 2) 165; Mitchell, Mitchell and Watterson (n 3) ch 11; G Virgo, *The Principles of the Law of Restitution* (Oxford, OUP, 2015) ch 11.

[35] *Swynson* (n 1) [118].

[36] ibid.

[37] ibid [30] (Lord Sumption).

For Lord Neuberger, subrogation is governed by the same rules as direct claims, one of which barred C's claim. On this view, subrogation is redundant as it duplicates a direct claim.

Lord Neuberger also said that he did 'not see any significant variation in the reasoning of Lord Sumption and Lord Mance …. However, given the ability of ingenious lawyers to identify possible differences between concurring judgments,' he agreed only with Lord Sumption.[38] Ultimately, then, four members of the Court endorsed Lord Sumption's judgment, which suggested that subrogation and direct claims are governed by different rules for determining whether there is an unjust factor and that subrogation has an idiosyncratic unjust factor: 'defeat of an expectation of benefit'.[39] It is this defeated expectations approach which has been subsequently applied at first instance[40] and the following sections will show that it fits the reasoning and results of previous lending cases better than the unjust factors of mistake and failure of basis.

IV. Reasoning

Giving the leading judgment in *Menelaou*, Lord Clarke stated that:

> the unjust factor or ground for restitution is usually identified in subrogation cases as being, either (1) that the lender was acting pursuant to the mistaken assumption that it would obtain security which it failed to obtain or (2) failure of consideration.
>
> On the facts here [C] expected to have a first legal charge over Great Oak Court securing the debts of [D's] parents … but, as events turned out, it did not ….[41]

Swadling[42] and Virgo[43] have each observed that this reasoning is inconsistent with the rules which restrict the unjust factors of mistake and failure of basis in direct claims. A lender's 'mistaken assumption that it would obtain security'[44] is

[38] ibid [121].
[39] ibid [30] (Lord Sumption).
[40] *Re CC Automotive Group Ltd* [2019] EWHC 2771 (Ch) [59]–[82] (HH Judge Klein).
[41] *Menelaou v Bank of Cyprus UK Ltd* [2015] UKSC 66, [2016] AC 176 [21]–[22] (citations omitted). For the facts, see ch 2, s V(B) above.
[42] W Swadling, 'In Defence of Formalism' in A Robertson and J Goudkamp (eds), *Form and Substance in the Law of Obligations* (Oxford, Hart Publishing, 2019) 116–17.
[43] G Virgo, 'Restitution and Unjust Enrichment in the Supreme Court: Reflections on *Bank of Cyprus UK Ltd v Menelaou*' University of Cambridge Faculty of Law Research Paper No 10/2016, ssrn.com/abstract=2724024, 11–12.
[44] *Menelaou* (n 41) [21] (Lord Clarke).

a misprediction about the future and so would not operate as an unjust factor in a direct claim. Furthermore, a lender's 'mistaken assumption that it would obtain security'[45] is not enough to establish the unjust factor of failure of basis. That C's payment was conditional must be shared with D. Some authorities say that C's basis must be communicated to D[46] whereas others go further and require D to agree to C's basis.[47] In *Menelaou*, D 'was not aware of [C's] intention to take any charge over Great Oak Court'[48] and so this condition had not been communicated to C, still less agreed to by her. Accordingly, Lord Clarke's suggestion that the unjust factor was C's 'mistaken assumption that it would obtain security' is inconsistent with the rules applicable to the unjust factors of failure of basis and mistake. By contrast, it accords with Lord Sumption's unjust factor: 'the defeat of an expectation of benefit'.[49]

Mitchell identifies a mistake about the present which could have served as the unjust factor in a direct claim: C 'mistakenly believed at the time when it released the charges on [Rush Green Hall] that D was aware of her parents' arrangements, and was willing to grant [C] a new charge over [Great Oak Court]'.[50] Thus, the result of *Menelaou* is consistent with the rules applicable to the unjust factors of failure of basis and mistake, even though Lord Clarke's unjust factor reasoning is not.

The same can be said of *Filby v Mortgage Express (No 2) Ltd*.[51] Mr and Mrs Filby owned a house, subject to X's mortgage. Mr Filby remortgaged the property with C, forging Mrs Filby's signature. This forgery meant that Mrs Filby was not bound by C's mortgage. However, May LJ, giving the judgment of the Court of Appeal, held that C was subrogated to X's extinguished personal rights against Mrs Filby.

May LJ said that the unjust factor was that C 'mistakenly believed that their advance was to be secured by a first legal charge'.[52] Just as in *Menelaou*, this is a misprediction of the future, so would not establish the unjust factor of mistake in a direct claim. But this reasoning fits with Lord Sumption's unjust factor: 'the defeat of an expectation of benefit'.[53]

[45] ibid (Lord Clarke).
[46] *Burgess v Rawnsley* [1975] Ch 429 (CA) 442C (Browne LJ); *Giedo van Der Garde BV v Force India Formula One Team Ltd* [2010] EWHC 2373 (QB) [286] (Stadlen J); *Lissack v Manhattan Loft Corp Ltd* [2013] EWHC 128 (Ch) [88] (Roth J).
[47] *Barnes* (n 8) [106], [115] (Lord Toulson); *Spaul v Spaul* [2014] EWCA Civ 679 [46]–[47] (Rimer LJ); *Swynson* (n 1) [30] (Lord Sumption).
[48] *Menelaou* (n 41) [5] (Lord Clarke).
[49] *Swynson* (n 1) [30].
[50] C Mitchell, 'Current Issues in Unjust Enrichment: The "Time Value" of Money and Proprietary Remedies for Failure of Basis' (2017) ssrn.com/abstract=3055715, 10.
[51] *Filby v Mortgage Express (No 2) Ltd* [2004] EWCA Civ 759.
[52] ibid [48].
[53] *Swynson* (n 1) [30].

Once again, Mitchell and Watterson identify a mistake about the past which could have served as the unjust factor in a direct claim: 'unknown to [C], the consent of [Mrs Filby] … was forged'.[54] Like *Menelaou*, then, the result fits the rules applicable to the unjust factor of mistake, even if the Court's reasoning does not.

Defeated expectations also feature in the House of Lords' reasoning in *BFC*.[55] Some passages suggest that the unjust factor was a mistake about present facts: C mistakenly believed that Mr Herzig had authority to bind OOL to the postponement letter.[56] But other passages suggest that the unjust factor was a defeated expectation about the future: C expected that OOL would become bound by the postponement letter. For instance, Lord Steyn said that:

> [C] expected that they would obtain a form of security sufficient to postpone repayment of loans by [OOL] until repayment of [C]'s loan. … Restitutionary liability is triggered by a range of unjust factors or grounds of restitution. Defeated bilateral expectations are a prime source of such liability. But sometimes unilateral defeated expectations may be sufficient.[57]

Similarly, Lord Hoffmann explained that the unjust factor was that C 'advanced the [loan] upon the mistaken assumption that it was obtaining a postponement letter'.[58] Lord Hutton said that C was entitled to subrogation because it '*expected* to receive the form of security constituted by the postponement of the demands of OOL'.[59]

Walton J's classic statement in *Burston Finance* also refers to defeated expectations: 'subrogation … finds one of its chief uses in the situation where [C] advances money on the understanding that he is to have certain security for the money he has advanced, and, for one reason or another, he does not receive the promised security'.[60]

[54] Mitchell and Watterson (n 2) para 6.59. The authors also suggest failure of basis: para 6.82. However, like D in *Menelaou*, Mrs Filby was unaware of the transaction so did not share C's basis: *Filby* (n 51) [10] (May LJ).

[55] *BFC* (n 6). For the facts, see ch 2, s V(A) above.

[56] ibid 227E (Lord Steyn), 234G–35A (Lord Hoffmann).

[57] ibid 227D–F.

[58] ibid 234G.

[59] ibid 245H (emphasis added).

[60] *Burston Finance Ltd v Speirway Ltd* [1974] 1 WLR 1648 (Ch) 1652C approved *BFC* (n 6) 245C–D (Lord Hutton); *Appleyard* (n 16) [25] (Neuberger LJ); *Halifax Plc v Omar* [2002] EWCA Civ 121, [2002] 2 P&CR 26 [79]–[80] (Jonathan Parker LJ); *Filby* (n 51) [11] (May LJ); *Menelaou v Bank of Cyprus Plc* [2013] EWCA Civ 1960, [2014] 1 WLR 854 [16] (Floyd LJ); *Menelaou* (n 41) [111] (Lord Carnwath). See also *Eagle Star Insurance Co Ltd v Karasiewicz* [2002] EWCA Civ 940 [19] (Arden LJ).

In sum, the reasoning of previous cases supports Lord Sumption's suggestion that defeated unilateral expectations about the future can serve as the unjust factor for subrogation.

V. Results

Furthermore, there are some cases in which subrogation succeeded, even though it was difficult to establish the unjust factor of mistake or failure of basis. These cases do not seem to be governed by the rules which restrict the unjust factors of mistake and failure of basis in direct claims, but they are consistent with Lord Sumption's suggestion that a defeated unilateral expectation about the future can serve as the unjust factor.

A. *Reversion Fund and Insurance Co Ltd v Maison Cosway Ltd*

Hedley identifies *Reversion Fund* as an example.[61] The managing director of D, without authority, borrowed money from C on D's behalf. He used the loan monies to discharge D's debt to X. C knew that the managing director had no authority to borrow on D's behalf, but expected D to subsequently ratify the transaction. D never did. Some time later, C sought to recover the money from D. Given that D had not authorised the loan, D was not contractually obliged to repay it. Nevertheless, a majority of the Court of Appeal held that C acquired new rights against D with the same content as X's extinguished rights against D.[62]

C made no mistake here: C knew that the managing director had no authority to borrow on D's behalf.[63] C's expectation that D would later ratify the loan was a misprediction of the future, not a mistake as to the past or present.[64]

[61] S Hedley, *Restitution: Its Division and Ordering* (London, Sweet & Maxwell, 2001) 138, 140 citing *Reversion Fund and Insurance Co Ltd v Maison Cosway Ltd* [1913] 1 KB 364 (CA).

[62] The Court rejected the language of subrogation: ibid 377–80, 382 (Buckley LJ), 383 (Kennedy LJ). However, this reasoning is no longer persuasive and the case is best understood as an example of subrogation: see pages 135–136 below.

[63] C Mitchell, *The Law of Subrogation* (Oxford, Clarendon Press, 1994) 134–35, who therefore concludes that the case was wrongly decided and Vaughan Williams LJ's dissent is to be preferred. However, the majority decision was applied in *Rolled Steel Products (Holdings) Ltd v British Steel Corp* [1986] 1 Ch 246 (CA) 300A–D (Slade LJ), 307F (Browne-Wilkinson LJ), cf 302B (Slade LJ).

[64] Mitchell and Watterson (n 2) para 6.63.

Mitchell and Watterson argue that there was a failure of basis: C only advanced the money on the basis that D would be obliged to repay it and that basis failed.[65] However, there are difficulties in establishing that this basis was shared with D. On the one hand, if failure of basis only requires D to have knowledge of C's basis, then there may have been a failure of basis. Even though the managing director had no authority to contract on D's behalf, his knowledge of C's basis may be attributable to D.[66] On the other hand, if failure of basis requires D to agree to the basis, then it seems unlikely that there was a failure of basis. The managing director was unauthorised to contract on D's behalf, so it seems unlikely that he was authorised to non-contractually agree to C's basis on D's behalf.

In *Reversion Fund*, the Court awarded subrogation, assigning no importance to these difficulties in establishing the unjust factors of mistake or failure of basis. By contrast, this result is consistent with Lord Sumption's suggestion that defeated unilateral expectations about the future can render an enrichment unjust for the purposes of subrogation. The basis of C's consent to paying the loan monies was his defeated expectation that D would subsequently ratify the loan and become contractually obliged to repay it.

B. *National Westminster Bank Plc v Mayfair Estates Property Investments Ltd*

The difficulties in establishing the unjust factor of failure of basis have been magnified by another development. As Chapter 3 explained, *BFC* established that subrogation can reverse two enrichments.[67] Subrogation reverses D's primary enrichment: the release of D's duties and liabilities to X. Subrogation also reverses the secondary enrichment of D's junior creditors, whose security increases in value when X's senior security is discharged. For instance, in *BFC*, subrogation reversed OOL's secondary enrichment: the increase in value of OOL's second charge, following C mistakenly paying off part of X's first charge.[68]

In other cases, however, it is difficult to establish the unjust factors of mistake or failure of basis to render a secondary enrichment unjust. One illustration is

[65] ibid para 6.59 fn 100, para 6.82.

[66] *Meridian Global Funds Management Asia Ltd v Securities Commission* [1995] 2 AC 500 (PC); *Bilta (UK) Ltd v Nazir (No 2)* [2015] UKSC 23, [2016] AC 1.

[67] *BFC* (n 6); *Swynson* (n 1) [57] (Lord Mance); Mitchell and Watterson (n 2) ch 4 esp para 4.08; Burrows, *Restatement* (n 2) 174–75; Mitchell, Mitchell, and Watterson (n 3) para 39-27.

[68] ibid.

National Westminster Bank Plc v Mayfair Estates Property Investments Ltd.[69] There, D owned property, subject to X's first charge and Mayfair's second charge. C then made a loan to D, which was used to partially pay off X's charge. In exchange, D granted C a third charge. On the same day as the loan, C, D, and X entered into a 'Deed of Priority' under which C's charge 'shall rank in priority to' X's charge. The following year, C asked Mayfair to enter a similar Deed of Priority, giving C's charge priority over Mayfair's, but Mayfair refused.[70] Subsequently, the property was sold, but the proceeds were insufficient to satisfy all three charges. A priority dispute therefore arose between C and Mayfair.

The judge stated that Mayfair 'was not a party to the Deed of Priority and so was not bound by it in any way'.[71] However, C's loan had been used to partially pay off X's first charge, increasing the value of Mayfair's second charge. The judge said that 'this is just the sort of uncovenanted benefit to a second mortgagee that the equitable doctrine of subrogation is intended to counteract'.[72] Consequently, insofar as C's loan discharged X's first charge, C was entitled to be subrogated to X's first charge, giving it priority over Mayfair's second charge.[73] In other words, subrogation would have reversed Mayfair's secondary enrichment: the increase in value to Mayfair's second charge, caused by the partial discharge of X's first charge. However, the judge was unable to make an order to this effect, since the matter was res judicata.[74]

The judge did not consider what unjust factor rendered Mayfair's secondary enrichment unjust. It would have been difficult to establish the unjust factor of either mistake or failure of basis.

Turning first to mistake, C understood that Mayfair was not a party to the Deed of Priority and so was not bound by it.[75] Thus, it cannot be said that C had a mistaken belief that the Deed gave its charge priority over Mayfair's. C may have made its loan under the mistaken belief that its charge would rank first in priority. But that would be a misprediction as to the future, not an actionable mistake as to the past or present. Perhaps C mistakenly thought the law was such that,

[69] *National Westminster Bank Plc v Mayfair Estates Property Investments Ltd* [2007] EWHC 287 (Ch).
[70] ibid [18] (Sir Donald Rattee).
[71] ibid [4] (Sir Donald Rattee).
[72] ibid [24] (Sir Donald Rattee).
[73] ibid [24], [27] (Sir Donald Rattee).
[74] ibid [32] (Sir Donald Rattee).
[75] ibid [13] (Sir Donald Rattee).

if the transaction went ahead as planned, the law would give its charge priority over Mayfair's. However, there is no evidence of this mistaken belief.[76] Indeed, C initially accepted that its charge lacked priority over Mayfair's and only raised subrogation 'at a very late stage' in proceedings.[77]

As for failure of basis, the judge said that 'the bargain [C] intended to make … was that it should rank first in order of priority'.[78] However, it was difficult to establish that this basis was shared with Mayfair. If failure of basis requires agreement, Mayfair certainly did not agree that C's charge should have priority over its own. Even if failure of basis only requires knowledge of C's basis, it is unclear whether Mayfair was aware of the basis on which C acted, especially at the time when Mayfair was enriched. C only asked Mayfair to enter a Deed of Priority some six months after C's loan and the partial discharge of X's charge.[79]

To sum up, in *Mayfair*, the judge stated that, if the matter were not res judicata, C would have been entitled to subrogation to reverse Mayfair's secondary enrichment. However, it would have been difficult to use the unjust factors of mistake or failure of basis to render Mayfair's secondary enrichment unjust. By contrast, this result is again consistent with Lord Sumption's suggestion that defeated unilateral expectations about the future can render an enrichment unjust for the purposes of subrogation. The basis of C's consent to paying the loan monies was its defeated expectation that its charge would rank first in priority.

C. *Anfield (UK) Ltd v Bank of Scotland Plc*

A similar example concerning a secondary enrichment is *Anfield*.[80] To repeat the facts, D owned property, subject to X's first legal charge. C made a loan to D, who used it to redeem X's charge. In return, C acquired a new charge ('the 2006 charge') but failed to register it. Subsequently, Anfield obtained a charging order over the property and registered it, gaining priority over C's 2006 charge. However,

[76] cf *Nurdin & Peacock Plc v DB Ramsden & Co Ltd* [1999] 1 WLR 1249 (Ch), where C's mistake of law was induced by the advice of its solicitors, and so there was evidence of C's mistake: 1254D–F, 1256B (Neuberger J).

[77] *Mayfair* (n 69) [11]–[12] (Sir Donald Rattee).

[78] ibid [24] (Sir Donald Rattee). See also [26] (Sir Donald Rattee).

[79] ibid [2], [18] (Sir Donald Rattee).

[80] *Anfield (UK) Ltd v Bank of Scotland Plc* [2010] EWHC 2374 (Ch), [2011] 1 WLR 2414.

Proudman J held that C was entitled to be subrogated to X's extinguished charge, which had priority over Anfield's charge.

Mitchell, Mitchell, and Watterson take issue with the court's assumption that C's subrogated rights had priority over Anfield's registered charge.[81] However, the authors do not question that C was entitled to subrogation.

In reaching this conclusion, Proudman J treated subrogation as a remedy for unjust enrichment.[82] She said that Anfield was enriched because '[i]ntermediate lenders are necessarily enriched by the discharge of a prior security.'[83] She said this enrichment was 'unjust because [C] funded the repayment of the Halifax charge on the basis that it would obtain a legal charge. Because of the failure to register under the Land Registration Act 2002 it obtained only a subsequent equitable charge.'[84]

However, just like *Mayfair*, it is difficult to satisfy the rule that the basis must be shared with party whose unjust enrichment is being reversed. Anfield did not agree that C should obtain a legal charge. And, given that C's 2006 charge was not on the register, Anfield was likely unaware of C's loan and that C had made its loan on condition that it obtained a legal charge.

Nor can the unjust factor be recast as a mistake. C's expectation that it would obtain a legal charge was a misprediction of the future, not an actionable mistake about the past or present.

By contrast, the result and reasoning of *Anfield* is consistent with Lord Sumption's suggestion that defeated unilateral expectations about the future can render an enrichment unjust for the purposes of subrogation. Proudman J said that 'the factor that renders the enrichment unjust is the non-fulfilment of the lender's expectation as to the security, forming the basis of its decision to advance funds'.[85]

In short, it is often said that: (i) subrogation can be justified by reversing unjust secondary enrichments, and (ii) subrogation and direct claims are governed by the same rules and so subrogation is subject to the limits on the unjust factors of mistake and failure of basis. *Mayfair* and *Anfield* show that these two propositions

[81] S Watterson, 'Subrogation, Priority Disputes and Rectification: Mapping a Route Through the Thicket' [2016] *RLR* 1; Mitchell, Mitchell and Watterson (n 3) paras 39-97–39-104.

[82] *Anfield* (n 80) [10] (Proudman J).

[83] ibid [11] (Proudman J).

[84] ibid [36] (Proudman J).

[85] ibid [34] (Proudman J). See also [12].

are inconsistent, and so it is impossible to maintain both of them. Indeed, this book argues that subrogation is not a remedy for unjust enrichment and so both propositions are incorrect.

VI. Chapter Summary

In subrogation cases, C's defeated unilateral expectation about the future can render an enrichment unjust. In a direct claim, this is not so. Consequently, subrogation is available when a direct claim is not; subrogation does not duplicate a direct claim and subrogation is not redundant.

6

Defences

I. Introduction

This chapter argues that it is unclear whether subrogation and direct claims are susceptible to different defences. Section II shows that many direct unjust enrichment claims are susceptible to the change of position defence. Sections III and IV then show that there is no clear authority for the defence applying to subrogation.

II. Direct Claims

The change of position defence applies 'where an innocent [D]'s position is so changed that … the injustice of requiring him … to repay outweighs the injustice of denying [C] restitution'.[1] It is a pro tanto defence, in that D's duty to make restitution is reduced only to the extent that D has changed its position.[2] The change of position must be 'causally linked (at least on a "but for" test)' to D's enrichment.[3] The 'defence is not open to one who has changed his position in bad faith, as where [D] has paid away the money with knowledge of the facts entitling [C] to restitution'.[4]

It is sometimes said that all direct unjust enrichment claims are susceptible to the change of position defence. For example, in *Haugesund Kommune v Depfa ACS Bank*, Aikens LJ said that 'the defence of change of position is a general defence to all restitution claims (for money or other property) based on unjust enrichment'.[5]

[1] *Lipkin Gorman v Karpnale Ltd* [1991] 2 AC 548 (HL) 579F (Lord Goff).
[2] ibid 579G (Lord Goff).
[3] *Scottish Equitable Plc v Derby* [2001] EWCA Civ 369, [2001] 3 All ER 818 [31] (Robert Walker LJ).
[4] *Lipkin Gorman* (n 1) 580C (Lord Goff).
[5] *Haugesund Kommune v Depfa ACS Bank* [2010] EWCA Civ 579, [2012] QB 549 [122]. See also P Birks, 'Misnomer' in WR Cornish and others (eds), *Restitution Past, Present and Future: Essays in Honour of Gareth Jones* (Oxford, Hart Publishing, 1998) 24.

Burrows' textbook endorses this.[6] In the same vein, Mitchell, Mitchell, and Watterson state that change of position may 'defeat or limit any cause of action in unjust enrichment'.[7]

However, there is now authority establishing that the defence does not apply to *Woolwich* claims.[8] Despite their statements in the previous paragraph, Burrows and Mitchell, Mitchell, and Watterson suggest that there are other direct claims to which the defence does not apply.[9] At best, then, most direct claims are susceptible to the change of position defence. Thus, even if there is no authority for change of position applying to subrogation, this only proves that subrogation and most direct claims are susceptible to different defences.

III. Primary Enrichee

Mitchell, Mitchell, and Watterson state that:

> As an equitable remedy designed to reverse unjust enrichment, a [subrogation] claim … may be defeated or limited by any defence or bar that will defeat or limit any cause of action in unjust enrichment. These include [the defence] of change of position ….[10]

The authors suggest that change of position may operate as a defence for the primary enrichee (D) or for recipients of secondary enrichments.[11]

This chapter shows that there is no clear authority for the application of this change of position defence to subrogation. This section considers the primary enrichee, while the following section considers secondary enrichees.

Some cases explicitly state that the primary enrichee can raise change of position as a defence to subrogation.[12] However, most of these statements are obiter

[6] A Burrows, *The Law of Restitution* (Oxford, OUP, 2011) 544–45.

[7] C Mitchell, P Mitchell and S Watterson, *Goff and Jones: The Law of Unjust Enrichment* (London, Sweet & Maxwell, 2022) para 39-38. See also C Mitchell and S Watterson, *Subrogation: Law and Practice* (Oxford, OUP, 2007) para 7.68; S Watterson, 'Modelling Subrogation as an "Equitable Remedy"' (2016) 2 *CJCCL* 609, 619, 671.

[8] *Test Claimants in the FII Group Litigation v Revenue and Customs Commissioners* [2014] EWHC 4302 (Ch) [309]–[315] (Henderson J).

[9] Burrows, *Restitution* (n 6) 550; A Burrows, *A Restatement of the English Law of Unjust Enrichment* (Oxford, OUP, 2012) 122; Mitchell, Mitchell and Watterson (n 7) paras 27-64–27-83. See also G Virgo, *The Principles of the Law of Restitution* (Oxford, OUP, 2015) 695.

[10] Mitchell, Mitchell and Watterson (n 7) para 39-38. See also Mitchell and Watterson (n 7) para 7.69; Watterson (n 7) 619, 671.

[11] Mitchell and Watterson (n 7) para 7.69; Mitchell, Mitchell and Watterson (n 7) para 39-39.

[12] *Boscawen v Bajwa* [1996] 1 WLR 328 (CA) 341C–E (Millett LJ); *Niru Battery Manufacturing Co v Milestone Trading Ltd (No 2)* [2004] EWCA Civ 487, [2004] 1 CLC 882 [37], [60] (Clarke LJ); *Barons*

and so not authoritative. In fact, it seems that there are only two subrogation cases which, as part of their ratio, allow the primary enrichee the defence: *Re Diplock*,[13] an English case, and *Gertsch v Atsas*,[14] a case from New South Wales. These two cases will be considered in turn.

A. *Re Diplock*

In *Re Diplock*, a payment was made to D under a will. D used some of the money to pay off a charge over its property.[15] The will was then found to be invalid. C, the judicial trustee of the deceased's estate, sought to recover the money paid to D.

The Court of Appeal held that C was not entitled to be subrogated to the extinguished charge.[16] The Court's reasoning is difficult to follow.[17] In *Boscawen*, Millett LJ explained the result on the basis that D had changed its position. D 'had in all innocence used the money to redeem a mortgage held by its bank, which, no doubt, was willing to allow its advance to remain outstanding indefinitely', whereas C would enforce the subrogated charge and force the property to be sold.[18]

However, there are two reasons why *Re Diplock* is not a clear authority for change of position being a defence to subrogation. First, the judgment in *Re Diplock* did not use the language of change of position. Instead, this is an ex-post rationalisation of the result.

Second, in *Boscawen* Millett LJ conceded that change of position was not an entirely satisfactory explanation of *Re Diplock*. The defence 'did not require the withholding of any remedy [the result in *Re Diplock*], but only that the charge by subrogation should not be enforceable until [D] had had a reasonable opportunity to obtain a fresh advance on suitable terms from a willing lender'.[19]

As a result, *Re Diplock* is not compelling authority for the proposition that change of position is a defence to subrogation.

Finance Ltd v Kensington Mortgage Co Ltd [2011] EWCA Civ 1592 [28] (Tomlinson LJ); *Menelaou v Bank of Cyprus UK Ltd* [2015] UKSC 66, [2016] AC 176 [36] (Lord Clarke).

[13] *Re Diplock* [1948] 1 Ch 465 (CA).

[14] *Gertsch v Atsas* [1999] NSWSC 898.

[15] *Re Diplock* (n 13) 548 (Lord Greene MR, Wrottesley and Evershed LJJ).

[16] ibid 549–50 (Lord Greene MR, Wrottesley and Evershed LJJ).

[17] *Boscawen* (n 12) 340G–41B (Millett LJ). See also P Birks, *An Introduction to the Law of Restitution* (Oxford, Clarendon Press, 1989) 374–75.

[18] *Boscawen* (n 12) 341C–D. See also A Tettenborn, *The Law of Restitution in England and Ireland* (London, Cavendish, 2002) para 2-27.

[19] *Boscawen* (n 12) 341D (Millett LJ).

B. *Gertsch v Atsas*

In *Gertsch*, D received a legacy of AU$100,000 under a will.[20] The will was then shown to be a forgery. C, the executor and sole beneficiary of the deceased's intestate estate, sought to recover the legacy from D. Giving the judgment of the Supreme Court of New South Wales, Foster AJ held that D was liable to make restitution of her unjust enrichment.

However, D had been unaware that the will was a forgery and had spent the legacy. D had used AU$69,000 of the legacy to pay off her mortgage.[21] Prima facie, therefore, C was subrogated to the extinguished AU$69,000 charge.

Foster AJ, however, held 'that it is reasonable to regard [C's subrogation claim] … as being comprehended within claims relating to "unjust enrichment" and as being susceptible to defences appropriate to such claims'.[22] As a result, the defence of change of position was available to D.[23]

C argued that using the legacy to pay off the mortgage did not afford D a change of position defence, since D benefited from not having to repay the mortgage using her own funds.[24] Foster AJ rejected that argument. D had no funds with which to repay the legacy. To repay, she would have to sell her home, leaving her in financial hardship and with little money to find alternative accommodation. In these circumstances, paying off the mortgage amounted to a change of position.[25]

Had D not received the legacy, she would have only have paid off AU$10,000 of the mortgage. Thus, by paying off the whole AU$69,000 mortgage, she had changed her position to the extent of AU$59,000.[26] Consequently, AU$10,000 'represent[ed] the amount of her unjust enrichment'[27] and she was obliged to repay this sum.[28] Furthermore, Foster AJ held that C could be subrogated to the discharged mortgage and so he could make an order charging AU$10,000 (plus interest) upon D's home.

Gertsch is the strongest authority for change of position being a defence to subrogation. Nevertheless, an English court would not be bound to follow this

[20] *Gertsch* (n 14).
[21] ibid [16].
[22] ibid [22].
[23] ibid [22]–[23].
[24] ibid [95].
[25] ibid [90]–[92], [94]–[99].
[26] ibid [98].
[27] ibid.
[28] ibid [99].

decision of the Supreme Court of New South Wales. In fact, *Gertsch* may no longer be authoritative even in New South Wales. Foster AJ's conclusion that change of position was a defence to subrogation relied on the premiss that 'it is reasonable to regard [C's subrogation claim] … as being comprehended within claims relating to "unjust enrichment"'.[29] But ten years after *Gertsch* was decided, the High Court of Australia rejected this premiss.[30]

Furthermore, the discussion of change of position in *Gertsch* may have been obiter. Foster AJ's order was for monetary restitution.[31] He considered that subrogation allowed him to make a charging order and that change of position modified the quantum of that order. However, he did not actually make the charging order, instead granting C 'liberty to apply on 7 days' notice to seek [such] an order'.[32] Arguably, then, the application of change of position to subrogation was obiter.

To summarise, at least in England, there is no compelling authority for change of position being available as a defence to subrogation for the primary enrichee.

IV. Secondary Enrichees

Mitchell and Watterson also say that recipients of a secondary enrichment can raise the change of position defence:

> An example is where a junior secured creditor can make out the defence, on the basis that he made further advances in the belief that [X's] senior charge to which [C] seeks to be subrogated has been extinguished. In such cases, the most proportionate response in practice might be for the court to hold that [C]'s [subrogated] charge has priority to the junior chargee's claims only to the extent of the junior creditor's original advance. The further advance, made on the faith of the apparent discharge of [X's] senior charge, would have priority over [C]'s [subrogated] charge.[33]

There is, however, no clear authority allowing recipients of a secondary enrichment the defence.

[29] ibid [22]–[23].

[30] *Bofinger v Kingsway Group Ltd* [2009] HCA 44, (2009) 239 CLR 269 [90]–[98] (Gummow, Hayne, Heydon, Kiefel, and Bell JJ).

[31] *Gertsch* (n 14) [99], [144].

[32] ibid [100], [144].

[33] Mitchell and Watterson (n 7) para 7.85. See also paras 7.69, 7.78; Mitchell, Mitchell and Watterson (n 7) para 39-39.

A. *Redman v Rymer*

Mitchell and Watterson cite *Redman v Rymer* as an 'early English case which shows that the courts are sensitive to changes of position by' secondary enrichees.[34] The facts were complex, but at their simplest they were that a father's property was subject to X's £2000 mortgage. The father died and his will charged his estate with a legacy for his daughters. The father's sons and heirs, D, borrowed money from C and used it to discharge X's mortgage. To secure the loan, D purported to mortgage the property to C, with priority over the daughters' charge. A priority dispute then arose between C and the daughters.

Kekewich J held that D lacked the authority to give C priority over the daughters' charge. Prima facie, then, the daughters had priority over C. However, C's loan had been used to discharge X's £2000 mortgage so C was subrogated to this discharged mortgage. C therefore had priority over the daughters to the extent of £2000.

Kekewich J suggested that had the daughters 'made an advance or made a purchase on the faith of [X's £2000 mortgage] being paid off', C would not have been subrogated to X's mortgage.[35] Mitchell and Watterson interpret this as a recognition of the change of position defence for secondary enrichees (here, the daughters).[36] However, this was obiter: on the facts the daughters had not changed their position so had no defence.[37]

B. *Anfield (UK) Ltd v Bank of Scotland Plc*

The only other English recognition of change of position as a defence for recipients of a secondary enrichment came in *Anfield*.[38] Proudman J recognised that 'there may potentially be harm to third party lenders who can demonstrate reliance on the register' and that this might activate the 'change of position defence'.[39] She went on to say that 'any unfair consequences of subrogation can be dealt with by way of a defence founded on change of position'.[40] Again, however, this

[34] Mitchell and Watterson (n 7) para 7.71 citing *Redman v Rymer* (1889) 60 LT 385 (Ch).
[35] ibid 388.
[36] Mitchell and Watterson (n 7) paras 7.71–7.72.
[37] *Redman* (n 34) 388 (Kekewich J).
[38] *Anfield (UK) Ltd v Bank of Scotland Plc* [2010] EWHC 2374 (Ch), [2011] 1 WLR 2414. For the facts, see ch 4, s III(D)(i) above.
[39] ibid [31].
[40] ibid [38].

was obiter: the possibility of Anfield having a change of position defence was not raised.

V. Chapter Summary

This chapter showed that it is unclear whether direct claims and subrogation are subject to the same defences. Some direct claims are susceptible to a change of position defence. However, there is no clear authority for the defence applying to subrogation.

7

Effect

I. Introduction

This chapter argues that subrogation has a different effect compared to direct unjust enrichment claims. Section II shows that direct claims reverse a transaction whereas subrogation does not. Section III rebuts four objections to this argument. Accordingly, subrogation does not duplicate a direct claim and so subrogation is not redundant.

II. Reversing a Transaction

In *Swynson*, Lord Sumption stated that:

> the law of unjust enrichment is generally concerned to restore the parties to a normatively defective transfer to their pre-transfer position. Subrogation, however, does not restore the parties to their pre-transfer position.[1]

This can be illustrated by contrasting the cases of *Barclays Bank Ltd v WJ Simms Son & Cooke (Southern) Ltd*[2] and *B Liggett (Liverpool) Ltd v Barclays Bank Ltd*.[3]

[1] *Swynson Ltd v Lowick Rose LLP* [2017] UKSC 32, [2018] AC 313 [30]. See also *Challenger Managed Investments Ltd v Direct Money Corp Pty Ltd* [2003] NSWSC 1072 [50] (Bryson J); *Bofinger v Kingsway Group Ltd* [2009] HCA 44, (2009) 239 CLR 269 [97] (Gummow, Hayne, Heydon, Kiefel, and Bell JJ); *Investment Trust Companies v Revenue and Customs Commissioners* [2017] UKSC 29, [2018] AC 275 ('*ITC*') [42], [49] (Lord Reed); L Smith, 'Defences and the Disunity of Unjust Enrichment' in A Dyson, J Goudkamp and F Wilmot-Smith (eds), *Defences in Unjust Enrichment* (Oxford, Hart Publishing, 2016) 51; TRS Cutts, 'Modern Money Had and Received' (2018) 38 *OJLS* 1, 23; L Smith, 'Restitution: A New Start?' in P Devonshire and R Havelock (eds), *The Impact of Equity and Restitution in Commerce* (Oxford, Hart Publishing, 2019) 107–08.

[2] *Barclays Bank Ltd v WJ Simms Son & Cooke (Southern) Ltd* [1980] QB 677 (QB).

[3] *B Liggett (Liverpool) Ltd v Barclays Bank Ltd* [1928] 1 KB 48 (KB).

In *Simms*, the Royal British Legion Housing Association Ltd had an account with Barclays Bank.[4] Barclays mistakenly thought that it had authority to pay the company's debt to a creditor. In fact, Barclays paid the creditor without authority.

Robert Goff J reversed the transaction. He held that Barclays' payment had not discharged the company's debt to the creditor[5] and that Barclays had a direct claim against the creditor to recover its payment.

Compare the earlier case of *Liggett*, where B Liggett (Liverpool) Ltd had an account with Barclays Bank.[6] Barclays mistakenly thought that it had authority to pay the company's debts to creditors. In fact, Barclays paid the creditors without authority.

The facts of *Simms* and *Liggett* were therefore virtually indistinguishable; even the bank was the same. The law could have responded to the facts of *Liggett* in the same way as the facts of *Simms*. The court could have reversed the transaction by holding that the debts were not discharged and that Barclays had direct claims against the creditors to recover its payments.[7]

However, that was not how *Liggett* was decided. Wright J held that Barclays' payments discharged the company's debts and that Barclays was subrogated to the creditors' extinguished rights against the company.[8]

Simms and *Liggett* therefore represent two different ways in which the law can respond to the same facts. In *Simms*, the direct claim reversed the transaction by having the creditor repay Barclays. By contrast, in *Liggett*, the court upheld the transactions by holding that they were effective in discharging the company's debts, and instead subrogation gave Barclays rights against the company. While direct claims reverse transactions, subrogation does not. Subrogation therefore has a different effect to direct claims; subrogation does not duplicate direct claims and so subrogation is not redundant.

III. Objections

One might object to this argument in four ways.

1. *Simms* and *Liggett* can be distinguished.

[4] *Simms* (n 2).

[5] See also *Crantrave Ltd v Lloyds Bank Plc* [2000] QB 917 (CA) criticised by A Burrows, *The Law of Restitution* (Oxford, OUP, 2011) 159.

[6] *Liggett* (n 3).

[7] *Challenger* (n 1) [50] (Bryson J); *Bofinger* (n 1) [97] (Gummow, Hayne, Heydon, Kiefel, and Bell JJ); D Friedmann, 'Payment of Another's Debt' (1983) 99 *LQR* 534, 554–56; Smith, 'Restitution' (n 1) 107.

[8] *Liggett* (n 3) 64.

2. *Simms* and *Liggett* are inconsistent.
3. Direct claims and subrogation both reverse an enrichment so subrogation is redundant.
4. Direct claims and subrogation are both restitutionary so subrogation is redundant.

Each objection will be rejected in turn.

First, the cases are often distinguished on the basis that the payments in *Liggett* discharged the company's debts whereas in *Simms* the payment did not.[9] One might argue that this distinction, and not the difference between subrogation and direct claims, explains why the cases had different results.

However, whether or not a debt is discharged is not an immutable fact. Rather, the law must make a choice about if and when a mistaken payment of another's debt discharges that debt.[10] It is true that the debt was discharged in *Liggett* and not in *Simms*. But this is part of the way in which the law has a different effect in direct claim cases compared to subrogation cases, and so is part of the reason why subrogation is not redundant.

Second, one might argue that *Liggett* and *Simms* are 'inconsistent': in *Liggett* Barclays' unauthorised and mistaken payment discharged its customer's debts whereas in *Simms* it did not.[11] Accordingly, one of these cases is wrongly decided.

Even if this is true, subrogation and direct claims still have different effects. *Liggett* and *Simms* have substantially the same facts so comparing these cases makes the different effect of subrogation and direct claims obvious. But other cases could be chosen to show that subrogation and direct claims have different effects.[12]

[9] *Crantrave* (n 5); C Mitchell and S Watterson, *Subrogation: Law and Practice* (Oxford, OUP, 2007) para 2.06; Burrows, *Restitution* (n 5) 159; C Mitchell, P Mitchell and S Watterson, *Goff and Jones: The Law of Unjust Enrichment* (London, Sweet & Maxwell, 2022) para 5-68.

[10] *Butler v Rice* [1910] 2 Ch 277 (Ch) 282 (Warrington J); *Liggett* (n 3); *Simms* (n 2); *Crantrave* (n 5) 923G–H (Pill LJ); *Absa Bank Ltd v Moore* [2016] ZACC 34 [33] (Cameron J); P Birks and J Beatson, 'Unrequested Payment of Another's Debt' (1976) 92 *LQR* 188, 188–202; Friedmann (n 7); P Birks, *An Introduction to the Law of Restitution* (Oxford, Clarendon Press, 1989) 189–191; J Beatson, *The Use and Abuse of Unjust Enrichment: Essays on the Law of Restitution* (Oxford, Clarendon Press, 1991) 200–05; S Hedley, *Restitution: Its Division and Ordering* (London, Sweet & Maxwell, 2001) 140–44; Mitchell and Watterson (n 9) para 2.05; Burrows, *Restitution* (n 5) 460–68; A Burrows, *A Restatement of the English Law of Unjust Enrichment* (Oxford, OUP, 2012) 100; Mitchell, Mitchell and Watterson (n 9) para 5-55.

[11] Mitchell and Watterson (n 9) para 2.06; Mitchell, Mitchell and Watterson (n 9) para 5-68.

[12] eg *Cunliffe Brooks & Co v Blackburn and District Benefit Building Society* (1884) 9 App Cas 857 (HL); *ITC* (n 1); *Prudential Assurance Co Ltd v Revenue and Customs Commissioners* [2018] UKSC 39, [2018] 3 WLR 652.

Third, it is often said that both direct claims and subrogation reverse an enrichment.[13] Even if this is true, it does not follow that subrogation is redundant. Direct claims and subrogation reverse different enrichments of different parties in different ways.

In *Simms*, the court held that the debt was not discharged. As a result, the creditor was left factually enriched by Barclays' payment. The direct claim reversed the creditor's factual enrichment by imposing a duty on the creditor to repay Barclays.

By contrast, in *Liggett* the court held that the debts were discharged. In effect, the creditors exchanged their rights against the company for Barclays' payments and so the creditors were not enriched.[14] Instead, it was the company that was enriched: it was released from its duties to pay the creditors. Subrogation reversed that legal enrichment by imposing a duty on the company, owed to Barclays, with prima facie the same content as the duties that the company used to owe to the creditors.

As a result, it is true that both direct claims and subrogation have the effect of reversing an enrichment. But while a direct claim reverses X's factual enrichment, subrogation reverses D's legal enrichment. Thus, direct claims and subrogation reverse different enrichments of different parties in different ways. Subrogation does not have the same effect as a direct claim so subrogation is not redundant.

Finally, some say that direct claims and subrogation are both restitutionary.[15] Others object that subrogation is not restitutionary.[16] This is a barren semantic

[13] *Boscawen v Bajwa* [1996] 1 WLR 328 (CA) 335C–D (Millett LJ); *Banque Financière de La Cité SA v Parc (Battersea) Ltd* [1999] 1 AC 221 (HL) ('*BFC*') 231G–H (Lord Hoffmann); Mitchell and Watterson (n 9) chs 4, 8; Burrows, *Restitution* (n 5) 144–67; Mitchell, Mitchell and Watterson (n 9) ch 39; S Watterson, 'Modelling Subrogation as an "Equitable Remedy"' (2016) 2 *CJCCL* 609; S Watterson, 'Subrogation' in G Virgo and S Worthington (eds), *Commercial Remedies: Resolving Controversies* (Cambridge, CUP, 2017) 437–49.

[14] *Simms* (n 2) 695C–E (Robert Goff J).

[15] *BFC* (n 13) 232A–C, 234C (Lord Hoffmann); Birks (n 10) 96–97; Burrows, *Restitution* (n 5) 14–15, 439–40; AVM Lodder, *Enrichment in the Law of Unjust Enrichment and Restitution* (Oxford, Hart Publishing, 2012) 141–47; G Virgo, *The Principles of the Law of Restitution* (Oxford, OUP, 2015) 234; Watterson, 'Modelling Subrogation as an "Equitable Remedy"' (n 13) 617–18; Mitchell, Mitchell and Watterson (n 9) para 39-19.

[16] *Challenger* (n 1) [50] (Bryson J); *Bofinger* (n 1) [97] (Gummow, Hayne, Heydon, Kiefel, and Bell JJ); *ITC* (n 1) [49] (Lord Reed); J Edelman and E Bant, *Unjust Enrichment* (Oxford, Hart Publishing, 2016) 45, 50; Smith, 'Defences and the Disunity of Unjust Enrichment' (n 1) 51; Smith, 'Restitution' (n 1) 107–08.

debate. Different meanings can be given to the word 'restitution'; some of those meanings include subrogation whereas others do not. Nothing turns on this and it does not alter the point that direct claims reverse transactions whereas subrogation does not.

IV. Chapter Summary

A direct claim reverses a transaction whereas subrogation does not. Subrogation and direct claims therefore have different effects. Subrogation does not duplicate a direct claim and subrogation is not redundant.

PART III

Is Subrogation Justified?

8

Previous Attempts to Justify Subrogation

I. Introduction

Part II considered whether subrogation is redundant as a matter of authority. It showed that subrogation is available in different circumstances, and has a different effect, compared to a direct unjust enrichment claim. Accordingly, subrogation is not redundant.

Part III now turns to whether subrogation is justified as a matter of principle and, if so, when subrogation should occur and what rights it should create. This chapter clears the ground by rejecting four leading contenders for subrogation's justification: intention, unjust enrichment, unconscionability, and equity. Chapter 9 then considers the relationship between subrogation and tracing. It rejects the popular idea that subrogation has the same justification as trusts over traceably acquired rights. Chapters 10 and 11 then put forward two good justifications for subrogation.

II. Intention

Older cases justified subrogation on the basis of actual[1] or presumed[2] intention for C to acquire X's extinguished rights. Sometimes, the courts looked to C's intentions[3] whereas on other occasions they considered C and D's 'mutual intentions'.[4]

[1] *Patten v Bond* (1889) 60 LT 583 (Ch) 586 (Kay J).

[2] *Butler v Rice* [1910] 2 Ch 277 (Ch) 282–83 (Warrington J); *Ghana Commercial Bank v Chandiram* [1960] AC 732 (PC) 745 (Lord Jenkins); *Orakpo v Manson Investments Ltd* [1978] AC 95 (HL) 104G–05C (Lord Diplock).

[3] *Butler* (n 2) 282–83 (Warrington J); *Ghana Commercial Bank* (n 2) 745 (Lord Jenkins).

[4] *Orakpo* (n 2) 104G–05C (Lord Diplock); J Palmer, 'Unjust Enrichment, Proprietary Subrogation and Unsatisfactory Explanations' (2016) 28 *Singapore Academy of Law Journal* 955, para 45.

However, Mitchell and Watterson explain that if the parties want C to acquire X's rights then they can choose to transfer X's rights by assignment. Subrogation to extinguished rights is therefore 'an unnecessary complication' which parties never intend.[5] For instance, in *Butler v Rice*, Butler's actual intention was to acquire rights under a new legal mortgage.[6] It was fictional to say that Butler (C) intended to acquire rights resembling those the bank (X) had under its extinguished equitable charge.[7] Meanwhile, Mrs Rice (D) had no knowledge of Butler (C) and so no intention of Butler acquiring rights against her.[8] Thus, in *BFC*, the House of Lords rightly rejected intention as the justification for subrogation.[9]

Palmer offers a different intention-based theory. She argues that subrogation to proprietary rights is justified by D's intention to grant C a security interest.[10]

At the outset, it should be noted this does not fit the results or reasoning of the cases. For instance, Palmer treats the leading case of *Butler v Rice* as wrongly decided because in that case D had no intention of giving C rights.[11] Although some cases justify subrogation by reference to C and D's mutual intention,[12] *Boscawen* seems to be the only case which treated D's intention alone as decisive.[13]

Furthermore, Palmer's theory becomes fictitious:

> equity will not be limited only to [D's] actual or express intention. Equity requires of all parties that they act in good conscience. It may therefore deem [D] to have a certain intention. … Proprietary subrogation will also be available where equity deems [D] to have an intention to grant an interest to [C] in the particular circumstances despite [D]'s protestations. *Boscawen* is an example of this. Although [D] never intended that [C] would have a charge on his property had the transaction as planned been implemented, in the circumstances that did occur, [D] must in good conscience be taken to have intended to grant a security to [C]. [D] could not intend both to have the property unencumbered and the debt discharged. Again, the extinguished security interest of [X] serves as a useful evidential proxy for what [D] should have agreed to give [C].[14]

[5] C Mitchell and S Watterson, *Subrogation: Law and Practice* (Oxford, OUP, 2007) para 3.01.

[6] *Butler* (n 2). For the facts, see ch 1, s I above.

[7] *Halifax Mortgage Services Ltd v Muirhead* (1998) 76 P & CR 418 (CA) 425 (Evans LJ); C Mitchell, P Mitchell and S Watterson, *Goff and Jones: The Law of Unjust Enrichment* (London, Sweet & Maxwell, 2022) para 39-07.

[8] *Banque Financière de La Cité SA v Parc (Battersea) Ltd* [1999] 1 AC 221 (HL) ('*BFC*') 231D–34D (Lord Hoffmann) citing *Butler* (n 2).

[9] *BFC* (n 8) 231D–34D (Lord Hoffmann); 241D (Lord Hutton).

[10] Palmer (n 4) paras 44–54.

[11] ibid para 53 citing *Butler* (n 2). See also N Tamblyn, 'Separating Unjust Enrichment and Subrogation' (2017) 44 *Exeter LR* 1, 19. For the facts, see ch 1, s I above.

[12] *Orakpo* (n 2) 104G–05C (Lord Diplock).

[13] *Boscawen v Bajwa* [1996] 1 WLR 328 (CA) 337F–39H (Millett LJ); Palmer (n 4) para 46.

[14] Palmer (n 4) paras 47, 52 referring to *Boscawen* (n 13). For the facts of that case, see ch 4, s III(D) above.

As Palmer herself acknowledges, deeming D to have this intention is fictional.[15] In *Boscawen*, D had no intention of giving C rights. If subrogation is justified by D's deemed intention to give C rights, then the reason for so deeming is the justification for subrogation and clothing it in the language of D's intention is misleading and unnecessary. The reason why D 'could not' in 'good conscience … intend both to have the property unencumbered and the debt discharged' is the real reason for subrogation. This reason must be sought out, rather than clothed in a fictional intention.

One might therefore amend Palmer's theory by saying that subrogation is justified only by D's actual intention to give C security. However, this still faces two problems. First, it is unclear why subrogation should allow the parties to evade any formalities which would otherwise be required for D to give C security.[16]

Second, if D's intention is what matters, and D intended to give C greater rights than X, then C should acquire those greater rights. But subrogation describes giving C rights which have prima facie the same content as X's extinguished rights.[17] Consequently, even if D intended to give C greater rights than X, X's rights limit what subrogation gives to C.[18] D's intention cannot explain this, and so it cannot justify the form of rights created by subrogation.

III. Unjust Enrichment

Instead, orthodoxy says that subrogation is a remedy for unjust enrichment. Part II showed that subrogation is governed by different rules to direct unjust enrichment claims. Nevertheless, it is conceivable that subrogation may still be a remedy for unjust enrichment in another sense: that courts faced with a subrogation claim ought to ask the four unjust enrichment questions.[19] In *ITC*, Lord Reed stated that 'the questions are not themselves legal tests, but are signposts towards areas of

[15] Palmer (n 4) para 48.

[16] Law of Property Act 1925, ss 52, 53.

[17] See ch 1 above.

[18] *Re Manchester, Middleton, and District Tramways Company* [1893] 2 Ch 638 (Ch) 655 (Kekewich J); *Nottingham Permanent Benefit Building Society v Thurstan* [1902] 1 Ch 1 (CA) affd [1903] AC 6 (HL); *Ghana Commercial Bank* (n 2); *Muirhead* (n 7).

[19] *BFC* (n 8) 234B–G (Lord Hoffmann); *Niru Battery Manufacturing Co v Milestone Trading Ltd (No 2)* [2004] EWCA Civ 487, [2004] 1 CLC 882 [56] (Clarke LJ); *Menelaou v Bank of Cyprus Plc* [2013] EWCA Civ 1960, [2014] 1 WLR 854 [27] (Floyd LJ); *Sandher v Pearson* [2013] EWCA Civ 1822 [9] (Arden LJ); *Menelaou v Bank of Cyprus UK Ltd* [2015] UKSC 66, [2016] AC 176 ('*Menelaou (SC)*') [18] (Lord Clarke); *Swynson Ltd v Lowick Rose LLP* [2017] UKSC 32, [2018] AC 313 [56] (Lord Mance), [110] (Lord Neuberger); Mitchell and Watterson (n 5) paras 3.02–3.03; A Burrows, *The Law of*

inquiry involving a number of distinct legal requirements'.[20] Consequently, even if direct claims and subrogation raise the same four questions, the rules which govern the answers to the questions need not be the same for both.[21] However, even if subrogation is only a remedy for unjust enrichment in this looser sense, unjust enrichment remains an incomplete justification for subrogation in two ways.

First, even those who argue that subrogation is a remedy for unjust enrichment concede that something more is needed to justify subrogation's creation of proprietary rights. Mitchell and Watterson explain that the advantages of proprietary rights over personal rights mean that:

> further inquiry is required before the law affords [subrogation to proprietary rights]. It is not sufficient to conclude that [D] has been unjustly enriched at the expense of [C]. … This means in turn that it should always be necessary to address the following question, distinctly and directly, in cases where [C] seeks to acquire a security interest via subrogation: is it appropriate on these facts to reverse [D]'s unjust enrichment by awarding a proprietary restitutionary remedy rather than a personal restitutionary remedy?[22]

The authors suggest that the 'authorities reveal a surprising readiness to award proprietary subrogation',[23] since proprietary subrogation is more widely available than allowed for by the leading theories on when unjust enrichment should create proprietary rights.[24]

Similarly, Burrows writes that:

> subrogation is of central importance to the continuing debate and controversy over the extent of, and justification for, proprietary restitution. … Although subrogation to

Restitution (Oxford, OUP, 2011) 145; Mitchell, Mitchell and Watterson (n 7) para 39–25; S Watterson, 'Modelling Subrogation as an "Equitable Remedy"' (2016) 2 *CJCCL* 609, 618–19, 669–70.

[20] *Investment Trust Companies v Revenue and Customs Commissioners* [2017] UKSC 29, [2018] AC 275 [41].

[21] ibid [38], [50] (Lord Reed); *Prudential Assurance Co Ltd v Revenue and Customs Commissioners* [2018] UKSC 39, [2018] 3 WLR 652 [68] (Lord Mance, Lord Reed, and Lord Hodge); Burrows, *Restitution* (n 19) 51, 70, 75–85, 153 fn 48; A Burrows, *A Restatement of the English Law of Unjust Enrichment* (Oxford, OUP, 2012) 48–52; A Burrows, '"At the Expense of the Claimant": A Fresh Look' [2017] *RLR* 167; A Burrows, 'In Defence of Unjust Enrichment' (2019) 78 *CLJ* 521, 542; S Watterson, 'At the Claimant's Expense' in E Bant, K Barker and S Degeling (eds), *Research Handbook on Unjust Enrichment and Restitution* (Cheltenham, Edward Elgar Publishing, 2020); Mitchell, Mitchell and Watterson (n 7) paras 1-12, 6-07.

[22] Mitchell and Watterson (n 5) para 8.39. See also *Menelaou* (SC) (n 19) [130]–[132] (Lord Carnwath); D Winterton, 'Unjust Enrichment and Rough Justice' [2016] *RLR* 164, 169; S Watterson, 'Subrogation' in G Virgo and S Worthington (eds), *Commercial Remedies: Resolving Controversies* (Cambridge, CUP, 2017) 464; Mitchell, Mitchell and Watterson (n 7) para 39-41.

[23] Mitchell and Watterson (n 5) para 8.46.

[24] ibid paras 8.40–8.45.

> proprietary rights … is commonplace, this is generally difficult to justify because [C] has taken the risk of [D]'s … insolvency and therefore does not appear to merit priority over unsecured creditors.[25]

Second, there is a more fundamental problem with treating unjust enrichment as a justification. Mitchell, Mitchell, and Watterson write that:

> Whatever may be the underlying moral justifications for the award of restitution in these cases, the 'unjust' element in 'unjust enrichment' is simply a 'generalisation of all the factors which the law recognises as calling for restitution'. In other words, unjust enrichment is not an abstract moral principle to which the courts refer when deciding cases …. The reasons why the courts have held [D]'s enrichment to be unjust vary from one set of cases to another ….[26]

This was approved by the Supreme Court in *Barnes v Eastenders Cash & Carry plc*.[27]

Thus, unjust enrichment is not itself a justification for subrogation. However, the various unjust factors may justify subrogation. Mitchell and Watterson write that 'secondary liability, ignorance, mistake and failure of consideration … are the grounds which can most commonly support a subrogation claim in practice'.[28] In *Swynson*, Lord Sumption suggested that subrogation is instead triggered by a unique unjust factor: 'defeat of an expectation of benefit'.[29]

However, the following sections will argue that mistake, failure of basis, and defeated expectations all fail to justify the form of rights created by subrogation. The following chapter will argue that ignorance also fails to justify subrogation.[30] Chapter 10 will argue that almost all cases of subrogation are justified by the idea which is misleadingly labelled 'secondary liability', but this has nothing to do with unjust enrichment.

[25] Burrows, *Restitution* (n 19) 147, 167. See also 149–50.

[26] Mitchell, Mitchell and Watterson (n 7) paras 1-08–1-09 (footnotes omitted). See also C Webb, 'Property, Unjust Enrichment, and Defective Transfers' in R Chambers, C Mitchell and J Penner (eds), *Philosophical Foundations of the Law of Unjust Enrichment* (Oxford, OUP, 2009) 342–43; R Stevens, 'Is There a Law of Unjust Enrichment?' in S Degeling and J Edelman (eds), *Unjust Enrichment in Commercial Law* (Pyrmont, NSW, Lawbook Co, 2008) 15; C Webb, *Reason and Restitution: A Theory of Unjust Enrichment* (Oxford, OUP, 2016) chs 1–2.

[27] *Barnes v Eastenders Cash & Carry Plc* [2014] UKSC 26, [2015] AC 1 [102] (Lord Toulson).

[28] Mitchell and Watterson, (n 5) para 6.02. See also Burrows, *Restitution* (n 19) 147, 148, 167; Burrows, *Restatement* (n 21) 173; Watterson, 'Modelling Subrogation as an "Equitable Remedy"' (n 19) 619. cf Mitchell, Mitchell and Watterson (n 7) para 39-29.

[29] *Swynson* (n 19) [30].

[30] See ch 9, s IV below.

A. Mistake and Failure of Basis

Many lending cases rely on the unjust factors of mistake or failure of basis.[31] A mistake or failure of basis is a fact, not a justification. There are, however, many theories about why these facts render D's enrichment unjust, justifying giving C rights against D. This section will consider the two leading contenders: vitiated or qualified intention, and absence of basis. The merits of each theory have been debated extensively elsewhere.[32] Rather than rehashing those debates, this section will assume that each theory successfully justifies a direct unjust enrichment claim for mistake or failure of basis, and ask whether the theory can also justify subrogation.

The fundamental problem is that direct claims and subrogation take different forms, as the previous chapter showed. Direct claims reverse the transaction in which C unjustly enriched D. Subrogation does not, and instead gives C new rights with prima facie the same content as X's extinguished rights. Both the vitiated or qualified intention theory and the absence of basis theory fail to explain why direct claims and subrogation take these different forms. Accordingly, each theory fails to justify the form of rights created by subrogation. This will now be demonstrated for each theory in turn.

i. Vitiated Intention

The dominant view is that a mistake justifies a direct unjust enrichment claim because it vitiates C's intention to enrich D, while a failure of basis justifies a direct unjust enrichment claim because it qualifies C's intention to enrich D. For example, Birks wrote that:

> Where there is 'a non-voluntary transfer' so that the circumstance calling for restitution is 'a factor negativing voluntariness', the explanation of the response is always reducible in the simplest terms to the statement that [C] did not mean [D] to have

[31] See ch 5, s II above.

[32] *Deutsche Morgan Grenfell Group Plc v Inland Revenue Commissioners* [2006] UKHL 49, [2007] 1 AC 558 [21]–[22] (Lord Hoffmann), [158] (Lord Walker); P Birks, *Unjust Enrichment* (Oxford, OUP, 2005) chs 5–6; A Burrows, 'Absence of Basis: The New Birksian Scheme' in A Burrows and Lord Rodger of Earlsferry (eds), *Mapping the Law: Essays in Memory of Peter Birks* (Oxford, OUP, 2006); S Meier, 'No Basis: A Comparative View' in A Burrows and Lord Rodger of Earlsferry (eds), *Mapping the Law: Essays in Memory of Peter Birks* (Oxford, OUP, 2006); Stevens, 'Is There a Law of Unjust Enrichment?' (n 26); H Scott, *Unjust Enrichment in South African Law: Rethinking Enrichment by Transfer* (Oxford, Hart Publishing, 2013).

> the … enrichment … In [mistake cases, C's] judgement in forming the intent to transfer was vitiated …. In [failure of basis cases, C] … qualified his intention by specifying the event in which, or basis on which, he wanted [D] to have the benefit. Here the reason why we ultimately say the transfer was non-voluntary is that the specified event or basis failed to materialise: in the events which have occurred he did not want [D] to have the benefit.[33]

The form of the remedy (reversing the transaction) flows from its justification (impaired intention). As Scott explains:

> property passes by virtue of the transferor's intention to confer ownership on the recipient of the transfer and the recipient's corresponding intention to become owner; transfer is thus itself an exercise of the parties' autonomy …. But where the intention of [C] in conferring the benefit is impaired, for example, because he is mistaken about his liability, that autonomy is only imperfectly expressed …. It is this – the impairment of [C]'s autonomy in deciding to make the transfer – that provides the ethical justification for restitution ….[34]

Thus, impaired intention explains why direct claims reverse the transaction which C mistakenly entered. However, subrogation does not reverse this transaction. Instead, it grants C new rights with prima facie the same content as X's extinguished rights against D. It is difficult to see why C's impaired intention justified reversing the transaction in *Simms*, whereas C's impaired intention justified upholding the transaction and giving C new rights with prima facie the same content as X's extinguished rights in subrogation cases like *Liggett*.

Moreover, it is difficult to see how impaired intention justifies the form of the rights of created by subrogation. Subrogation does not undo the transaction to which C's consent was impaired. Nor does subrogation cure the defect in C's consent, making the world as if C were correct and not mistaken. Taking the classic case of *Butler v Rice* as an example, subrogation did not undo the transaction by reinstating the bank's mortgage and giving Butler his money back.[35] Nor did subrogation cure Butler's mistaken belief that Mr Rice owned the property by making Mr Rice the owner. Instead, subrogation left Mrs Rice as the owner and gave Butler a charge over her property.

[33] P Birks, *An Introduction to the Law of Restitution* (Oxford, Clarendon Press, 1989) 100–01. See also Burrows, *Restitution* (n 19) 86; Burrows, *Restatement* (n 21) 5, 30; G Virgo, *The Principles of the Law of Restitution* (Oxford, OUP, 2015) 121; Mitchell, Mitchell and Watterson (n 7) para 1-29.

[34] Scott, (n 32) 210 (footnotes omitted). See also Birks, *Introduction* (n 33) 100–01, 140; Virgo, *The Principles of the Law of Restitution* (n 33) 121.

[35] *Butler* (n 2). For the facts, see ch 1, s I above.

In short, even if impaired intention justifies a direct mistake claim, it is difficult to see how this can justify subrogation.

ii. Qualified Intention

The same point applies to qualified intention and failure of basis. Wilmot-Smith explains that when C 'performs some action with a conditional intention and the condition fails, the problem she faces … might be conceived of in one of two ways. First, one might regard the problem as being … [that] her action is not a reflection of her true intentions' and so the law should reverse that action. Alternatively, one might say that 'the problem is that the condition attached to her action has failed' and so the law should satisfy the condition.[36] There is also a third option: the law could do nothing. In direct claims the law takes the first approach whereas subrogation takes the second. Qualified intention cannot explain this difference, so cannot justify subrogation's form. Three cases illustrate this.

First, in *Cobbe v Yeoman's Row Management Ltd*, D orally agreed to sell a block of flats to C.[37] C therefore obtained planning permission to redevelop the flats. D then withdrew from the agreement. As the agreement to sell the flats was not in writing, it was unenforceable.[38]

The House of Lords held that D had been unjustly enriched by the planning permission.[39] The unjust factor was failure of basis: C obtained the planning permission on condition that D would sell the flats to him.[40]

The law could respond to this in one of three ways. First, the law could reverse the service to which the failed condition attached. Second, the law could fulfil the failed condition by enforcing the agreement to sell the flats to C. Third, the law could do nothing. The House chose the first response: C was entitled to recover the value of his services in obtaining the planning permission.[41]

Similarly, in *Guinness Mahon & Co Ltd v Kensington and Chelsea RLBC*, a bank entered an interest rate swap with a council.[42] At the end of the swap, the bank had

[36] F Wilmot-Smith, 'Failure of Condition' (DPhil thesis, University of Oxford 2013) ora.ox.ac.uk/objects/uuid:93ab182a-be71-489a-88e8-1479d9b8efb3, 167. See also 121–26; D Winterton and T Pilkington, '*Mann v Paterson Constructions Pty Ltd*: The Intersection of Debt, Damages and *Quantum Meruit*' (2020) 44 *Melbourne LR* 679, 710–11.

[37] *Cobbe v Yeoman's Row Management Ltd* [2008] UKHL 55, [2008] 1 WLR 1752.

[38] Law Reform (Miscellaneous Provisions) Act 1989, s 2(1).

[39] *Cobbe* (n 37) [40] (Lord Scott).

[40] ibid [43] (Lord Scott).

[41] ibid [41]–[44] (Lord Scott).

[42] *Guinness Mahon & Co Ltd v Kensington and Chelsea RLBC* [1999] QB 215 (CA). The same analysis applies to *Rover International Ltd v Cannon Film Sales Ltd* [1989] 1 WLR 912 (CA)(Cannon's Claim); *Goss v Chilcott* [1996] AC 788 (PC).

paid more to the council than the council had paid to the bank. It then transpired that the swap was ultra vires for the council and so void. The Court of Appeal held that the bank paid the council on condition that it had a contractual right to the council's counter-performance and that condition had failed.

Again, the law could respond to this in one of three ways. First, the law could reverse the payments to which the failed condition attached. Second, the law could fulfil the failed condition by imposing an obligation on the council to pay. Third, the law could do nothing. Again, the Court chose the first response: the bank could recover its payments to the council, less the council's payments to the bank.

Contrast these cases with *Lehman Commercial Mortgage Conduit Ltd v Gatedale Ltd*, a subrogation case which relies on failure of basis.[43] There, one company, Brookdane, owned another, D. C loaned money to Brookdane. Brookdane used the loan to discharge X's charge over D's property. C had contracted with Brookdane for a charge over D's property, and D executed a third party charge in favour of C. But legislation rendered this charge void. Prima facie, then, C was unsecured. However, Vos J held that D was unjustly enriched at C's expense because C 'bargained for the charge over the property but did not get it … [and] had made [the charge] a condition of the transaction'.[44]

Once again, the law could respond to this in one of three ways. First, the law could reverse the action to which the failed condition attached by undoing C's loan and reinstating X's charge. Second, the law could fulfil the failed condition by giving C its charge. Third, the law could do nothing. Vos J took the second route by holding that C was subrogated to X's extinguished charge.

Cobbe, *Guinness Mahon*, and *Lehman* are therefore all said to be failure of basis cases, but the law responds to this in opposite ways. In *Cobbe* and *Guinness Mahon* the law gave C a direct claim to reverse the action to which C's condition attached, whereas in *Lehman* the law used subrogation to satisfy the failed condition. Qualified intention cannot explain this difference, so cannot justify subrogation's form.

iii. Absence of Basis

In his later work, Birks changed his mind and thought that the justification for mistake and failure of basis claims was that: 'every enrichment at another's expense either has an explanation known to the law or has not. … An enrichment which

[43] *Lehman Commercial Mortgage Conduit Ltd v Gatedale Ltd* [2012] EWHC 848 (Ch).
[44] ibid [28] (Vos J).

turns out to have no such explanation is inexplicable and cannot be retained.'[45] Mistake and failure of basis were each ways of showing that there was no basis for D's enrichment.[46]

However, this comes no closer to solving the problem posed in the previous sub section. In direct claims, if an enrichment has no basis, then the transaction which enriched D is reversed. By contrast, in subrogation cases, if an enrichment has no basis, then C is given new rights with prima facie the same content as X's extinguished rights. It is difficult to see why the same justification (absence of basis) should lead to different outcomes in different cases. Accordingly, even if absence of basis justifies direct mistake and failure of basis claims, it does not justify subrogation.

iv. Different Enrichments

Watterson offers a potential solution to these difficulties. He suggests that direct claims and subrogation take different forms because they reverse different enrichments.[47] Direct claims reverse '"factual" enrichments: the receipt of value' by ordering D to pay 'a money sum reflecting the monetary value of [D]'s enrichment'.[48] By contrast, subrogation reverses a '"legal" enrichment … the release of [X's] rights … by substantially recreating the released liabilities/rights in favour of C'.[49]

However, in both direct claims and subrogation, the law reverses both types of enrichment, so the distinction between different enrichments cannot explain why direct claims and subrogation take different forms. In the direct claim in *Simms*, Robert Goff J held that D's debt was not discharged by C's payment.[50] This prevented D being factually or legally enriched. In the subrogation case of *Liggett*, Wright J held that D's debts were discharged by C's payments.[51] D was factually and legally enriched by this, but both enrichments were reversed by subrogation recreating the debts in C's favour. Thus, direct claims and subrogation take different forms, but in both the law ensures that D is not factually or legally enriched.

[45] Birks, *Unjust Enrichment* (n 32) 102–03.

[46] Birks, *Unjust Enrichment* (n 32) chs 5–6.

[47] Watterson, 'Subrogation' (n 22) 439–48; Watterson, 'Modelling Subrogation as an "Equitable Remedy"' (n 19) 615–17. See also AVM Lodder, *Enrichment in the Law of Unjust Enrichment and Restitution* (Oxford, Hart Publishing, 2012) 141–47.

[48] Watterson, 'Subrogation' (n 22) 440 (emphasis omitted), 438.

[49] ibid 440–41 (emphasis omitted).

[50] *Barclays Bank Ltd v WJ Simms Son & Cooke (Southern) Ltd* [1980] QB 677 (QB).

[51] *B Liggett (Liverpool) Ltd v Barclays Bank Ltd* [1928] 1 KB 48 (KB).

The distinction between factual and legal enrichment does not explain why direct claims and subrogation take different forms.

v. Summary

In sum, whatever the justification is for direct mistake and failure of basis claims, it cannot justify subrogation too. There is no explanation for why the same justification supports reversing C's actions in direct claims but giving C rights with prima facie the same content as X's extinguished rights in subrogation cases.

B. Defeated Expectations

Giving the leading judgment in *Swynson*, Lord Sumption suggested that subrogation is triggered by a different unjust factor to direct claims. He said:

> The cases on the use of equitable subrogation to prevent or reverse unjust enrichment are all cases of defective transactions. They were defective in the sense that [C] paid money on the basis of an expectation which failed. … [T]he real basis of [subrogation] is the defeat of an expectation of benefit which was the basis of [C]'s consent to the payment of the money for the relevant purpose.
>
> … [T]he role of the law of unjust enrichment in such cases is to characterise the resultant enrichment of [D] as unjust, because the absence of the stipulated benefit disrupted a relevant expectation about the transaction under which the money was paid.[52]

Chapter 5 explained that C's defeated expectation cannot be the justification for 'all cases' of subrogation as Lord Sumption suggested,[53] but that it does fit the reasoning and results of lending cases. However, as a matter of principle, Lord Sumption's defeated expectation approach is problematic because it seems to treat like cases inconsistently.[54] Lord Sumption stated that 'failure of basis … ordinarily requires that the expectation should be mutual [between C and D], whereas this is not a requirement for equitable subrogation'.[55] Thus, Chapter 5 explained that if C's defeated unilateral expectation about the future leads to the discharge of D's obligation to X, then C is subrogated to X's extinguished rights against D. But

[52] *Swynson* (n 19) [30]–[31].
[53] ibid [30].
[54] Mitchell, Mitchell and Watterson (n 7) paras 39-21, 39-35–39-37.
[55] *Swynson* (n 19) [30].

if C's defeated unilateral expectation about the future leads to D being enriched in any other way, then C has no claim against D. Lord Sumption does not justify this difference, so his justification for subrogation appears to treat like cases inconsistently.

Mitchell, Mitchell and Watterson suggest that this difference 'might be supportable' because, in subrogation cases, 'there is no injustice, in so far as [D] is a volunteer and the subrogation remedy does no more than reinstate the position they were in before they received the unbargained windfall of the release of their liabilities at another's expense'.[56] The problem is that this applies equally to cases where D is enriched in another way, such as receipt of money. The remedy of restitution 'does no more than reinstate the position they were in before they received the unbargained windfall' of receiving the money. As a result, it remains difficult to see why subrogation is special and can be justified a defeated unilateral expectation about the future, whereas a direct unjust enrichment claim cannot.

IV. Unconscionability

Some cases suggest that subrogation may be justified to prevent unconscionable behaviour. For instance, in *Boscawen*, Millett LJ said that subrogation occurs when it is 'unconscionable for [D] to deny the proprietary interest claimed by [C]'.[57]

Virgo suggests that conscience can be interpreted in four different ways:

> [There is] a fundamental distinction between [D]'s conscience and the conscience of the court. … When [D]'s conscience is assessed, a further distinction needs to be drawn between conscience as a state of [D]'s mind and conscience as an assessment of [D]'s behaviour, which essentially reflects subjective and objective interpretations of conscience. … Conscience alternatively refers to the conscience of the court. This can be interpreted as the exercise either of principled or unprincipled discretion.[58]

On any of Virgo's interpretations, unconscionability is not a sufficient justification for subrogation. As for the first interpretation – 'conscience as a state of [D]'s mind' – it has already been shown that subrogation cannot be justified by D's intention to

[56] Mitchell, Mitchell and Watterson (n 7) para 39-37.

[57] *Boscawen* (n 13) 335D (Millett LJ). See also *Cochrane v Cochrane* (1985) 3 NSWLR 403 (NSWSC) 405C–E (Kearney J).

[58] G Virgo, 'Whose Conscience? Unconscionability in the Common Law of Obligations' in A Robertson and M Tilbury (eds), *Divergences in Private Law* (Oxford, Hart Publishing, 2016) 309–10.

grant C rights.[59] For the second interpretation – 'conscience as an assessment of [D]'s behaviour' – the standard by which D's behaviour is to be assessed needs to be articulated and justified.

Moving ahead to the fourth interpretation – conscience as an exercise of unprincipled discretion – Virgo rightly argues that this is indefensible. He argues that principles are needed to guide the discretion to ensure that the law is 'predictable' and that 'like cases are treated alike'.[60]

The third interpretation – conscience as an exercise of principled discretion – fits with Millett LJ's suggestion that:

> subrogation … is not a remedy which the court has a general discretion to impose whenever it thinks it just to do so. The equity arises from the conduct of the parties on well settled principles and in defined circumstances which make it unconscionable for [D] to deny the proprietary interest claimed by [C].[61]

This also fits the position of the High Court of Australia. In *Bofinger v Kingsway Group Ltd*, the Court quoted Millett LJ's dictum with approval[62] and stated that:

> whether a particular case [justifies subrogation] is determined by reference to well developed principles, both specific and flexible in character. It is to those principles that the court has first regard rather than entering into the case at that higher level of abstraction involved in notions of unconscientious conduct in some loose sense where all principles are at large.[63]

However, Virgo argues that, where the courts have a principled discretion, the principles which govern the exercise of this discretion need to be articulated.[64] These principles may be enough to justify the law, leaving 'unconscionability' doing no justificatory work.[65]

[59] See ch 8, s II above.

[60] Virgo, 'Whose Conscience?' (n 58) 310. See also P Birks, 'Annual Miegunyah Lecture: Equity, Conscience, and Unjust Enrichment' (1999) 23 *Melbourne University LR* 1, 20–22.

[61] *Boscawen* (n 13) 335C–E.

[62] *Bofinger v Kingsway Group Ltd* [2009] HCA 44, (2009) 239 CLR 269 [94] (Gummow, Hayne, Heydon, Kiefel, and Bell JJ). See also [8] (Gummow, Hayne, Heydon, Kiefel, and Bell JJ).

[63] ibid [81] (Gummow, Hayne, Heydon, Kiefel, and Bell JJ) quoting *Tanwar Enterprises Pty Ltd v Cauchi* [2003] HCA 57, (2003) 217 CLR 315 [20] (Gleeson CJ, McHugh, Gummow, Hayne, and Heydon JJ). See generally *Bofinger* (n 62) [78]–[82] (Gummow, Hayne, Heydon, Kiefel, and Bell JJ).

[64] Virgo, 'Whose Conscience?' (n 58) 314–15, 319. See also R Havelock, 'Rivalry over Liability for Defective Transfers' in P Devonshire and R Havelock (eds), *The Impact of Equity and Restitution in Commerce* (Oxford, Hart Publishing, 2019) 133–38.

[65] J Edelman and E Bant, *Unjust Enrichment* (Oxford, Hart Publishing, 2016) 27; Virgo, 'Whose Conscience?' (n 58) 314–16, 319–20. cf S Agnew, 'The Meaning and Significance of Conscience in Private Law' (2018) 77 *CLJ* 479.

This is the case for subrogation. For example, in *Bofinger*, D owed a debt to X. C guaranteed that debt. D defaulted, so C paid the debt. The Court held that C was subrogated to X's extinguished rights because D had 'ultimate liability' for the debt, whereas C had only 'secondary liability'.[66] Chapter 10 endorses this as a good justification for subrogation. However, it leaves unconscionability as a conclusory label which does no work justifying subrogation.

V. Equity

In *Bofinger*, the High Court of Australia stated that subrogation is governed by 'principles of equity'.[67] Just as with conscience, these principles need to be articulated. Chapter 10 will show that, once these principles are articulated, they complete the task of justifying subrogation, leaving 'equity' with no justificatory work to do. Indeed, 'equity' can be defined in different ways; this section will consider three leading definitions and show that each is an insufficient justification for subrogation.

Maitland's definition was that 'Equity now is that body of rules administered by our English courts of justice which, were it not for the operation of the Judicature Acts, would be administered only by those courts which would be known as Courts of Equity'.[68] Subrogation certainly fits that definition. However, this is a historical description rather than a justification for subrogation.[69]

A second view is that equity represents a discretionary power for judges to mitigate harsh Common Law rules. However, this has not been true since Lord Nottingham LC's regularisation of equity in the seventeenth century. Milsom wrote that the Common Law and Equity then became 'two systems of certainty, two systems of law'.[70] While equitable defences and remedies are often said

[66] *Bofinger* (n 62) [7]–[8] (Gummow, Hayne, Heydon, Kiefel, and Bell JJ).

[67] ibid [89] (Gummow, Hayne, Heydon, Kiefel, and Bell JJ). See also *Challenger Managed Investments Ltd v Direct Money Corp Pty Ltd* [2003] NSWSC 1072 [50] (Bryson J).

[68] FW Maitland, *Equity: Also the Forms of Action at Common Law* (Cambridge, CUP, 1909) 1. See also P Birks, 'Equity in the Modern Law: An Exercise in Taxonomy' (1996) 26 *University of Western Australia LR* 1, 9; A Burrows, 'We Do This at Common Law but That in Equity' (2002) 22 *OJLS* 1, 2; B McFarlane, *The Structure of Property Law* (Oxford, Hart Publishing, 2008) 66; J McGee, *Snell's Equity* (London, Sweet & Maxwell, 2020) para 1-003; A Burrows, *Remedies for Torts, Breach of Contract, and Equitable Wrongs* (Oxford, OUP, 2019) 10–11, 544.

[69] Maitland (n 68) 1–2; McFarlane, *The Structure of Property Law* (n 68) 68; B McFarlane and R Stevens, 'The Nature of Equitable Property' (2010) 4 *J Eq* 1, 9; McGee (n 68) para 1-031.

[70] SFC Milsom, *Historical Foundations of the Common Law* (London, Butterworths, 1981) 95. See also Burrows, 'We Do This at Common Law but That in Equity' (n 68) 2; McGee (n 68) para 1-013;

to be discretionary, these discretions are bound by rules just as much as Common Law defences and remedies. To repeat, in *Boscawen*, Millett LJ stated that 'subrogation … is not a remedy which the court has a general discretion to impose whenever it thinks it just to do so. The equity arises from the conduct of the parties on well settled principles and in defined circumstances'.[71]

A third view is that:

> a distinctive feature of equity … [is] its secondary or supplementary nature. Equitable intervention presupposes the existence of primary rules of positive law. The effect of equity is to qualify the enforcement of the positive law to ensure a more complete standard of justice than the law itself would attain.[72]

In particular, McFarlane and Stevens argue that '[e]quitable rights concern rights in relation to other rights. … [They allow C] to control the [D]'s acquisition or enforcement of a particular right'.[73]

Subrogation to proprietary rights may be equitable in this sense. A charge created by subrogation is dependent on the law's prior recognition of the right which is charged,[74] and the charge restricts the chargor's ability to exercise the right which is charged.[75] But it is more difficult to see subrogation to personal rights as dependent upon Common Law rights.

Burrows, *Remedies for Torts, Breach of Contract, and Equitable Wrongs* (n 68) 11; J Nadler, 'What Is Distinctive about the Law of Equity?' (2021) 41 *OJLS* 854, 856–57.

[71] *Boscawen* (n 13) 335C–D (Millett LJ). See also *BFC* (n 8) 237D–E (Lord Clyde); *Filby v Mortgage Express (No 2) Ltd* [2004] EWCA Civ 759 [67] (May LJ).

[72] McGee (n 68) para 1-002. See also S Hedley, 'Rival Taxonomies Within Obligations: Is There a Problem?' in S Degeling and J Edelman (eds), *Equity in Commercial Law* (Pyrmont, NSW, Lawbook Co, 2005) 77, 85; HE Smith, 'Equitable Defences as Meta-Law' in PS Davies, S Douglas and J Goudkamp (eds), *Defences in Equity* (Oxford, Hart Publishing, 2018) 18–27. cf Nadler (n 70) 855.

[73] B McFarlane and R Stevens, 'What's Special about Equity? Rights about Rights' in D Klimchuk, I Samet and HE Smith (eds), *Philosophical Foundations of the Law of Equity* (Oxford, OUP, 2020) 191–92. See also B McFarlane, 'Unjust Enrichment, Property Rights and Indirect Recipients' [2009] *RLR* 37, 42, 55; McFarlane, *The Structure of Property Law* (n 68); LD Smith, 'Trust and Patrimony' (2008) 38 *Revue Générale de Droit* 379; McFarlane and Stevens, 'The Nature of Equitable Property' (n 69); Burrows, *Restitution* (n 19) 191–93; R Stevens, 'When and Why Does Unjustified Enrichment Justify the Recognition of Proprietary Rights?' (2012) 92 *BULR* 919; J Edelman, 'Two Fundamental Questions for the Law of Trusts' (2013) 129 *LQR* 66; R Stevens, 'Floating Trusts' in PS Davies and J Penner (eds), *Equity, Trusts and Commerce* (Oxford, Hart Publishing, 2017) 114–17; NJ McBride, *The Humanity of Private Law: Part I: Explanation* (Oxford, Hart Publishing, 2019) 77; B McFarlane, 'Form and Substance in Equity' in A Robertson and J Goudkamp (eds), *Form and Substance in the Law of Obligations* (Oxford, Hart Publishing, 2019); D Klimchuk, 'Unjust Enrichment and the Forms of Justice' in E Bant, K Barker and S Degeling (eds), *Research Handbook on Unjust Enrichment and Restitution* (Cheltenham, Edward Elgar Publishing, 2020) 196–98; B McFarlane, 'Equity and the Justification of Private Rights' in S Degeling, M Crawford and N Tiverios (eds), *Justifying Private Rights* (Oxford, Hart Publishing, 2020) 222–23.

[74] R Stevens, 'Set-Off and the Nature of Equity' in PS Davies, S Douglas and J Goudkamp (eds), *Defences in Equity* (Oxford, Hart Publishing, 2018) 43–44.

[75] McFarlane and Stevens, 'The Nature of Equitable Property' (n 69) 22–26; Stevens, 'Set-Off and the Nature of Equity' (n 74) 44.

More importantly, on this third view, equitable rights are united by their form, not their justification.[76] Even is subrogation is equitable in this third sense, this does not in itself provide a justification for subrogation.

Consequently, on each of these three interpretations, equity is an insufficient justification for subrogation.

VI. Chapter Summary

This chapter argued that four leading attempts to justify subrogation are unsatisfactory because they fail to justify the form of rights created by subrogation.

[76] Stevens, 'Set-Off and the Nature of Equity' (n 74) 42; McFarlane and Stevens, 'What's Special about Equity?' (n 73) 191–94.

9

Subrogation and Tracing

I. Introduction

This chapter examines the relationship between subrogation and tracing. Many subrogation cases invoke the rules of tracing,[1] and section II will show that there is a striking factual similarity between cases which have awarded subrogation to traceably discharged debts and cases which have recognised trusts over traceably acquired rights. As a result, it is commonly thought that subrogation to traceably discharged debts is subject to the same conditions, and is justified by the same reason, as trusts over traceably acquired rights. However, there is fierce disagreement over what that justification is. Sections III to VI consider four leading contenders and show that each fails to justify the form of rights created by subrogation.

II. The Analogy

Tracing is:

> the process by which [C] demonstrates what has happened to his property, identifies its proceeds and the persons who have handled or received them, and justifies his claim that the proceeds can properly be regarded as representing his property.[2]

Say a trustee holds title to cash on trust and without authorisation spends the cash. If tracing shows that the trustee exchanged title to the cash for title to a car, then

[1] eg *Boscawen v Bajwa* [1996] 1 WLR 328 (CA); *Banque Financière de La Cité SA v Parc (Battersea) Ltd* [1999] 1 AC 221 (HL) ('*BFC*') 235C (Lord Hoffmann); *Filby v Mortgage Express (No 2) Ltd* [2004] EWCA Civ 759 [28]–[31] (May LJ); *Menelaou v Bank of Cyprus UK Ltd* [2015] UKSC 66, [2016] AC 176 [100]–[104] (Lord Neuberger), [118]–[140] (Lord Carnwath).

[2] *Foskett v McKeown* [2001] 1 AC 102 (HL) 128D (Lord Millett).

the trustee holds title to the car on trust.[3] Alternatively, if tracing shows that the trustee exchanged title to the cash for the discharge of her mortgage, then the beneficiaries are subrogated to the extinguished mortgage.[4]

The only difference in the facts of these two scenarios is that in the first the trustee acquires a right, whereas in the second the trustee discharges its debt. The overwhelmingly dominant view is that this factual difference is normatively insignificant: subrogation to traceably discharged debts is subject to the same conditions, and is justified by the same reason, as trusts over traceably acquired rights.[5] For example, Mitchell writes that:

> only [the] obscure language [of subrogation] conceals the fact that, if a successful tracing exercise identifies, not shares or a yacht, but an extinguished security interest, the conditions which dictate the transfer of the shares or the yacht will be the same conditions as will justify giving [C] a new security interest that mirrors the extinguished charge.[6]

A number of cases support this analogy between traceably discharged debts and traceably acquired rights.

A. *Boscawen v Bajwa*

In *Boscawen v Bajwa*, Millett LJ said that:

> If [C] succeeds in tracing his property … into the hands of [D], and overcomes any defences which are put forward on [D]'s behalf, he is entitled to a remedy. … [C] will generally be entitled to a personal remedy; if he seeks a proprietary remedy he must usually prove that the property to which he lays claim is still in the ownership of [D]. If he succeeds in doing this the court will treat [D] as holding the property on a constructive trust for [C] and will order [D] to transfer it in specie to [C]. … If … [C]'s money has been used to discharge a mortgage on [D]'s land, then the court may achieve a similar result by treating the land as subject to a charge by way of subrogation in favour of [C].[7]

[3] *Foskett* (n 2).

[4] *Boscawen* (n 1).

[5] ibid 334B–35F (Millett LJ); *Swynson Ltd v Lowick Rose LLP* [2017] UKSC 32, [2018] AC 313 [58]–[61] (Lord Mance); P Birks, *An Introduction to the Law of Restitution* (Oxford, Clarendon Press, 1989) 84, 96, 390; A Tettenborn, *The Law of Restitution in England and Ireland* (London, Cavendish, 2002) para 2-27; P Birks, *Unjust Enrichment* (Oxford, OUP, 2005) 298–99; NJ McBride, *The Humanity of Private Law: Part I: Explanation* (Oxford, Hart Publishing, 2019) 218.

[6] C Mitchell, 'Unjust Enrichment' in A Burrows (ed), *English Private Law* (Oxford, OUP, 2013) para 18.282; C Mitchell, 'Unjust Enrichment' in A Burrows (ed), *Principles of the English Law of Obligations* (Oxford, OUP, 2015) para 3.282.

[7] *Boscawen* (n 1) 334H–35C. See also 341F–42C (Millett LJ). For the facts, see ch 4, s III(D) above.

B. *Patten v Bond*

Attempts to analogise between traceably acquired rights and traceably discharged debts date back to at least 1889 and the case of *Patten v Bond*.[8] James Patten was a trustee of two trusts: the Bond trust and the Dixon trust. X had a mortgage of title to a house, securing a £1000 debt. As trustee of the Bond trust, Patten held the equity of redemption. As trustee of the Dixon trust, Patten held £600. In breach of the Dixon trust, Patten paid the £600 to X, partially discharging X's mortgage.

Nine years later, the beneficiaries of the Bond trust paid X £400 and obtained a transfer of X's mortgage. They refused to repay £600 to the Dixon trustees. The Dixon trustees therefore claimed that they were subrogated to X's mortgage, insofar as Patten's payment of £600 extinguished it.

Kay J allowed the claim. His reasoning drew a parallel between trusts over traceably acquired rights and subrogation to traceably discharged debts. He cited *Taylor v Plumer*,[9] a case of a trust over a traceably acquired right,[10] and then said that the 'money, to the knowledge of all concerned, was trust money, and persons have a right to follow it where it has gone'.[11] He explained that, if the Bond trustees had made the payment of £600 to X, then they would be subrogated to X's mortgage insofar as their payment had extinguished it.[12] Instead, Patten made the payment in his capacity as trustee of the Dixon trust. So, by analogy, the Dixon trustees were subrogated to X's extinguished mortgage, which they held under the Dixon trust.[13]

C. *Gertsch v Atsas*

The analogy between traceably acquired rights and traceably discharged debts has also been invoked where D did not agree to be an express trustee. *Gertsch* provides a good example.[14] There, D received a legacy of AU$100,000 under a will. D used AU$69,000 of the legacy to pay off her mortgage[15] and spent the balance on

[8] *Patten v Bond* (1889) 60 LT 583 (Ch).

[9] ibid 585 citing *Taylor v Plumer* (1815) 3 M 562, 105 ER 721.

[10] *Trustee of the Property of FC Jones & Sons (a Firm) v Jones* [1997] Ch 159 (CA) 169E–F (Millett LJ) citing LD Smith, 'Tracing in *Taylor v Plumer*: Equity in the Court of King's Bench' [1995] *LMCLQ* 240.

[11] *Patten* (n 8) 586.

[12] ibid 585.

[13] ibid 585–86.

[14] *Gertsch v Atsas* [1999] NSWSC 898.

[15] ibid [16] (Foster AJ).

various other things, including acquiring title to Nike shoes.[16] It then transpired that the will was a forgery. C, the executor and sole beneficiary of the deceased's intestate estate, sought to recover the money.

Giving the judgment of the Supreme Court of New South Wales, Foster AJ said that:

> the moneys [D] received under the Will were not paid to her as the result of a genuine legacy. They were moneys which should have passed on intestacy to [C]. Accordingly, [C] is prima facie entitled to recover them … through tracing them as trust money ….[17]

AU$69,000 of the legacy could be traced into the discharge of the mortgage and so C was entitled to be subrogated to the extinguished mortgage,[18] subject to the defence of change of position.[19]

The quote above suggests that C was also entitled to recover the remaining AU$31,000 'through tracing them as trust moneys'.[20] This would imply that D was under a duty to restore title to the Nike shoes to the estate.[21] Unsurprisingly, this was not pleaded[22] and the only order made in respect of the AU$31,000 was an order for personal restitution of D's unjust enrichment,[23] subject to the change of position defence.[24] In principle, however, the Court treated the traceably acquired rights in the same way as the traceably discharged mortgage.

D. *Re Diplock*

However, not all cases support the analogy between traceably acquired rights and traceably discharged debts. In *Boscawen*, Millett LJ treated subrogation as a remedy for unjust enrichment[25] but then, as Lord Millett in *Foskett v McKeown*, stated that trusts over traceably acquired rights are not remedies for unjust enrichment.[26]

[16] ibid [17] (Foster AJ).
[17] ibid [59].
[18] ibid [19], [100] (Foster AJ).
[19] ibid [22], [98]–[100] (Foster AJ). For discussion, see ch 6, s III(B) above.
[20] ibid [59].
[21] *Foskett* (n 2).
[22] *Gertsch* (n 14) [18] (Foster AJ).
[23] ibid [93] (Foster AJ). See also [144] (Foster AJ).
[24] ibid [22], [93] (Foster AJ).
[25] *Boscawen* (n 1) 335C–F.
[26] *Foskett* (n 2) 127E–F, 129D–H, 132A–B (Lord Millett); S Watterson, 'Subrogation' in G Virgo and S Worthington (eds), *Commercial Remedies: Resolving Controversies* (Cambridge, CUP, 2017) 452.

Furthermore, in *Re Diplock*, payments were made to various charities under a will.[27] The will was then found to be invalid. C, the judicial trustee of the deceased's estate, sought to recover the payments.

One charity used its payment to purchase a bond and the Court of Appeal held that C had a charge over the bond.[28] Another charity used its payment to purchase 'War Stock' and the Court held that C had a charge over the stock.[29]

A third charity used its payment to pay off X's charge over its property.[30] However, the Court held that C was not subrogated to X's extinguished charge.[31] The Court therefore allowed the claim to the traceably acquired right and denied the claim to be subrogated to the traceably discharged debt. In *Boscawen*, Millett LJ suggested that subrogation failed because of the change of position defence[32] but there are difficulties with this explanation.[33]

In summary, many cases support the idea that subrogation to traceably discharged debts is subject to the same conditions, and is justified by the same reason, as trusts over traceably acquired rights. However, some cases doubt this. The following sections will show that the doubts are justified: whatever the justification is for trusts over traceably acquired rights, it cannot justify the form of rights created by subrogation.

III. Fiduciary Duty

One possible justification for trusts over traceably acquired rights is a fiduciary's voluntarily assumed duty to act exclusively in the interests of their principal.[34] This argument runs roughly as follows. A fiduciary undertakes to act exclusively in the

[27] *Re Diplock* [1948] 1 Ch 465 (CA).
[28] ibid 552–54, 557 (Lord Greene MR, Wrottesley and Evershed LJJ).
[29] ibid 554–57 (Lord Greene MR, Wrottesley and Evershed LJJ).
[30] ibid 548 (Lord Greene MR, Wrottesley and Evershed LJJ).
[31] ibid 549–50 (Lord Greene MR, Wrottesley and Evershed LJJ).
[32] *Boscawen* (n 1) 341B–F.
[33] See ch 6, s III(A) above.
[34] S Worthington, 'Justifying Claims to Secondary Profits' in EJH Schrage (ed), *Unjust Enrichment and the Law of Contract* (London, Kluwer Law International, 2001) 466–72; TRS Cutts, 'The Role of Tracing in Claiming' (DPhil thesis, University of Oxford 2015) ora.ox.ac.uk/objects/ora:12239, 154–55; L Smith, 'Equity Is Not a Single Thing' in D Klimchuk, I Samet and HE Smith (eds), *Philosophical Foundations of the Law of Equity* (Oxford, OUP, 2020) 162–66; S Worthington, 'The Myth of Common Law Tracing' in C Mitchell and S Watterson (eds), *The World of Maritime and Commercial Law: Essays in Honour of Francis Rose* (Oxford, Hart Publishing, 2020) 322; C Mitchell, P Mitchell and S Watterson, *Goff and Jones: The Law of Unjust Enrichment* (London, Sweet & Maxwell, 2022) para 8-163.

interests of their principal, to the exclusion of their own interests.[35] Consequently, if a fiduciary acquires a right within the scope of their fiduciary duty, they must use that right for the benefit of their principal, to the exclusion of their own interests. Thus, the fiduciary must hold the right on trust for their principal.[36] A trustee is a fiduciary[37] so, if a trustee uses a right held on trust to traceably acquire another right, then they acquire a right within the scope of their fiduciary duty, and so they must hold that right on trust for their beneficiaries. This justifies why a trustee holds a traceably acquired right on trust.

However, Smith explains that this account cannot be extended to justify subrogation to traceably discharged debts:

> If someone pays my debt of £10, I am £10 better off; my bottom line or patrimony is that much larger. Nonetheless, it might be the case that nowhere is there the £10 by which I am enriched. … Although tracing might be required to prove that the plaintiff's value was used to pay the debt, nonetheless any consequent claim based upon reviving subrogation is not a claim to the traceable proceeds of the plaintiff's value. It follows that claims based upon … subrogation require a theoretical foundation which is independent from that which underlies claims to the traceable proceeds of value.[38]

In other words, when a trustee traceably acquires a right, the trustee comes under a duty to hold that specific right on trust. By contrast, when a trustee traceably discharges its debt, the trustee does not acquire a specific right, so there is nothing for them to hold on trust. Instead, the trustee is released from the duty to pay the debt. One might therefore think that the trustee should hold the release of this specific duty on trust. But it is difficult to see how this can be done.

One might think that the trustee could be subrogated to their creditor's extinguished rights and required to hold these rights on trust. But subrogating the trustee to the creditor's extinguished rights against the trustee would amount to the trustee owing a debt to itself: a conceptual impossibility, leaving no right for the trustee to hold on trust.

Alternatively, one might think that the beneficiaries should be subrogated to the creditor's extinguished rights. But then the trustee would simply owe a debt to

[35] *Bristol and West Building Society v Mothew* [1998] 2 Ch 1 (CA) 18A–C (Millett LJ); *Al Nehayan v Kent* [2018] EWHC 333 (Comm), [2018] 1 CLC 216 [159] (Leggatt LJ); *Children's Investment Fund Foundation (UK) v Attorney General* [2020] UKSC 33, [2022] AC 155 [44]–[45] (Lady Arden).

[36] *Boardman v Phipps* [1967] 2 AC 46 (HL); *Murad v Al-Saraj* [2005] EWCA Civ 959; *FHR European Ventures LLP v Cedar Capital Partners LLC* [2014] UKSC 45, [2015] AC 250.

[37] *Al Nehayan* (n 35) [157] (Leggatt LJ).

[38] LD Smith, 'Tracing into the Payment of a Debt' (1995) 54 *CLJ* 290, 299–04 (footnotes omitted). See also LD Smith, *The Law of Tracing* (Oxford, Clarendon Press, 1997) 151–52.

the beneficiaries. Beyond the simple case of a bare trust, this creates insurmountable obstacles. In a charitable trust, there is no beneficiary who can be subrogated to the creditor's extinguished rights. In a discretionary trust, it is unclear who should be subrogated to the creditor's extinguished rights. One might suggest the whole class of discretionary beneficiaries. But this would mean that the trustee owed a debt to the whole class, so the right to the debt would be equally divided between the beneficiaries. This would effectively convert the discretionary trust into a fixed sum of money, allowing the terms of the trust to be disregarded.

In short, when a trustee traceably acquires a right, their fiduciary obligation requires them to hold that specific right on trust. By contrast, when a trustee traceably discharges its debt, there is no specific right which can be held on trust. Consequently, their fiduciary obligation cannot justify the form of rights created by subrogation.

Even if these obstacles could be overcome, a further limitation of this account is that it can only explain a narrow range of cases. As Mitchell, Mitchell, and Watterson explain, this justification is premised on 'the duties which the trustee voluntarily assumed when he took office'[39] and so it can only justify rights against those who have 'voluntarily assumed a fiduciary position and associated duties'.[40] This account therefore fails to justify the vast majority of cases of subrogation, including *Butler v Rice*,[41] *Boscawen v Bajwa*,[42] and *Gertsch v Atsas*.[43] Against those who have not voluntarily assumed a fiduciary office, the authors instead justify trusts over traceably acquired rights and subrogation to traceably discharged debts as a remedy for unjust enrichment.[44]

IV. Unjust Enrichment

The view of Birks, Burrows, and (where D did not voluntarily assume a fiduciary relationship to C) Mitchell, Mitchell, and Watterson is that trusts over traceably acquired rights are remedies for unjust enrichment:

1. D is enriched by the traceably acquired right.
2. This is at C's expense because C can trace into it.

[39] Mitchell, Mitchell and Watterson (n 34) para 8-163.
[40] ibid para 8-164.
[41] *Butler v Rice* [1910] 2 Ch 277 (Ch).
[42] *Boscawen* (n 1).
[43] *Gertsch* (n 14).
[44] Mitchell, Mitchell and Watterson (n 34) paras 8-145–8-149, 39-31.

3. The unjust factor is variously identified as C's 'ignorance' of the transaction in which D acquired the right, C's 'powerlessness' to prevent the transaction, C's 'lack of consent' to the transaction, or a fiduciary's 'want of authority' to enter the transaction.[45]

Burrows, Mitchell, and Watterson suggest that the same unjust factor can trigger subrogation as a remedy for unjust enrichment:

1. D is enriched by the discharge of its debt to X.
2. This is at C's expense because C can trace into the payment that discharged D's debt to X.
3. Again, the unjust factor is variously identified as C's 'ignorance' of the transaction in which D's debt was discharged,[46] C's 'lack of consent' to the transaction, or a fiduciary's 'want of authority' to enter the transaction.[47]

However, no subrogation case has explicitly relied upon this unjust factor[48] and, even beyond the subrogation cases, it seems that only first instance decisions have relied on this unjust factor.[49]

As a matter of principle, commentators have offered many objections to the view that unjust enrichment justifies trusts over traceably acquired rights.[50]

[45] Birks, *Introduction* (n 5) 140–146; A Burrows, 'Proprietary Restitution: Unmasking Unjust Enrichment' (2001) 117 *LQR* 412; R Chambers and J Penner, 'Ignorance' in S Degeling and J Edelman (eds), *Unjust Enrichment in Commercial Law* (Pyrmont, NSW, Lawbook Co, 2008); A Burrows, *The Law of Restitution* (Oxford, OUP, 2011) 169, ch 6, ch 16; A Burrows, *A Restatement of the English Law of Unjust Enrichment* (Oxford, OUP, 2012) 92–98; Mitchell, Mitchell and Watterson (n 34) paras 8-153–8-166. L Smith, 'Unjust Enrichment, Property and the Structure of Trusts' (2000) 116 *LQR* 412, 415–28.

[46] C Mitchell and S Watterson, *Subrogation: Law and Practice* (Oxford, OUP, 2007) paras 6.42–6.50; Burrows, *Restitution* (n 45) 167.

[47] Mitchell, Mitchell and Watterson (n 34) paras 8-145–8-149, 39-31.

[48] Mitchell and Watterson (n 46) para 6.43 citing *Primlake Ltd v Matthews Associates (No 1)* [2006] EWHC 1227 (Ch), [2007] 1 BCLC 666 [340] (Lawrence Collins J).

[49] *Relfo Ltd v Varsani* [2012] EWHC 2168 (Ch) [88] (Sales J); *Scott v Bridge* [2020] EWHC 3116 (Ch) [139]–[140] (HHJ Paul Matthews). On the lack of other authority, see *Farah Constructions Pty Ltd v Say-Dee Pty Ltd* [2007] HCA 22, (2007) 230 CLR 89 [156] (Gleeson CJ, Gummow, Callinan, Heydon and Crennan JJ); Worthington, 'Justifying Claims to Secondary Profits' (n 34) 459–60; Mitchell and Watterson (n 46) paras 6.44, 6.48; Chambers and Penner (n 45) 253; W Swadling, 'Ignorance and Unjust Enrichment: The Problem of Title' (2008) 28 *OJLS* 627, 630; L Smith, 'Philosophical Foundations of Proprietary Remedies' in R Chambers, C Mitchell and J Penner (eds), *Philosophical Foundations of the Law of Unjust Enrichment* (Oxford, OUP, 2009) 298–99; Burrows, *Restitution* (n 45) 403; Burrows, *Restatement* (n 45) 93; Mitchell, Mitchell and Watterson (n 34) paras 8-05–8-06; G Virgo, *The Principles of the Law of Restitution* (Oxford, OUP, 2015) 152, 565.

[50] Worthington, 'Justifying Claims to Secondary Profits' (n 34) 455–60; RB Grantham and CEF Rickett, 'Property Rights as a Legally Significant Event' (2003) 62 *CLJ* 717; Chambers and Penner (n 45); Swadling, 'Ignorance and Unjust Enrichment' (n 49); W Swadling, 'Policy Arguments for Proprietary Restitution' (2008) 28 *LS* 506; B McFarlane, 'Unjust Enrichment, Property Rights and

Perhaps the biggest problem is that D is not enriched at C's expense.[51] Say that D holds shares on trust for C. In breach of trust, D transfers the shares to X in exchange for title to £100 in cash. X knows that the transaction is a breach of trust. In this situation, C can elect between a trust over X's shares and a trust over D's traceably acquired title to the £100.[52]

D has been enriched by the title to the £100. But this enrichment has not come at C's expense since C is still entitled to have the shares held on trust. Accordingly, it is difficult to see the trust over the traceably acquired right to the £100 as a remedy for D's unjust enrichment at C's expense.

The example can be modified to make the same point for subrogation. Say that D holds shares on trust for C. In breach of trust, D transfers the shares to X in exchange for the discharge of D's £100 debt to X. X knows that the transaction is a breach of trust. In this situation, C can elect between a trust over X's shares[53] and subrogation to X's traceably discharged right to £100 from D.[54]

D has been enriched by the discharge of its debt. But this enrichment has not come at C's expense since C is still entitled to have the shares held on trust. Accordingly, it is difficult to see subrogation as a remedy for D's unjust enrichment at C's expense.

One might object that C must elect between subrogation and the trust of the shares.[55] In order to be subrogated, C must relinquish any entitlement to a trust of the shares, so the discharge of D's debt does come at C's expense, and subrogation reverses D's unjust enrichment at C's expense. However, this makes the argument circular. It is premised on C having an election between subrogation and a trust of the shares. But the availability of subrogation is exactly what unjust enrichment is trying to explain.

Indirect Recipients' [2009] *RLR* 37; Smith, 'Philosophical Foundations of Proprietary Remedies' (n 49) 298–304; B McFarlane, 'Unjust Enrichment, Rights and Value' in D Nolan and A Robertson (eds), *Rights and Private Law* (Oxford, Hart Publishing, 2012); W Swadling, 'The Nature of "Knowing Receipt"' in PS Davies and J Penner (eds), *Equity, Trusts and Commerce* (Oxford, Hart Publishing, 2017) 317–22; TRS Cutts, 'Modern Money Had and Received' (2018) 38 *OJLS* 1; J English and MJ Hafeez-Baig, *The Law of Tracing* (Alexandria, NSW, Federation Press, 2021) paras 2.25–2.43.

[51] L Smith, 'Tracing' in A Burrows and Lord Rodger of Earlsferry (eds), *Mapping the Law: Essays in Memory of Peter Birks* (Oxford, OUP, 2006) 120–124; Swadling, 'Ignorance and Unjust Enrichment' (n 49); McFarlane, 'Unjust Enrichment, Property Rights and Indirect Recipients' (n 50); Smith, 'Philosophical Foundations of Proprietary Remedies' (n 49); McFarlane, 'Unjust Enrichment, Rights and Value' (n 50) 587; Swadling, 'The Nature of "Knowing Receipt"' (n 50) 318–21; Cutts, 'Modern Money Had and Received' (n 50); English and Hafeez-Baig (n 50) paras 2.29–2.33.

[52] *Foskett* (n 2).

[53] ibid.

[54] *Boscawen* (n 1).

[55] P Birks, 'Receipt' in P Birks and A Pretto (eds), *Breach of Trust* (Oxford, Hart Publishing, 2002) 232; Birks, *Unjust Enrichment* (n 5) 66–69.

Burrows' response is that whether D is enriched at C's expense 'is assessed factually and not in terms of legal entitlement'.[56] Applied to the examples above, the argument is that as a matter of fact C lost the shares because they are no longer held by D, even though C can still elect to have X hold the shares on trust.

English and Hafeez-Baig doubt that this works where C only ever had a beneficial interest under a trust, in their example a trust of a title to a car:

> [C] never had a right to or against the car, or a right to immediate possession of the car, in the first place. It cannot be said … that [C] has been deprived of possession of the car. To say that 'at [C]'s expense' is assessed factually in this example simply does not work.[57]

Moreover, as Chapter 3 explained, a factual assessment of enrichment makes it is difficult to explain why subrogation gives C rights with prima facie the same content as X's extinguished rights.[58] Watterson explains that the 'natural restitutionary response'[59] to factual enrichments is 'an order to pay a money sum reflecting the monetary value of [D]'s enrichment'.[60] Consequently, if enrichment is assessed factually, it is difficult to explain why subrogation gives C new (proprietary) rights with prima facie the same content as X's extinguished rights.

Unjust enrichment theorists are therefore on the horns of a dilemma. On the one hand, if whether D is enriched at C's expense is assessed legally, then any enrichment does not come at C's expense. On the other hand, if whether D is enriched at C's expense is assessed factually, then it is difficult to explain the form of the rights created by subrogation.

Unjust enrichment theorists might respond by saying that whether D is enriched is assessed legally, and whether that came at C's expense is assessed factually. This is implicitly the position taken by Watterson in a chapter in an edited collection. In the first half of the chapter, Watterson argues that subrogation is 'addressed to the release of D's liabilities, conceived as a "legal" enrichment'.[61] Then, in the second half of the chapter, Watterson shows that

[56] A Burrows, 'The Relationship Between Unjust Enrichment and Property: Some Unresolved Issues' in S Degeling and J Edelman (eds), *Unjust Enrichment in Commercial Law* (Pyrmont, NSW, Lawbook Co, 2008) 335; Burrows, *Restitution* (n 45) 195. See also Burrows, 'Proprietary Restitution' (n 45) 419; Burrows, *Restitution* (n 45) 194–98, 408; Mitchell, Mitchell and Watterson (n 34) paras 8-16–8-19.

[57] English and Hafeez-Baig (n 50) para 2.33.

[58] See ch 3, s III above.

[59] Watterson, 'Subrogation' (n 26) 440.

[60] ibid 438.

[61] ibid 441.

subrogation does not depend upon C tracing into the payment which discharged D's debt.[62] In Watterson's account, therefore, whether D is enriched is assessed legally and whether that enrichment came at C's expense is assessed factually. The test for whether D is enriched is divorced from the test for whether that enrichment came at C's expense.

The problem with divorcing these tests is that it becomes difficult to explain why subrogation gives C rights against D. That D is unjustly legally enriched by the release from its duty to X may explain why a new duty should be imposed on D with prima facie the same content as D's extinguished duty to X. But this does not explain why D's new duty should be owed to C. Conversely, the fact that C is unjustly factually worse off may explain why C should be given a right to a sum of money. But this does not explain why C's right should be against D. The argument that D is legally enriched, and that C is factually worse off, does not explain why the law should respond to this by subrogation, rather than giving C rights against the state and the state rights against D.[63]

In sum, the idea that subrogation to traceably discharged debts is a remedy for unjust enrichment does not explain why subrogation gives C (and not anyone else) rights against D (and not anyone else) with prima facie the same content as X's extinguished rights against D.

V. Property

A third view is that trusts over traceably acquired rights are justified to vindicate C's property rights. In *Foskett*, the House of Lords declared that the 'transmission of a claimant's property rights from one asset to its traceable proceeds is part of our law of property'.[64] Similarly, Virgo argues that trusts over traceably acquired

[62] ibid 448–64. See also Mitchell and Watterson (n 46) paras 5.48–5.50; S Watterson, '"Direct Transfers" in the Law of Unjust Enrichment' (2011) 64 *CLP* 435, 464–65.

[63] NJ McBride and P McGrath, 'The Nature of Restitution' (1995) 15 *OJLS* 33, 34; EJ Weinrib, *Corrective Justice* (Oxford, OUP, 2012) 6; F Wilmot-Smith, 'Should the Payee Pay?' (2017) 37 *OJLS* 844, 845; R Stevens, *The Laws of Restitution* (Oxford, OUP, 2023) 20.

[64] *Foskett* (n 2) 127E–F (Lord Millett). See also 108F–G (Lord Browne-Wilkinson), 112H (Lord Steyn), 115G (Lord Hoffmann), 126C–F (Lord Hope), 129D–H, 132A–B (Lord Millett); P Millett, 'Proprietary Restitution' in S Degeling and J Edelman (eds), *Equity in Commercial Law* (Pyrmont, NSW, Lawbook Co, 2005); P Millett, '*Jones v Jones*: Property or Unjust Enrichment?' in A Burrows and Lord Rodger of Earlsferry (eds), *Mapping the Law: Essays in Memory of Peter Birks* (Oxford, OUP, 2006).

rights[65] and subrogation both 'vindicate [C]'s equitable property rights'.[66] Three cases also suggest that the justification for subrogation is linked to property.

Most notably, in *Menelaou*, Lord Carnwath stated that 'there is a clear distinction of principle between a claim to enforce property rights and a claim for unjust enrichment' and '[s]ubrogation to a vendor's lien is a claim to a property right'.[67] By contrast, the rest of the Supreme Court treated subrogation as a remedy for unjust enrichment.[68] Lord Clarke said that this made it 'unnecessary' to consider Lord Carnwath's approach, although there was 'much to be said' for it.[69] Meanwhile, Lord Neuberger was 'attracted to the view that [subrogation] could be justified on the alternative basis of an orthodox proprietary claim rather than on unjust enrichment'[70] and to this extent agreed with Lord Carnwath.[71]

Second, in *Halifax Plc v Omar*, Jonathan Parker LJ said that:

> In the *BFC Case*, the House of Lords fashioned the restitutionary remedy of subrogation to meet a situation in which … property rights were not in issue. It did so by the application of the wider doctrine of unjust enrichment, so as to confer personal rights (as opposed to property rights) on [C] …. The instant case, on the other hand, does not require the remedy of subrogation to be fashioned in that special way. In my judgment, the instant case is a straightforward case involving property rights, calling into play well-settled principles.[72]

Subsequently, in *Eagle Star Insurance Co Ltd v Karasiewicz*, Arden LJ said that:

> the *Halifax* decision … explains that what might be described as the more usual case of subrogation is where money is lent to pay off a secured claim. The effect of the *Halifax* decision is that in that situation [C] is given the remedy by way of satisfaction of a pre-existing equitable proprietary right which is vindicated by the order for subrogation.[73]

[65] Virgo, *The Principles of the Law of Restitution* (n 49) 11–17, 152–53, 557–65, 631. See also Grantham and Rickett (n 50).

[66] Virgo, *The Principles of the Law of Restitution* (n 49) 637. See also G Virgo, 'Restitution and Unjust Enrichment in the Supreme Court: Reflections on *Bank of Cyprus UK Ltd v Menelaou*' [2016] University of Cambridge Faculty of Law Research Paper No 10/2016, ssrn.com/abstract=2724024; G Virgo, 'Unjust Enrichment' in W Day and S Worthington (eds), *Challenging Private Law: Lord Sumption on the Supreme Court* (Oxford, Hart Publishing, 2020) 179.

[67] *Menelaou* (n 1) [108].

[68] ibid [18], [37], [49]–[50] (Lord Clarke), [61]–[99] (Lord Neuberger), [141] (Lord Kerr and Lord Wilson).

[69] ibid [53]–[54].

[70] ibid [59].

[71] ibid [100]–[104].

[72] *Halifax Plc v Omar* [2002] EWCA Civ 121, [2002] 2 P&CR 26 [71] referring to *BFC* (n 1).

[73] *Eagle Star Insurance Co Ltd v Karasiewicz* [2002] EWCA Civ 940 [19].

Birks made two criticisms of the view that property justifies trusts over traceably acquired rights.[74] First, he said that the view makes a '[c]ategorical error': property is one of the law's responses to an event, not an event to which the law responds.[75] Those who treat property as a justification therefore mistake the thing that needs to be explained for its explanation. Second, Birks said that this error was concealed by the 'fiction of persistence' in which C's 'original right in the original asset simply persisted in, or was transmitted to, the substitute'.[76] This is fiction because the 'right in the substitute is not the same right, and … [its existence] has to be fully explained'.[77]

Grantham, Rickett, and Virgo respond to these criticisms by explaining that a trust over a traceably acquired right is not the persistence of C's original right. Instead, it is a new right justified by, and created in response to the event of, D's interference with the original right.[78]

However, this still does not justify why the law responds to this interference by imposing a trust over the traceably acquired right, rather than responding in another way such as giving C a right to compensation from D.[79] As Mitchell, Mitchell, and Watterson put it:

> there is nothing inherent in the concept of ownership which dictates that the owner of an asset must also own its unauthorised substitute. If an owner is afforded such rights, it is a contingent choice which our system has made, which must itself be justified.[80]

The same applies to subrogation. C's property rights need not be vindicated by subrogation.[81] The law could vindicate C's property rights in another way, such as by giving C a right to compensation.[82] As a result, property does not justify subrogation's form.

[74] Birks, 'Receipt' (n 55) 215–22; Birks, *Unjust Enrichment* (n 5) 21–38; Millett, '*Jones v Jones*' (n 64) 270–72. See also Burrows, 'Proprietary Restitution' (n 45); R Chambers, 'Tracing and Unjust Enrichment' in JW Neyers, M McInnes and SGA Pitel (eds), *Understanding Unjust Enrichment* (Oxford, Hart Publishing, 2004) 264–65, 272–78; Mitchell and Watterson (n 46) para 6.50; Burrows, *Restitution* (n 45) 183–91; Mitchell, Mitchell and Watterson (n 34) paras 8-156–8-159, 39-24.

[75] Birks, *Unjust Enrichment* (n 5) 32–33.

[76] ibid 35.

[77] Birks, 'Receipt' (n 55) 216.

[78] Grantham and Rickett (n 50); Virgo, *The Principles of the Law of Restitution* (n 49) 15, 563.

[79] English and Hafeez-Baig (n 50) para 2.20.

[80] Mitchell, Mitchell and Watterson (n 34) para 8-157. See also Worthington, 'Justifying Claims to Secondary Profits' (n 34) 458–66; Birks, 'Receipt' (n 55) 219; B McFarlane, *The Structure of Property Law* (Oxford, Hart Publishing, 2008) 328; Burrows, *Restitution* (n 45) 183, 186; Cutts, 'The Role of Tracing in Claiming' (n 34) 121–26; Watterson, 'Subrogation' (n 26) 463; English and Hafeez-Baig (n 50) paras 2.12–2.20.

[81] Watterson, 'Subrogation' (n 26) 463.

[82] English and Hafeez-Baig (n 50) para 2.20.

VI. Next Best

Stevens offers a fourth possible justification for trusts over traceably acquired rights:

> The trustee's duty here is one of next best compliance. The reasons justifying the original obligation [to hold the original right on trust] do not disappear when they can no longer be perfectly complied with. The reasons persist and create a new obligation. He ought not to have exchanged the [original right] but, given that he has, he ought now to do the nearest thing to complying with his original duty. This duty includes, at the beneficiaries' option, not using the right he has obtained in exchange for his own benefit. … Once the reasons for the creation of a trust have been established, those reasons will suffice to generate a trust over substitute rights.[83]

In some cases,[84] Stevens argues that this can also justify subrogation to traceably discharged debts:

> Just as where the trustee has substituted trust rights for new rights, his duties as trustee justify the creation of a new duty upon him equivalent to the one that he has discharged. … Given the breach of trust, this is the 'next best' equivalent to his having complied with his original duty that is now available.[85]

A. Problem 1: Form

The fundamental problem with this account is that it does not explain the form of rights created by subrogation, since it is not clear why subrogation 'is the "next best" equivalent to [D] having complied with his original duty'. D's original duty was to hold the original right on trust. A trust over the traceably acquired right might be said to be the next best equivalent to D's performance of its original duty,

[83] Stevens (n 63) 243–45. See also S Agnew and B McFarlane, 'The Paradox of the Equitable Proprietary Claim' in S Agnew and B McFarlane (eds), *Modern Studies in Property Law: Volume 10* (Oxford, Hart Publishing, 2019) 304–07; B McFarlane and R Stevens, 'What's Special about Equity? Rights about Rights' in D Klimchuk, I Samet and HE Smith (eds), *Philosophical Foundations of the Law of Equity* (Oxford, OUP, 2020) 204; English and Hafeez-Baig (n 50) paras 2.5, 2.44–2.65.

[84] Specifically, those 'where the debt is discharged not by a payment by [C] himself but instead with money in relation to which he has an entitlement, either at law or in equity': Stevens (n 63) 253. In cases where C pays D, Stevens argues that subrogation has a different justification: 252–53. That other justification will be considered by ch 10 below.

[85] Stevens (n 63) 253–54.

since it takes the same form as the original duty: a duty to hold a right on trust. However, the same argument cannot justify subrogation. Subrogation does not require D to hold a right on trust, and so it takes a different form to the original duty to hold a right on trust.

Instead, Stevens suggests that subrogation is the '"next best" equivalent to [D] having complied with his original duty' because:

> The position we are seeking as nearly as possible to put the parties into is one where the money that had been held on trust for [C] had not been used to discharge a debt owed by D. Given the discharge of D's obligation to X, how can this position now be most closely replicated? The answer … is that the next best position achievable is for an identical debt to the one D owed to X now to be owed to [C], on both the same terms and subject to the same security ….[86]

However, the discharge of D's obligation to X is not a 'given'. As Chapter 7 showed, the law could say that D's debt to X was not discharged and impose an obligation on X to repay D. This would have the effect of reversing the transaction, putting all parties back into their original positions, including reinstating D's original duty. This would be the 'best', perfect equivalent of D's original duty, rather than merely the 'next best'. Accordingly, this account fails to explain why subrogation gives C new rights with prima facie the same content as X's extinguished rights, rather than reversing the transaction which discharged X's rights.

Even if the discharge of D's obligation were taken as a 'given', there are many other possible duties that the law could impose on D. The law could instead require D to pay compensation to C or require D to pay a penalty to C or to the state. It is unclear why subrogation (and not these other duties) is the next best equivalent to D having complied with its original duty.

B. Problem 2: Scope

A second issue is that this account has a more limited scope than Stevens claims for it. If subrogation is the next best equivalent to D's original duty to hold a right on trust, then subrogation can only be justified where D had a duty or liability[87] to hold a right on trust. It therefore cannot justify subrogation in two types of case.

[86] ibid 254.
[87] ibid 254.

The first is where D acquires a right, but is never under a duty or liability in relation to that right. Chapter 4 used the case of *Anfield* as an example.[88] D owned property, subject to X's first legal charge. C made a loan to D, who used it to redeem X's charge. In return, C acquired a new charge ('the 2006 charge') but failed to register it. Subsequently, Anfield obtained a charging order over the property and registered it, gaining priority over C's 2006 charge. The court held that C was entitled to be subrogated to X's extinguished charge, which had priority over Anfield's charge.

When C paid the loan monies to D, C lost any entitlement in relation to them. D acquired title to the loan monies free from any trust or mere equity. Accordingly, D was never under a duty or liability to hold any right on trust, and so subrogation cannot be justified as the 'next best equivalent' to such a duty.

Furthermore, this account cannot justify subrogation where D never acquires a right so never comes under a duty or liability to hold a right on trust. This is so where it is not D but a fourth party who pays X, discharging D's debt, such as in *Boscawen*.[89] D owned a house subject to X's charge. D agreed to sell the property to purchasers. C agreed to loan the purchasers funds for the purchase, in exchange for a charge over the property. C paid the loan to the purchasers' solicitors, who paid it to D's solicitors. D's solicitors were authorised to pay the monies to X on completion of the sale of the property. However, D's solicitors acted too soon, and paid the monies to X before completion, partially discharging X's charge.

The sale then fell through and completion never took place. This left D with unencumbered title to the house. Meanwhile, C had paid out the loan monies but had not received any security. To remedy this, Millett LJ held that C was subrogated to X's extinguished charge.

Here, the loan monies were never paid to D. Accordingly, D never acquired a right,[90] so never came under any duty or liability to hold a right on trust. Nevertheless, Stevens stretches his account to encompass *Boscawen* by saying that D 'ought to reverse what has occurred, just as much as someone who has acquired a specific right transferred in breach of trust should do so'.[91] However, if a duty or liability to hold a right on trust is what justifies subrogation, and D was never under such duty or liability, then this account offers no reason for why D 'ought

[88] *Anfield (UK) Ltd v Bank of Scotland Plc* [2010] EWHC 2374 (Ch), [2011] 1 WLR 2414. See ch 4, s III(D)(i) above.

[89] *Boscawen* (n 1). Ch 4, s III(A) above referred to these cases as Type 1, 3, and 4 cases.

[90] *Russell Gould Pty Ltd v Ramangkura* [2014] NSWCA 310, (2014) 87 NSWLR 552 [36] (Barrett JA); Smith, 'Tracing into the Payment of a Debt' (n 38) 298; Smith, *The Law of Tracing* (n 38) 150.

[91] Stevens (n 63) 254.

to reverse what has occurred'. The failure of this account to explain *Boscawen* is particularly notable, given that Millett LJ's judgment is one of the most prominent examples of the analogy between trusts over traceably acquired rights and subrogation to traceably discharged debts.[92]

In short, even if subrogation were justified as the next best equivalent of D's duty or liability to hold a right on trust, this can only justify subrogation where D had such a duty or liability. It cannot justify subrogation where D never acquires a right (such as in *Boscawen*) or acquires a right free from any duty or liability in relation to it (such as in *Anfield*).

VII. Chapter Summary

This chapter evaluated the popular view that trusts over traceably acquired rights and subrogation to traceably discharged debts share the same justification. It considered four possible justifications for trusts over traceably acquired rights and showed that each fails to justify the form of rights created by subrogation. It is mistaken to think that, just because trusts over traceably acquired rights and subrogation to traceably discharged debts both use the rules of tracing, they must have the same justification. Instead, the following chapter argues that the distinctive form of rights created by subrogation reflects a distinctive justification.

[92] See s II(A) above.

10

Properly Distributing the Burden of a Debt

I. Introduction

This chapter[1] argues that subrogation's distinctive form reflects a distinctive justification. Subrogation is justified by ensuring that the burden of debts are distributed as they should be. If C bears the burden of D's debt to X and this burden should have been borne by D, then the burden needs to be lifted from C and reinstated upon D. Subrogation achieves this by reinstating the debt and having D now owe the debt to C. Thus, the particular form of rights created by subrogation reflects subrogation's particular role in ensuring interpersonal justice. Subrogation gives C new rights against D with prima facie the same content as X's extinguished rights against D because this ensures that the burden of D's extinguished debt to X is distributed as it should be.

For example, in *Forbes v Jackson*, a debtor borrowed £200 from a creditor, secured by a mortgage over the debtor's property.[2] A surety guaranteed the debt. The debtor defaulted so the surety paid £200 to the creditor, discharging the debtor's debt and the mortgage. Hall VC held that the debtor owed £200 to the surety and that the surety was 'entitled to have all [X's] securities preserved for him' including the mortgage.[3]

This can be justified as an instance of subrogation properly distributing the burden of a debt. The debtor agreed to mortgage his property as security for the creditor's loan. Consequently, the debtor agreed that his title to the property would be encumbered until the loan was repaid. A surety agrees to pay if the

[1] Elements of this chapter were published as R Gregson, 'Subrogation, Marshalling, and Property' in N Mrockova, A Nair and L Rostill (eds), *Modern Studies in Property Law Volume 12* (Oxford, Hart Publishing, 2023).

[2] *Forbes v Jackson* (1882) 19 ChD 615 (Ch).

[3] ibid 621.

principal debtor cannot so, as between the debtor and the surety, the debtor agreed to bear the burden of repaying the loan and releasing the mortgage. Meanwhile, the debtor's other voluntary creditors did not bargain for security over the property. They therefore agreed not to have recourse to the property until the debtor had borne the burden of the debts secured over the property.[4]

The surety then paid the creditor, discharging the debt and the mortgage. The surety therefore bore the burden of discharging the debt and the mortgage, whereas this burden should have been borne by the debtor. The other creditors now had recourse to the property, whereas they should not have done before the debtor had borne the burden of the debt which had been secured over the property.

To put all this right, the surety was subrogated to creditor's extinguished mortgage. This lifted the burden of discharging the debt and the mortgage from the surety and reinstated it upon the debtor. It denied the other creditors recourse to the property, until the debtor had borne the burden of the debt which had been secured over the property. Thus, subrogation was justified by properly distributing the burden of a debt. As Smith puts it:

> The surety has guaranteed the risk of non-payment by the debtor to the creditor. He has not guaranteed any larger risk. If the creditor has real security for the debt, then the creditor's risk is reduced; so then should be the surety's. The only way to ensure that the surety's risk is no greater than the risk taken by the creditor is to provide that the surety shall have the benefit of any security, once he has paid the creditor.[5]

This justification is also reflected in the reasoning of many cases.[6] For example, in *Duncan Fox & Co v North & South Wales Bank*, Lord Selborne LC said that subrogation is justified when

[4] *Drew v Lockett* (1863) 32 Beav 499, 505, 55 ER 196, 198 (Sir John Romilly MR); C Rotherham, 'Subrogation' in S Hedley and M Halliwell (eds), *The Law of Restitution* (London, Butterworths, 2002) para 8.14.

[5] L Smith, 'Book Review' (1995) 9 *TLI* 133, 134. See also L Smith, 'Security' in A Burrows (ed), *English Private Law* (Oxford, OUP, 2013) para 5.178.

[6] *Yonge v Reynell* (1852) 9 Hare 809, 818–19, 68 ER 744, 748–49 (Sir GJ Turner VC); *Re Downer Enterprises* [1974] 1 WLR 1460 (Ch) 1468C–69A (Pennycuick VC); *Bofinger v Kingsway Group Ltd* [2009] HCA 44, (2009) 239 CLR 269 [7]–[8] (Gummow, Hayne, Heydon, Kiefel, and Bell JJ). See also C Mitchell, *The Law of Contribution and Reimbursement* (Oxford, OUP, 2003) paras 1.01, 1.09, 1.11, 3.28–3.29; JA Dieckmann, 'Scots Influence on English Law: The Guarantor's Right to Derivative Recourse (Subrogation)' (2004) 8 *Edinburgh LR* 329, 343–45, 349–54; JA Dieckmann, 'The Normative Basis of Subrogation and Comparative Law: Select Explanations in the Common Law, Civil Law and in Mixed Legal Systems of the Guarantor's Right to Derivative Recourse' (2012) 27 *Tulane European & Civil Law Forum* 49, 76–83; JA Dieckmann, 'The Province of Subrogation Determined: Some Corrections – a Functional Analysis of the Guarantor's Right to Derivative Recourse, Comprising a Critique of the Restitutionary Thesis' (2012) 20 *ERPL* 989, 1041; R Stevens, 'The Unjust Enrichment Disaster' (2018) 134 *LQR* 574, 588; NJ McBride, *The Humanity of Private Law: Part I: Explanation* (Oxford, Hart Publishing, 2019) 212–13; L Smith, 'Restitution: A New Start?' in P Devonshire and

> there is a primary and a secondary liability of two persons for one and the same debt, the debt being, as between the two, that of one of those persons only, and not equally of both, so that the other, if he should be compelled to pay it, would be entitled to reimbursement from the person by whom (as between the two) it ought to have been paid.[7]

The remainder of this chapter will develop this justification for subrogation in greater detail. Section II considers why D ought to bear the burden of a debt. Section III clears up some terminology associated with this justification. Section IV considers when C bears the burden of a debt. Section V considers the rule that subrogation will not give C more than it bargained for. It explains this rule on the basis that subrogation is not justified insofar as C consents to bearing the burden of D's debt. Finally, section VI considers what rights subrogation should create.

II. Why Should D Bear the Burden?

The reason why, and extent to which, D ought to bear the burden of a debt varies from case to case.[8] In some cases, there is an agreement about where the burden should fall. In *Forbes*, for example, the parties agreed who was the guarantor and who was the principal debtor, making it clear that the burden of the debt should fall on the principal debtor.[9]

This agreement need not be between C and D. For instance, in *Deering v Earl of Winchelsea*, Sir Edward Deering, Lord Winchelsea, and Sir John Rous each stood surety for a principal debtor.[10] The debtor went insolvent, and the creditor obtained judgment against Sir Edward Deering. The Court of Exchequer held that Deering was entitled to contribution from the other two sureties. Here, there was no agreement between the sureties. But each had agreed with the principal debtor to be a surety, so each had agreed that the burden of the debt ought to fall on the principal debtor, and that they would pay if the principal debtor could

R Havelock (eds), *The Impact of Equity and Restitution in Commerce* (Oxford, Hart Publishing, 2019) 106–08; R Stevens, *The Laws of Restitution* (Oxford, OUP, 2023) 253–54.

[7] *Duncan Fox & Co v North & South Wales Bank* (1880) 6 App Cas 1 (HL) 11.

[8] Mitchell, *The Law of Contribution and Reimbursement* (n 6), ch 10; Smith, 'Restitution' (n 6) 107; C Mitchell, 'Other Reasons for Restitution' in E Bant, K Barker and S Degeling (eds), *Research Handbook on Unjust Enrichment and Restitution* (Cheltenham, Edward Elgar Publishing, 2020) 391; Stevens, *The Laws of Restitution* (n 6) 154; C Mitchell, P Mitchell and S Watterson, *Goff and Jones: The Law of Unjust Enrichment* (London, Sweet & Maxwell, 2022) paras 20-87–20-110.

[9] *Forbes* (n 2) 621 (Hall VC).

[10] *Deering v Earl of Winchelsea* (1787) 2 Bos & Pul 270, 126 ER 1276.

not. Consequently, as between the sureties, the burden of the debt ought to be shared equally. Lord Chief Baron Eyre said 'as between themselves they are in aequali jure, and … ought to contribute in equal shares'.[11]

In other cases, a debt is assumed involuntarily and so there is no agreement about where its burden should fall. In *Niru Battery Manufacturing Co v Milestone Trading Ltd (No 2)*, X was a victim of a fraud which was caused by C's negligent misrepresentation, and which left D unjustly enriched at X's expense.[12] X obtained judgment against C and D. C owed X a duty to compensate X for the losses caused by its negligence, while D owed X a duty to make restitution of its unjust enrichment at X's expense. C and D were therefore jointly and severally indebted to X under a court judgment. C paid the whole of the judgment, discharging both parties' debt to X. C then sought to be subrogated to X's extinguished rights against D.

Here, no agreement decided who should bear the burden of the debt. Instead, the Court of Appeal explained that if the burden of the debt remained with C, this 'would leave [D] holding monies which, if acting in good faith, it would have repaid to [X]'.[13] By contrast, 'if [D] had paid back the money [to X] …, as it ought to have done and as it would have done if it had been acting in good faith, [X] would have suffered no loss and [C] would not have been liable to [X]'.[14] The Court therefore held that the burden of the debt ought to fall on D not C, and so C was subrogated to X's extinguished rights against D.

III. Terminology

Unjust enrichment theorists often label this justification 'legal compulsion' or 'secondary liability'. However, these labels are distracting and unnecessary.

A. Legal Compulsion

Birks argued that, where C pays C and D's common debt to X, subrogation was justified to reverse D's unjust enrichment. D was enriched at C's expense because

[11] *Deering v Earl of Winchelsea* (1787) 2 Bos & Pul 270, 274, 126 ER 1276, 1278–79.

[12] *Niru Battery Manufacturing Co v Milestone Trading Ltd (No 2)* [2004] EWCA Civ 487, [2004] 1 CLC 882 ('*Niru Battery* (CA)'). See also *Brook's Wharf & Bull Wharf Ltd v Goodman Bros* [1937] 1 KB 534 (CA).

[13] *Niru Battery* (CA) (n 12) [30] (Clarke LJ).

[14] ibid [29] (Clarke LJ).

C paid X, discharging D's debt to X. D's enrichment was rendered unjust by the unjust factor of 'legal compulsion': C was under a duty to pay X so the legal system compelled C to pay X, vitiating C's intention to enrich D.[15]

However, legal compulsion is not unjust. As Hilliard explained, a 'threat to have recourse to legal process is not objectionable, quite the reverse in fact'.[16] Mitchell gives an example:

> People routinely bind themselves by contract to perform obligations, and no question arises of their recovering the value of their performance via an action in unjust enrichment on the ground that their performance was compelled by the law of contract.[17]

As a result, Burrows writes that 'legal compulsion is better viewed as a policy-motivated unjust factor designed to ensure that liability is ultimately borne by the appropriate party in the appropriate amount'.[18] Burrows therefore endorses the idea that subrogation can be justified by C bearing the burden of a debt which ought to have been borne by D.[19] However, labelling this idea 'legal compulsion' is misleading given that this compulsion is not unjust and it plays no role in justifying subrogation.

B. Secondary Liability

Mitchell, Mitchell, and Watterson label the same idea 'secondary liability':

> [D] is the person who should ultimately bear some or all of the burden of paying [X]: in the language of the cases, because [D] is 'primarily' and [C] only 'secondarily' liable for [D]'s share of their common obligation.[20]

Mitchell, Mitchell, and Watterson therefore also endorse the idea that subrogation can be justified by C bearing the burden of a debt which ought to have been borne by D.[21]

[15] P Birks, *An Introduction to the Law of Restitution* (Oxford, Clarendon Press, 1989) 185–93. See also *Samsoondar v Capital Insurance Company Ltd* [2020] UKPC 33, [2021] 2 All ER 1105 [21] (Lord Burrows); G Virgo, *The Principles of the Law of Restitution* (Oxford, OUP, 2015) 233–53.

[16] J Hilliard, 'A Case for the Abolition of Legal Compulsion as a Ground of Restitution' (2002) 61 *CLJ* 551, 553. See also Dieckmann, 'The Province of Subrogation Determined' (n 6) 1031–33; Stevens, *The Laws of Restitution* (n 6) 169.

[17] Mitchell, *The Law of Contribution and Reimbursement* (n 6) para 3.27.

[18] A Burrows, *The Law of Restitution* (Oxford, OUP, 2011) 437. See also A Burrows, *A Restatement of the English Law of Unjust Enrichment* (Oxford, OUP, 2012) 99.

[19] Burrows, *Restitution* (n 18) 148; Burrows, *Restatement* (n 18) 173.

[20] Mitchell, Mitchell and Watterson (n 8) para 19-01. See also *Niru Battery Manufacturing Co v Milestone Trading Ltd (No 2)* [2003] EWHC 1032 (Comm), [2003] 2 All ER (Comm) 365 [31] (Moore-Bick J).

[21] C Mitchell and S Watterson, *Subrogation: Law and Practice* (Oxford, OUP, 2007) para 6.04; Mitchell, Mitchell and Watterson (n 8) para 39-30.

Calling this idea 'secondary liability' works well in cases like *Forbes* where C and D shared a common debt which arose under an agreement.[22] D agreed to take primary responsibility for paying X and C agreed to take secondary responsibility by agreeing to pay X if D failed to do so. The reason for subrogation was enforcing this agreement about who had 'primary' and 'secondary liability' for the burden of a common debt.

However, the language of 'secondary liability' is less apt in cases like *Niru Battery* where no agreement decided who had 'primary' and 'secondary liability' for the debt.[23] Instead, the reason that D ought to bear the burden of the debt to X, and thus the reason for subrogation, was to ensure that both D's unjust enrichment at X's expense, and X's loss caused by C's negligence, were reversed.[24] This led the Court to describe D as primarily and C as secondarily liable for the debt. But this was merely a conclusory label which did no justificatory work.[25]

As such, this book agrees with the substance of Burrows' and Mitchell, Mitchell, and Watterson's position: subrogation can be justified by ensuring that the burdens of debts are distributed as they should be. However, labelling this justification 'legal compulsion' or 'secondary liability' is inaccurate and unnecessary.

IV. Did C Bear the Burden of D's Debt?

It is often thought that properly distributing the burden of a debt can only justify subrogation where C was obliged to pay D's debt,[26] such as the guarantor case of *Forbes*.[27] This section challenges that assumption in three steps. First, it argues that the justification extends to cases where C pays D's debt, even though C was not obliged to do so. Second, it pushes this justification further still, arguing that it also operates where C does not pay D's debt but C can trace into the payment

22 *Duncan Fox* (n 7); *Forbes* (n 2).

23 *Niru Battery* (CA) (n 12). Burrows, *Restatement* (n 18) 99.

24 *Niru Battery* (CA) (n 12) [29]–[30] (Clarke LJ); Stevens, *The Laws of Restitution* (n 6) 172.

25 *Niru Battery* (CA) (n 12) [69] (Clarke LJ), [85] (Sedley LJ).

26 *Samsoondar* (n 15) [21] (Lord Burrows); Mitchell and Watterson (n 21) para 6.07; Burrows, *Restitution* (n 18), ch 17; Burrows, *Restatement* (n 18) 98–99; Mitchell, Mitchell and Watterson (n 8) paras 20-01–20-02.

27 *Forbes* (n 2).

which discharged D's debt. Finally, it argues that this justification does not extend to cases where C merely causes the discharge of D's debt.

A. C Pays D's Debt, Even Though C was not Obliged to do So

Turning first to cases where C pays D's debt, even though C was not obliged to do so, two questions must be distinguished:

1. Did C's payment to X discharge D's debt?
2. If so, is C subrogated to X's extinguished rights against D?

As to first question, the rules are complex and controversial:

- C's payment discharges D's debt if D authorises or subsequently ratifies it.[28]
- C's payment also discharges D's debt if it is made to recover C's property.[29] In *Exall v Partridge*, D owed rent to X.[30] C's carriage was on D's land and X distrained it for D's arrears. To recover the carriage, C paid D's rent to X. The Court of King's Bench held that C could recover this payment from D. This seems to assume that C's payment extinguished D's debt to X.[31]
- If C's payment was induced by a mistake, Chapter 7 showed that the authorities are divided on how the law should respond. Some cases, like *Barclays Bank Ltd v WJ Simms Son & Cooke (Southern) Ltd*, hold that D's debt is not discharged, and C has a claim against X for restitution of its mistaken payment.[32] Others, like *Butler v Rice* and *B Liggett (Liverpool) Ltd v Barclays Bank Ltd*, hold that C's payment discharges D's debt to X, and C is subrogated to X's extinguished rights against D.[33]

[28] *Belshaw v Bush* (1851) 11 CB 191, 206–07, 138 ER 444, 450–51 (Maule J); *Simpson v Eggington* (1855) 10 Ex 845, 847–48, 156 ER 683, 684 (Parke B).

[29] Burrows, *Restitution* (n 18) 440–41.

[30] (1799) 8 TR 308, 101 ER 1405.

[31] Birks, *Introduction* (n 15) 186–87; Burrows, *Restitution* (n 18) 440–41; Mitchell and Watterson (n 21) para 2.10, fn 15; Mitchell, Mitchell and Watterson (n 8) para 5-72 fn 150.

[32] *Barclays Bank Ltd v WJ Simms Son & Cooke (Southern) Ltd* [1980] QB 677 (QB). See also *Crantrave Ltd v Lloyds Bank Plc* [2000] QB 917 (CA) 923G–H (Pill LJ).

[33] *Butler v Rice* [1910] 2 Ch 277 (Ch) 282 (Warrington J); *B Liggett (Liverpool) Ltd v Barclays Bank Ltd* [1928] 1 KB 48 (KB); PG Watts, '"Unjust Enrichment" – the Potion That Induces Well-Meaning Sloppiness of Thought' (2016) 69 *CLP* 289, 307.

As a matter of principle, many – though not all[34] – writers argue that D's debt should be discharged whenever C pays X with the intention of discharging D's debt.[35] This is the position taken by South African law.[36]

In deciding whether English law should follow suit, there are a myriad of relevant considerations. On the one hand, a rule that says 'D's debt is discharged whenever C pays X with the intention of discharging D's debt' has the merit of simplicity,[37] giving parties certainty about their legal rights and obligations. It also protects X's security of receipt.[38]

On the other hand, one might take the view that C and X should not be able to change D's legal duties without D's consent.[39] Another concern is malicious intervenors. There are some English cases,[40] but the classic example is the American case of *Norton v Haggett*.[41] Following two arguments, Norton was 'desirous of harming' Haggett.[42] Norton paid off a bank's mortgage over Haggett's home, then sought to be subrogated to the bank's mortgage. The Supreme Court of Vermont held that the bank's mortgage was extinguished but denied Norton's claim to be subrogated to it. The Court explained that Norton 'was an intermeddler, and officiousness is not to be encouraged' and that Norton's 'good faith was apparently questionable'.[43]

Alternatively, a legal system could respond to a malicious intervenor like Norton by preventing his payment from discharging the debt in the first place. This is one argument for rule that says that C's payment to X cannot discharge D's debt to X unless C was obliged to pay D's debt or authorised by D to do so.[44]

In sum, when deciding when an unauthorised intervenor's payment should discharge another's debt, there are many factors in play. As a result, a legal system

[34] P Birks and J Beatson, 'Unrequested Payment of Another's Debt' (1976) 92 *LQR* 188, 188–202; P Watts, 'Mistaken Payment of Another's Debt – a Brief Defence of the Orthodox View' [1993] *NZ Recent LR* 248; J Beatson, *The Use and Abuse of Unjust Enrichment: Essays on the Law of Restitution* (Oxford, Clarendon Press, 1991) 200–05; Stevens, *The Laws of Restitution* (n 6) 160–61.

[35] Birks, *Introduction* (n 15) 189–191; Mitchell and Watterson (n 21) para 2.05; Burrows, *Restitution* (n 18) 460–68; Burrows, *Restatement* (n 18) 100; Mitchell, Mitchell and Watterson (n 8) para 5-62. cf D Friedmann, 'Payment of Another's Debt' (1983) 99 *LQR* 534.

[36] *Absa Bank Ltd v Moore* [2016] ZACC 34 [33] (Cameron J).

[37] Birks, *Introduction* (n 15) 189–91; Mitchell and Watterson (n 21) para 2.05; Mitchell, Mitchell and Watterson (n 8) para 5-62.

[38] Friedmann (n 35) 547–54.

[39] *Norton v Haggett* 117 Vt 130, (1952) 85 A 2d 571, 574 (Blackmer J); Watts, 'Mistaken Payment of Another's Debt' (n 34) 249; Stevens, *The Laws of Restitution* (n 6) 160–61.

[40] *Exall v Partridge* (1799) 8 TR 308, 310, 101 ER 1405, 1406 (Lord Kenyon CJ); *Owen v Tate* [1976] 1 QB 402 (CA).

[41] *Norton* (n 39).

[42] ibid 573 (Blackmer J).

[43] ibid (Blackmer J).

[44] Birks and Beatson (n 34) 206; Beatson (n 34) 202–03; Stevens, *The Laws of Restitution* (n 6) 161.

may reasonably choose one of a range of options on this matter[45] and so this book does not take a position on the first of the two questions stated above. Instead, it argues that the answer to the second question is 'yes': if D's debt is discharged, subrogation can be justified whenever C bore the burden of a debt which ought to have been borne by D, even if the debt was D's alone and C was not obliged to pay it.

This is illustrated by *Cunliffe Brooks & Co v Blackburn and District Benefit Building Society*.[46] There, the Blackburn Building Society had an overdrawn account at its bank. The Society instructed the bank to pay the Society's creditors and the bank did so, making the Society's account further overdrawn. It then transpired that the Society had acted ultra vires in borrowing from the bank, so was not contractually obliged to repay the bank. Nevertheless, the House of Lords held that the Society was obliged to repay the bank 'as far as it can be made out that the moneys which were advanced by the bankers simply went to pay the legitimate debts and liabilities of the society'.[47]

Importantly, the bank was not indebted to the Society's creditors. The Society and the bank did not share a common debt to the creditors. Nevertheless, the House assumed without discussion that the bank's payments had extinguished the Society's debts, and held that the Society was obliged to repay the bank. Lord Blackburn said that 'Any person, whether the bankers or any one else, might pay off the creditors and stand in the shoes of the creditor who is paid off'.[48]

Similarly, in the Court of Appeal Lord Selborne LC said that:

> those who pay legitimate demands which they are bound in some way or other to meet, and have had the benefit of other people's money advanced to them for that purpose, shall not retain that benefit so as, in substance, to make those other people pay their debts.[49]

Lord Selborne LC's reasoning echoes his judgment two years earlier in *Duncan Fox*. In *Duncan Fox*, C paid C and D's common debt to X. Lord Selborne LC justified subrogation on the basis that C was 'entitled to reimbursement from

[45] S Hedley, *Restitution: Its Division and Ordering* (London, Sweet & Maxwell, 2001) 140–44.

[46] *Cunliffe Brooks & Co v Blackburn and District Benefit Building Society* (1884) 9 App Cas 857 (HL) ('*Blackburn* (HL)'). See also *Re Wrexham Mold & Connah's Quay Railway Co* [1899] 1 Ch 440 (CA); *Brocklesby v Temperance Permanent Building Society* [1895] AC 173 (HL).

[47] *Blackburn Building Society v Cunliffe Brooks & Co* (1882) 22 ChD 61 (CA) ('*Blackburn* (CA)') 71 (Lord Selborne LC) affd *Blackburn* (HL) (n 46).

[48] *Blackburn* (HL) (n 46) 866.

[49] *Blackburn* (CA) (n 47) 71 (Lord Selborne LC).

the person by whom … [the debt] ought to have been paid'.[50] In *Blackburn*, the bank paid the Society's debts, even though the bank was not indebted to the creditors. Lord Selborne LC justified subrogation on much the same basis: the Society 'shall not … make those other people pay their debts'.[51] Thus, Lord Blackburn and Lord Selborne LC recognised that subrogation is justified whenever C pays a debt which D ought to bear the burden of, and that this justification is not limited to cases where the debt is C and D's common debt.

Lord Selborne LC's judgment in *Blackburn* was applied in many subsequent cases.[52] However, the judgment is now largely forgotten and an error has crept in, saying that properly distributing the burden of a debt can only justify subrogation where C was obliged to pay D's debt.[53] This is for two reasons.

First, the dispute in *Blackburn*, and almost all the cases which applied Lord Selborne LC's reasoning, arose because a company borrowed money ultra vires. Legislation now provides that the 'validity of an act done by a company shall not be called into question on the ground of lack of capacity'[54] so these cases no longer arise. Understandably, the treatises tend to relegate these cases to footnotes and omit their reasoning.[55]

Second, there was confusion over whether *Blackburn* was a subrogation case. The judgments in *Blackburn* did not explicitly use the language of 'subrogation', though Lord Blackburn said that the bank 'might … stand in the shoes of the creditor who is paid off'.[56] In *Wenlock*, the Court of Appeal applied Lord Selbourne LC's reasoning and held that C was 'entitled to be subrogated to the rights of [the] creditors'.[57] However, subsequent cases distinguished subrogation from the ultra vires borrowing principle in *Blackburn*, because it was feared that subrogation could 'place the lender in a better position than that in which he would have been if his loan had not been prohibited'.[58] Ultimately, these fears were unfounded: it is

[50] *Duncan Fox* (n 7) 11.

[51] *Blackburn* (CA) (n 47) 71.

[52] *Baroness Wenlock v River Dee Co (No 2)* (1887) 19 QBD 155 (CA) 165 (Lord Esher MR, Fry and Lopes LJJ); *Re Wrexham* (n 46) 451 (Rigby LJ), 461 (Vaughan Williams LJ); *Bannatyne v d&c MacIver* [1906] 1 KB 103 (CA) 108 (Collins MR); *Reversion Fund and Insurance Co Ltd v Maison Cosway Ltd* [1913] 1 KB 364 (CA) 376–77 (Buckley LJ); *Liggett* (n 33) 60–61 (Wright J).

[53] *Samsoondar* (n 15) [20] (Lord Burrows); Mitchell and Watterson (n 21) para 6.07; Burrows, *Restitution* (n 18), ch 17; Burrows, *Restatement* (n 18) 98–99; Mitchell, Mitchell and Watterson (n 8) paras 20-01–20-02.

[54] Companies Act 2006, s 39(1).

[55] Mitchell and Watterson (n 21) para 5.76, para 6.59, fn 99, para 6.59, fn 100, para 6.63, fn 124, para 6.82, fn 169, para 6.82, fn 170; Burrows, *Restitution* (n 18) 155, fn 57, 157, fn 65; Mitchell, Mitchell and Watterson (n 8) para 39-45, fn 120. cf Burrows, *Restitution* (n 18) 156–57.

[56] *Blackburn* (HL) (n 46) 866.

[57] *Wenlock* (n 52) 166 (Lord Esher MR, Fry and Lopes LJJ).

[58] *Re Wrexham* (n 46) 447 (Lindley MR). See also 455 (Rigby LJ), 464 (Vaughan Williams LJ); *Reversion Fund* (n 52) 377–82 (Buckley LJ); *Liggett* (n 33) 61 (Wright J).

now well-established that subrogation will not give a lender more than it bargained for.[59] In fact, *Blackburn* and the cases which applied it fit the definition of subrogation: C's new rights against D had prima facie the same content as X's extinguished rights against D.

Nevertheless, the damage was done. Lord Selbourne LC's judgment – once a leading authority – has now faded into obscurity, dealing with a problem – companies borrowing ultra vires – that no longer troubles the courts. This has obscured the judgment's significance for subrogation more generally: that subrogation is justified whenever C bears the burden of a debt which ought to be borne by D, even if C was not obliged to do so.

Again, the reason why D ought to bear the burden of the debt is the same reason why D was originally indebted to X. In *Blackburn*, the Society's debts paid by the bank included 'the payment of members who had given notice of withdrawal, and the balance in payment of salaries of officers or legal expenses'.[60] The Society's debts to its members and staff had been assumed voluntarily so the Society had consented to bearing the burden of these debts. The same might be true of the 'legal expenses' if they were debts to the Society's lawyers. Alternatively, the 'legal expenses' may have arisen under a court order to pay costs, in which case the court order would be the reason why the Society ought to bear the burden of this debt.

Blackburn provides a further argument against using the labels 'legal compulsion' or 'secondary liability' to describe the idea that C bore the burden of a debt which ought to be borne by D. The bank had no duty or liability to pay the Society's creditors; it is inaccurate to say that the bank was 'legally compelled' or had 'secondary liability' to pay. Nevertheless, subrogation was justified because the bank bore the burden of debts which ought to have been borne by the Society. The labels 'legal compulsion' and 'secondary liability' are therefore under-inclusive: they do not capture all the cases in which subrogation is justified because C bore the burden of a debt which ought to have been borne by D.

In sum, there is good reason for subrogation whenever C pays D's debt, even if the debt was not C and D's common debt.

[59] eg *Re Wrexham* (n 46); *Paul v Speirway* [1976] Ch 220 (Ch) 233B (Oliver J); *Banque Financière de La Cité SA v Parc (Battersea) Ltd* [1999] 1 AC 221 (HL) ('*BFC*') 235D (Lord Hoffmann), 237H (Lord Clyde), 242F–G (Lord Hutton); *Cheltenham & Gloucester Plc v Appleyard* [2004] EWCA Civ 291 [38], [41] (Neuberger LJ); *Swynson Ltd v Lowick Rose LLP* [2017] UKSC 32, [2018] AC 313 [31]–[34] (Lord Sumption), [86] (Lord Mance).

[60] *Blackburn* (CA) (n 47) 64.

B. C can Trace into the Payment which Discharged D's Debt

In fact, this justification may be pushed even further, beyond cases where C pays X, and to cases where C can trace into the payment which discharged D's debt to X. The previous chapter argued that subrogation to traceably discharged debts does not have the same justification as trusts over traceably acquired rights. Instead, tracing plays a different role in subrogation cases: it shows that C bore the burden of D's debt.

For example, in *Boscawen v Bajwa*, Bajwa owned a house subject to the Halifax's charge.[61] Bajwa agreed to sell the property to purchasers. The Abbey National agreed to loan the purchasers funds for the purchase, in exchange for a charge over the property. The Abbey National paid the loan to the purchasers' solicitors, who paid it to Bajwa's solicitors. Bajwa's solicitors were authorised to pay the monies to the Halifax on completion of the sale of the property. However, Bajwa's solicitors acted too soon and paid the monies to the Halifax before completion, partially discharging the Halifax's charge.

The sale then fell through and completion never took place. This left Bajwa with unencumbered title to the house. Meanwhile, the Abbey National had paid out the loan monies but had not received any security. To remedy this, Millett LJ held that the Abbey National was subrogated to the Halifax's extinguished charge.

Unlike the bank in *Blackburn*, the Abbey National had not itself paid the defendant's debt. Instead, it was Bajwa's solicitors who had made the payment to the Halifax. Nevertheless, the Abbey National still bore the burden of Bajwa's secured debt, and so subrogation was still justified, because the Abbey National could trace into the payment which discharged the secured debt. Millett LJ explained that when the Abbey National paid the loan monies to the purchasers' solicitors, the solicitors held the monies on trust for the Abbey National.[62] The Abbey National could then trace the monies from the purchasers' solicitors, through Bajwa's solicitors, and into the payment to the Halifax.[63] This enabled the Abbey National to show that it had borne the burden of Bajwa's secured debt to the Halifax. As a result, the Abbey National was subrogated to the Halifax's extinguished charge.[64]

[61] *Boscawen v Bajwa* [1996] 1 WLR 328 (CA).
[62] ibid 332F.
[63] ibid 335F–338A.
[64] ibid 334B–35F.

Many other cases support the idea that C bears the burden of D's debt where C can trace into the payment which discharged D's debt. The courts frequently justify subrogation on the basis that C's 'money' was used to discharge D's debt, even where it was not C who paid X.[65] In *Baroness Wenlock*, the Court of Appeal sought to 'follow the [loan] money into a debt or liability of the company … whether that pursuit be through one or more hands and by one or many steps'.[66] In *Bannatyne v D&C MacIver*, Romer LJ said that the rule in *Clayton's Case* must be applied to determine which debts had been discharged using C's loan.[67]

However, there are also cases in which the court awarded subrogation even though it did not investigate whether C could trace into the payment which discharged D's debt.[68] The results of many of these cases are defensible because, if the court were to conduct this investigation, C would be able to trace into the payment which discharged D's debt.

Butler v Rice illustrates this.[69] Mrs Rice (D) owned a house subject to a bank's (X's) charge. Acting behind his wife's back, Mr Rice asked Butler (C) for a loan to pay off the bank's charge. Butler thought that Mr Rice owned the house, so agreed to the loan in exchange for a mortgage over the house. Butler therefore paid the loan monies to Mr Rice, who paid the bank, discharging the bank's charge. When Mrs Rice discovered the arrangement, she refused to execute a mortgage in favour of Butler. The court held that Butler was subrogated to the bank's extinguished charge.

Unlike *Blackburn*, then, Butler did not himself pay the debt. Unlike *Boscawen*, the court did not investigate whether Butler could trace into the payment which discharged the debt. Nevertheless, had the court conducted this investigation, Butler would have been able to trace. As Birks explained, Mr Rice misrepresented to Butler that he, and not his wife, owned the house.[70] Butler therefore had a mere equity to rescind the contract with Mr Rice, allowing Butler to trace any monies paid under the contract.[71] Butler could therefore trace through Mr Rice's payment

[65] *Re Cork and Youghal Railway Co* (1868–69) LR 4 Ch App 748 761 (Lord Hatherley LC); *Bannatyne* (n 52) 108 (Collins MR), 109–110 (Romer LJ); *Reversion Fund* (n 52) 379; *Liggett* (n 33) 58 (Wright J); *Burston Finance Ltd v Speirway Ltd* [1974] 1 WLR 1648 (Ch) 1652 (Walton J).

[66] *Wenlock* (n 52) 166 (Lord Esher MR, Fry and Lopes LJJ).

[67] *Bannatyne* (n 52) 110 (Romer LJ) citing *Clayton's Case* (1816) 1 Mer 572, 35 ER 781.

[68] S Watterson, '"Direct Transfers" in the Law of Unjust Enrichment' (2011) 64 *CLP* 435, 464; S Watterson, 'Subrogation' in G Virgo and S Worthington (eds), *Commercial Remedies: Resolving Controversies* (Cambridge, CUP, 2017) 459–61.

[69] *Butler* (n 33). See also *Chetwynd v Allen* [1899] 1 Ch 353 (Ch).

[70] Birks, *Introduction* (n 15) 392–93; P Birks, *Unjust Enrichment* (Oxford, OUP, 2005) 97. See also B McFarlane, 'Unjust Enrichment, Property Rights and Indirect Recipients' [2009] *RLR* 37, 49.

[71] *Banque Belge Pour L'Etranger v Hambrouck* [1921] 1 KB 321 (CA); *El Ajou v Dollar Land Holdings Plc (No 1)* [1993] 3 All ER 717 (Ch) 734C–E (Millett J); Birks, *Introduction* (n 15) 392–93; Birks, *Unjust Enrichment* (n 70) 97.

to the bank, and into the payment which discharged the bank's charge. This showed that Butler bore the burden of Mrs Rice's debt to the bank, entitling Butler to subrogation. *Butler* was therefore correctly decided, albeit incorrectly reasoned as it justified subrogation by fictionally treating Butler as intending to keep the bank's charge alive.[72]

C. C Caused the Discharge of D's Debt

On the other hand, merely causing the discharge of D's debt is not enough to justify subrogation. For instance, say my son pays your creditor, discharging your debt. But for my actions, my son would not have been born, so my son would not have paid your creditor and your debt would not be discharged. However, nobody would say that I bore the burden of your debt or that I should be subrogated to your creditor's extinguished rights. Causing the discharge of D's debt is not enough to justify subrogation.

D. Summary

Subrogation is prima facie justified whenever C bears the burden of a debt which ought to have been borne by D. It is uncontroversial that this justifies subrogation where C pays X, discharging C and D's common debt to X. This section pushed that justification further, arguing that it can also justify subrogation in two further scenarios. First, the justification applies where C pays D's debt to X, even though C was not obliged to do so. Second, the justification applies even where C did not pay X, so long as C can trace into the payment which discharged D's debt to X.

V. Did C Consent to Bearing the Burden of D's Debt?

A. Countervailing Considerations

The previous section argued that properly distributing the burden of a debt provides a reason for subrogation whenever C can trace into the payment which

[72] See ch 8, s II above.

discharged D's debt to X. Nevertheless, this does not necessarily mean that subrogation will be awarded. The availability of subrogation may be cut back by countervailing considerations. Two examples illustrate this.

First, a legal system may choose to have a rule against malicious intervenors. This could take one of many different forms. It could be a rule that C's payment to X *cannot discharge* D's debt to X unless C was obliged to pay D's debt or authorised by D to do so.[73] It could be a rule that, if C pays X intending to discharge D's debt to X, D's debt is discharged *unless* C is a malicious intervenor. Or it could be a rule that a malicious intervenor may discharge D's debt to X, but *cannot be subrogated* to X's extinguished rights against D: the result reached in *Norton v Haggett*[74] and supported by the English cases.[75]

A second restriction is the rule that, in lending cases, subrogation will not give C more than it bargained for.[76] This section considers that rule in detail. It explains why this rule applies to lending cases but not to common liability cases. It then explains why subrogation is not constrained by the rules applicable to the unjust factors of mistake and failure of basis. Finally, it considers the related issue of whether subrogation ought to be available to a negligent lender.

B. Lending Cases

Stevens argues that, across private law, if C consented to the position they now find themselves in, then 'there is no reason for the law to come to his aid'.[77] He suggests that this idea travels under different labels – *volenti non fit injuria* in the law of torts and waiver in the law of contract – and that it also applies to restitution claims,[78] and claims to properly distribute the burden of a debt. He writes that 'someone who has voluntarily performed an obligation knowing that it is owed by another should not be able to obtain recovery. They have consented

[73] Birks and Beatson (n 34) 206; Beatson (n 34) 202–03; Stevens, *The Laws of Restitution* (n 6) 161.

[74] *Norton* (n 39).

[75] *Exall v Partridge* (1799) 8 TR 308, 310, 101 ER 1405, 1406 (Lord Kenyon CJ); *Owen* (n 40); Beatson (n 34) 204; Burrows, *Restitution* (n 18) 461; Burrows, *Restatement* (n 18) 100.

[76] eg *Re Wrexham* (n 46); *Paul* (n 59) 233B (Oliver J); *BFC* (n 59) 235D (Lord Hoffmann), 237H (Lord Clyde), 242F–G (Lord Hutton); *Appleyard* (n 59) [38], [41] (Neuberger LJ); *Swynson* (n 59) [31]–[34] (Lord Sumption), [86] (Lord Mance).

[77] R Stevens, 'Private Law and the Form of Reasons' in A Robertson and J Goudkamp (eds), *Form and Substance in the Law of Obligations* (Oxford, Hart Publishing, 2019) 138; Stevens, *The Laws of Restitution* (n 6) 76.

[78] Stevens, *The Laws of Restitution* (n 6) 73.

to the position they now find themselves in.'[79] This also explains the rule that subrogation will not give C more than it bargained for.

Swynson is a good example. There, the Supreme Court denied subrogation because C 'got precisely what he thought he was getting from the transaction in question, namely repayment to [X] of the original loan, and a right to recover the new loan from EMSL.'[80] In other words, C consented to make the loan to EMSL in exchange for a right to repayment from EMSL. C had that right to repayment from EMSL. Subrogation would therefore relieve C of a burden that it consented to bearing and so the Court would not come to C's aid.

Things become more complicated if C bargained for rights in exchange for bearing the burden of D's debt. The bargain evidences that C did not unconditionally consent to bearing the burden of D's debt. If C does not get the rights that it bargained for, then C is not in a situation that it consented to. Accordingly, there is no objection to subrogation and so subrogation succeeds.

But once C has the rights that it bargained for, C in a position that it consented to. If subrogation gave C more than it bargained for, C would be relieved of a burden that it consented to bearing. Thus, subrogation cannot give C more than it bargained for.

These principles are illustrated by *Re Wrexham Mold & Connah's Quay Railway Co.*[81] The Wrexham Railway Company had three classes of stockholders: A, B, and C. Each was entitled to interest, but the A stockholders had priority over the B and C stockholders, and the B stockholders had priority over the C stockholders. The North and South Wales Bank made an unsecured loan to the Company by paying the interest due to the A stockholders. However, this loan was ultra vires the Company and void, so the Company was not contractually obliged to repay the Bank. The Court of Appeal held that the Bank was subrogated to the A stockholders' personal rights against the Company, but not their priority over the other stockholders. Accordingly, the Bank could recover from the Company, but the B stockholders had priority over the Bank.

This was the correct result. The Bank paid the A stockholders, discharging the Company's debt to them. Accordingly, the Bank bore the burden of a debt which should have been borne by the Company. The Bank had consented to this in exchange for a right to repayment from the Company. The Bank had not got that right and so it was not in a position that it consented to. Consequently, there

[79] ibid 162.
[80] *Swynson* (n 59) [119] (Lord Neuberger). See also [33]–[34] (Lord Sumption), [87] (Lord Mance).
[81] *Re Wrexham* (n 46).

was no objection to subrogation properly distributing the burden of the debt by reinstating the Company's personal obligation to pay the A stockholders, and having the Company now owe that obligation to the Bank.

However, once the Bank had its personal right to repayment, it was in the situation that it consented to. The Bank bore the burden of discharging the A stockholders' priority debt, but the Bank consented to doing so in exchange for rights without priority. To subrogate the Bank to the A stockholders' priority would relieve the Bank of a burden which it consented to bearing. For this reason, Lindley MR was justified in saying that subrogation cannot 'place the lender in a better position than that in which he would have been if his loan had not been prohibited'.[82]

C. Common Liability Cases

In common liability cases, the rule that subrogation cannot give C more than it bargained for does not apply. In these cases, C may be subrogated to X's extinguished security, even if C did not bargain for any security.[83] This difference between lending and common liability cases is generally thought to be unjustifiable,[84] but it is in fact defensible.

The previous section argued that the rule that subrogation cannot give C more than it bargained for is best understood as a rule that subrogation should not relieve C of a burden that it consented to bearing. In a common liability case, C always has an easy way of showing that it did not consent to bearing the burden of the common debt. C can show that it paid X in order to discharge itself from the common debt and not because it consented to bearing the burden of D's share of the debt.[85] The fact that C failed to bargain for rights in exchange for discharging D's debt does not show that C consented to bearing the burden of D's share of the debt. Accordingly, subrogation is justified in giving C more than it bargained for in common liability cases.

[82] ibid 447. See also 449, 455 (Rigby LJ).

[83] *Mayhew v Crickett* (1818) 2 Swans 185, 191, 36 ER 585, 587; *Duncan Fox* (n 7); *Forbes* (n 2) 621 (Hall VC); *Insol Funding Co Ltd v Cowlam* [2017] EWHC 1822 (Ch) [120] (Master Bowles).

[84] *Duncan Fox* (n 7) 20–21 (Lord Blackburn); C Mitchell, *The Law of Subrogation* (Oxford, Clarendon Press, 1994) 59, 66; Rotherham, 'Subrogation' (n 4) para 8.38; A Tettenborn, *The Law of Restitution in England and Ireland* (London, Cavendish, 2002) para 2-39; Mitchell and Watterson (n 21) paras 8.39–8.60; Burrows, *Restitution* (n 18) 149–50. cf C Rotherham, *Proprietary Remedies in Context* (Oxford, Hart Publishing, 2002) 262–67; Rotherham, 'Subrogation' (n 4) paras 8.34–8.35, 8.38.

[85] Hilliard (n 16) 551; Burrows, *Restatement* (n 18) 55; W Day, '"At the Expense of" in Unjust Enrichment: Causal, Direct or Intentional Transfers of Value?' [2017] *LMCLQ* 588, 594; Smith, 'Restitution' (n 6) 99.

By contrast, in lending cases, C's payment of D's debt might suggest that C consented to bearing the burden of D's debt and so subrogation should be denied. C cannot remove this objection by saying that it paid in order to discharge itself from a debt, because C did not owe any debt. Instead, C must produce some other evidence to show that it did not consent to bearing the burden. Typically, C does this by showing that it bargained for rights in exchange for causing the discharge of D's debt. But once C has the rights that it bargained for, it consents to bearing the burden of D's debt. Thus, subrogation cannot give C more than it bargained for in lending cases.

In short, common liability and lending cases reveal different ways for C to show that it did not consent to bearing the burden of D's debt. This explains why the rule that subrogation cannot give C more than it bargained for applies only to lending cases and not common liability cases.

D. Mistake and Failure of Basis

This also explains why subrogation may succeed even if there is no mistake or failure of basis. Chapter 5 used the example of *Reversion Fund*.[86] The managing director of D, without authority, borrowed money from C on D's behalf. He used the loan monies to discharge D's debt to X. C knew that the managing director had no authority to borrow on D's behalf, but expected D to subsequently ratify the transaction. D never did. Some time later, C sought to recover the money from D. Given that D had not authorised the loan, D was not contractually obliged to repay it.

The Court of Appeal awarded subrogation, despite the difficulties in establishing a mistake or failure of basis.[87] Buckley LJ cited Lord Selborne LC's reasoning in *Blackburn*[88] and said that:

> there is, in substance, no borrowing; there is merely the replacement of one debt by another of the same amount. The existence or non-existence of borrowing power is, therefore, not material, and, consequently, [C's] knowledge as to its non-existence is not material.[89]

[86] *Reversion Fund* (n 52).
[87] See ch 5, s V(A) above.
[88] *Reversion Fund* (n 52) 376–77 citing *Blackburn* (CA) (n 47) 71 (Lord Selborne LC).
[89] *Reversion Fund* (n 52) 373.

Thus, Buckley LJ recognised that the justification for subrogation does not depend upon C's knowledge or mistake. Instead, the justification for subrogation was that C bore the burden of a debt which should have been borne by D. To put the burden back where it should be, C was subrogated to X's extinguished rights against D. C would not be entitled to subrogation if it consented to bearing the burden of D's debt. But C's expectation of obtaining a contractual right to repayment from D showed that C did not consent to bearing the burden, even though this unilateral expectation about the future did not establish the unjust factor of mistake or failure of basis.[90]

Thus, a mistake, failure of basis, or defeated expectation can show that C did not consent to bearing the burden of D's debt, so there is no objection to subrogation.[91] This explains why the concepts of mistake, failure of basis, and defeated expectation feature prominently in the reasoning of lending cases,[92] even though they cannot justify subrogation on their own.[93]

E. Negligence

The logic behind the rule that subrogation will not give C more than it bargained for should be pushed further, to deny subrogation to a lender whose lack of security is due to its own negligence. This used to be the law, as is shown by *Capital Finance Co Ltd v Stokes*[94] and *Burston Finance Ltd v Speirway Ltd.*[95] In each case, C provided a loan to D, a company, to fund the purchase of land from X. In exchange, D granted C a first legal charge over their title to the land. However, section 95(1) of the Companies Act 1948 provided that a charge created by a company was void against the liquidator and any creditor of the company, unless it was registered. The charge was not registered and D went into liquidation, so C could not rely on their charge.

C sought to be subrogated to X's extinguished unpaid vendor's lien. D's liquidators (in the latter case ably represented by Peter Millett QC and Leonard Hoffmann) sought to resist subrogation on the ground that subrogation would

[90] Stevens, *The Laws of Restitution* (n 6) 163.
[91] Stevens, 'Private Law and the Form of Reasons' (n 77) 138; Stevens, *The Laws of Restitution* (n 6) 162, 369–70.
[92] See ch 5.
[93] See ch 8, s III above.
[94] *Capital Finance Co Ltd v Stokes* [1969] 1 Ch 261 (CA).
[95] *Burston* (n 65).

give C more than it bargained for. In both cases, the court accepted that argument and denied subrogation. In *Burston Finance*, Walton J explained that, because D granted C a charge, 'there is no doubt that [C] got what they bargained for. They were merely lax in not taking steps to ensure that what they bargained for remained good against the world.'[96]

This can be understood as an extension of the principle that the courts will not rescue C from a position that they consented to. If C consents to bearing the burden of D's debt, then the law of subrogation will not come to C's aid. By analogy, one might say that if C's negligence causes it to bear the burden of D's debt, then it does not deserve the law of subrogation coming to its aid. As Dixon puts it, why should lenders enjoy subrogation:

> when its own lending practices have led it into the problem? It is lenders in these cases who can preserve the priority of their mortgages by adopting good lending practices. … [S]ubrogation should not rescue re-mortgagees from the folly of their own incompetent lending practices.[97]

Indeed, in *Burston Finance*, Walton J suggested that C had waived their right to subrogation, saying that C 'must deliberately be intending to replace his vendor's lien by th[e first legal charge], and that accordingly, … by presumed intention to waive the unpaid vendor's lien, that lien has gone'.[98]

Unfortunately, the law was changed in *BFC*.[99] There, C lacking its intended priority over OOL 'was due entirely to the failure of [C] to take the normal, indeed elementary, precautions' in verifying that Mr Herzig had authority to bind OOL to the postponement letter.[100] For the Court of Appeal, this was a reason for denying C's subrogation claim. The House of Lords disagreed and allowed C's subrogation claim. Lord Hoffmann, effectively reversing his victory as counsel in *Burston Finance*,[101] said:

> there is, so far as I know, no case in which it has been held that carelessness is a ground for holding that a consequent enrichment is not unjust. No doubt Mr Mynors

[96] ibid 1657F.
[97] M Dixon, 'Equitable Co-Ownership: Proprietary Rights in Name Only?' in E Cooke (ed), *Modern Studies in Property Law, Volume 4* (Oxford, Hart Publishing, 2007) 37, 46.
[98] *Burston* (n 65) 1653C.
[99] *BFC* (n 59). For the facts, see ch 2, s V(A) above.
[100] *Banque Financière de La Cité SA v Parc (Battersea) Ltd* (1999-11-29) (CA)(Morritt LJ).
[101] *Appleyard* (n 59) [39] (Neuberger LJ).

> (in *Chetwynd v Allen*) and Mr Butler (in *Butler v Rice*) were careless in parting with their money without bothering to inspect the borrower's title deeds. They relied upon Mr Chetwynd and Mr Rice as [C] relied upon Mr Herzig. But that did not entitle Mrs Chetwynd or Mrs Rice to be enriched as a result of their mistakes.[102]

This reasoning is problematic, since the point that subrogation should be denied because of C's carelessness was not argued in either *Chetwynd* or *Butler*. Cases are only authority for points argued before the court,[103] and so *Chetwynd* and *Butler* are not authority for the point that Lord Hoffmann cited them for.

Similarly, Lord Steyn said that 'the neglect of BFC is akin to the carelessness of a mistaken payor: it does not by itself undermine the ground of restitution'.[104] This reasoning is also problematic. Part II of this book showed that subrogation is governed by different rules to direct unjust enrichment claims. Negligence does not bar a direct claim for restitution on the ground of mistake,[105] but this says nothing about the rules which should apply to subrogation.

Despite these problems, the decision in *BFC* that a lender's negligence will not bar their subrogation claim has subsequently been applied by lower courts. For instance, in *Anfield*, C's 2006 charge would have had priority over Anfield's charging order, but for C's negligent failure to register the 2006 charge.[106] But Proudman J held that this did not prevent C being subrogated to X's extinguished charge. She said that the decisions in *Capital Finance* and *Burston Finance* 'cannot survive' after *BFC*.[107]

In summary, subrogation used to be denied if C's lack of security was due to its own negligence. This rule was subsequently abandoned in *BFC*, but the reasoning behind this was flawed. The better view is that if C's lack of security is due to its own negligence, then it does not deserve the courts coming to its aid. For this reason, the decisions in *Capital Finance* and *Burston Finance* should be preferred, and subrogation should not have been awarded in *BFC* and *Anfield*.

[102] *BFC* (n 59) 235E–G (Lord Hoffmann, citations omitted) citing *Chetwynd* (n 69); *Butler* (n 33).

[103] *Dunnachie v Kingston Upon Hull CC* [2004] EWCA Civ 84, [2004] ICR 481 [61] (Evans-Lombe LJ), [77]–[83] (Brooke LJ); affd [2004] UKHL 36; [2005] 1 AC 226 [11]–[13] (Lord Steyn); R Cross and JW Harris, *Precedent in English Law* (Oxford, Clarendon Press, 1991) 158–61.

[104] *BFC* (n 59) 227H (Lord Steyn).

[105] *Kelly v Solari* (1841) 9 M&W 54, 59, 152 ER 24, 26 (Parke B).

[106] *Anfield (UK) Ltd v Bank of Scotland Plc* [2010] EWHC 2374 (Ch), [2011] 1 WLR 2414. For the facts, see ch 4, s III(D)(i) above. See also *Appleyard* (n 59) [39], [71]–[75] (Neuberger LJ).

[107] *Anfield* (n 106) [30].

VI. What Rights Should Subrogation Create?

In addition to these implications for when subrogation should occur, the account given in this chapter also has implications for what rights subrogation should create. This section explains why the quantum of the rights created by subrogation are capped by C's loss, and why subrogation can give C legal (and not merely equitable) security. It then argues that the controversial awards of subrogation in *BFC* and *Menelaou* were unjustified. Finally, it argues that subrogation extends beyond debts, to properly distributing the burden of other obligations.

A. Quantum Capped by C's Loss

Chapter 3 showed that, in cases where D's gain exceeds C's loss, C's subrogation claim is capped by C's loss. This is difficult to explain if subrogation is a remedy for unjust enrichment, but it is consistent with the account given in this chapter. Where C bore the burden of a debt which ought to have been borne by D, that burden needs to be lifted from C and reinstated upon D. Accordingly, there is only an injustice insofar as C bore the burden of D's debt. Once C's loss is compensated, this burden is lifted from C, and so there is no justification for giving C a right to a greater sum.[108]

B. Legal Security

Where X had legal security, there is debate over whether subrogation gives C legal security or equitable security.[109] The explanation in this chapter justifies giving C legal security in this situation. In *Forbes*, by mortgaging his legal title, D agreed not to redeem his legal title until he had borne the burden of repaying the loan. In fact, this burden was borne by C. To put the burden where it should be, subrogation gave C a legal mortgage over D's property.[110] This prevented D from redeeming his legal title until he had borne the burden,

[108] Stevens, *The Laws of Restitution* (n 6) 168.
[109] See ch 2, s VI above.
[110] *Forbes* (n 2) 622–23 (Hall VC).

just as he had agreed. Far from being a legislative aberration,[111] Section 5 of the Mercantile Law Amendment Act 1856 is entirely justified in providing that a surety is subrogated to legal rights.

Nevertheless, even where X had legal security, two other rules may prevent subrogation giving C legal security. First, in lending cases, subrogation will not give C more than it bargained for. Second, subrogation may be prevented from creating legal security by formality requirements. For instance, sections 27(1) and 27(2)(f) of the Land Registration Act 2002 provide that 'the grant of a legal charge' of land 'does not operate at law until' it is 'completed by registration'. By itself, subrogation does not change the register, so on its own subrogation cannot create a legal charge. However, subrogation can give C an entitlement to a legal charge, which C can then complete by registration. Some cases have held exactly that.[112]

C. *BFC*

It was argued above that C's negligence should have prevented subrogation in *BFC*.[113] Another problem with the case was the unusual effect of subrogation, which is difficult to justify.

To repeat the facts, D owned property subject to X's first charge and OOL's second charge. C agreed to loan money to D – via an intermediary – to partially pay off X's charge, provided that OOL was bound by a 'postponement letter'. Under that letter, OOL would not demand repayment of its loan until C had been repaid. C performed its side of the bargain before discovering that the postponement letter did not bind OOL. A priority dispute then arose between C and OOL. As the postponement letter did not bind OOL, C could not rely on it to obtain priority. Instead, C sought to be subrogated to X's extinguished first charge.

The Court of Appeal denied subrogation and held that OOL's charge allowed it to recover ahead of C. The Court explained that C bargained for priority over

[111] S Watterson, 'Subrogation, Priority Disputes and Rectification: Mapping a Route Through the Thicket' [2016] *RLR* 1, 11 fn 52.

[112] *Castle Phillips Finance v Piddington* (1995) 70 P & CR 592 (CA) 602 (Peter Gibson LJ); *Appleyard* (n 59) [23], [69]–[74] (Neuberger LJ); *Primlake Ltd v Matthews Associates (No 2)* [2009] EWHC 2774 (Ch) [17](c), [27] (Jeremy Cousins QC); *Anfield* (n 106) [6], [40] (Proudman J). *Boscawen* (n 61) 341A–B, 342D (Millett LJ); *Day v Tiuta International Ltd* [2014] EWCA Civ 1246 [41]–[43] (Gloster LJ); Watterson, 'Subrogation, Priority Disputes and Rectification' (n 111) 12–14.

[113] *BFC* (n 59). See ch 10, s V(E) above.

OOL, but not for any security interest. As a result, subrogating C to X's extinguished first charge would give C more than it bargained for.

This was correct. C had consented to bear the burden of discharging X's proprietary rights in exchange for personal rights. Subrogating C to proprietary rights would therefore relieve C of a burden that it consented to bearing.

In the House of Lords, C modified its claim. C conceded that it was not entitled to recover ahead of all D's other creditors. Instead, C sought, and the House awarded, subrogation to X's extinguished rights only as against OOL and not as against D's other creditors.[114] This was novel: in all other cases of subrogation to extinguished security, subrogation allowed C to recover ahead of D's unsecured creditors.[115]

The House of Lords justified this as a remedy for OOL's unjust enrichment,[116] with the unjust factor described as either C's mistake[117] or defeated expectation.[118] However, this reasoning fails to justify subrogation.[119]

Moreover, the result cannot be justified on the basis that C bore the burden of a debt which should have been borne by D. It is D who figures in this justification; it is a justification for subrogation to rights against D and not a justification for subrogation against one of D's creditors like OOL.

One might think that this justification can be modified to explain the result in *BFC*. In *Forbes*, part of the reason that C was subrogated to X's extinguished mortgage was that D's voluntary unsecured creditors had not bargained for security over the property. They had therefore consented to not having recourse to the property until D had borne the burden of his debts secured over the property.

Similarly, in *BFC*, OOL had bargained for a second charge. OOL had therefore agreed not to have recourse to the property until D had borne the burden of the debts secured by the first charge. However, C (and not D) had borne the burden of partially discharging X's first charge. This gave OOL recourse to the property before D had borne the full burden of the debt which had been secured by the first charge. OOL had recourse to the property sooner than it had agreed; OOL had more than it had bargained for. To put this right, C was subrogated, as against OOL, to X's first charge insofar as it was discharged. OOL therefore got

[114] ibid 228B–F (Lord Steyn), 229B–D, 236H–37D (Lord Hoffmann), 237G–38A (Lord Clyde), 242F–H (Lord Hutton).
[115] Mitchell and Watterson (n 21) paras 8.54–8.55; Mitchell, Mitchell and Watterson (n 8) para 39-64.
[116] *BFC* (n 59) 226F–28F, 231H (Lord Hoffmann), 238H (Lord Clyde).
[117] ibid 227E (Lord Steyn), 234G–35A (Lord Hoffmann).
[118] ibid 227D–F (Lord Steyn), 234G (Lord Hoffmann), 235H (Lord Hutton), 237D–G (Lord Clyde).
[119] See ch 8, s III above.

only what it had bargained for: recourse to the property after D had borne the full burden of the debt secured by the first charge.

In *Forbes*, D's other creditors were relevant as part of the justification for subrogation to a secured debt against D. However, the previous paragraph takes a further step and allow a free-standing claim against those creditors. Armstrong and Cerfontaine observe that this creates a problem: a circular system of priorities.[120] C was only subrogated to X's extinguished rights as against OOL. Consequently, subrogation gave C priority over OOL but not D's other creditors, so D's preferred creditors had priority over C. Meanwhile, OOL's charge allowed it to recover ahead of D's other creditors, including the preferred creditors. Thus, C had priority over OOL, who could recover ahead of D's preferred creditors, who had priority over C. This is a circular system of priorities, making it impossible to know who should be paid first.[121]

In sum, the unusual effect of subrogation in *BFC* cannot be supported by the Law Lords' reasoning, or by the justification for subrogation offered by this chapter.

D. *Menelaou*

Similarly, the award of subrogation in *Menelaou* is difficult to justify.[122] To recap, the facts were that Mr and Mrs Menelaou had title to Rush Green Hall, which was subject to C's two charges. Mr and Mrs Menelaou decided to sell Rush Green Hall and use the proceeds to buy a new property, Great Oak Court, from X. C released its charges over Rush Green Hall in exchange for a new charge over Great Oak Court. However, Mr and Mrs Menelaou registered Great Oak Court in the name of D, their daughter. D had not consented to C's new charge, which was therefore invalid.

C could show that it bore the burden of discharging X's unpaid vendor's lien. As Lord Carnwath explained, the parents' solicitor held the proceeds of the sale of Rush Green Hall under a *Quistclose* trust for C.[123] C could therefore trace

[120] M Armstrong and A Cerfontaine, 'Subrogation, Unjust Enrichment and Insolvency: A French View of *Banque Financière de La Cité SA v Parc (Battersea) Ltd*' in F Rose (ed), *Restitution and Insolvency* (London, Mansfield Press, 2000) 103–04.

[121] ibid 103–04; Mitchell and Watterson (n 21) para 8.144.

[122] *Menelaou v Bank of Cyprus UK Ltd* [2015] UKSC 66, [2016] AC 176.

[123] ibid [133]–[139] citing *Barclays Bank Ltd v Quistclose Investments Ltd* [1970] AC 567 (HL). See also *Buhr v Barclays Bank Plc* [2001] EWCA Civ 1223; *Menelaou* (n 122) [53] (Lord Clarke), [104] (Lord Neuberger), [133] (Lord Carnwath); M Raczynska, *The Law of Tracing in Commercial Transactions* (Oxford, OUP, 2018) para 4.02.

through the payment of the proceeds to X, and into the discharge of X's unpaid vendor's lien.[124]

The difficulty with justifying subrogation in *Menelaou* is showing that D ought to have borne the burden of this. This will be illustrated in two stages. First, it is not clear that D should have borne the burden of paying the purchase price of Great Oak Court. Second, it is not clear that D should have borne the burden of extinguishing X's lien.

Turning first to the debt, on the one hand, D contracted with X to purchase Great Oak Court so – as between D and X – D agreed to bear the burden of paying the purchase price. On the other hand, D agreed on the basis that the property was a gift from her parents so – as between D and her parents – D had *not* agreed to bear the burden of paying the purchase price. Which of these constructions should govern the relationship between D and C? For the purposes of C's subrogation claim, had D agreed to bear the burden of paying the purchase price?

Ultimately, a personal claim was not pursued in *Menelaou*; C only sought subrogation to X's unpaid vendor's lien.[125] It is unclear whether the burden of discharging this lien should have been borne by D. On the one hand, the unpaid vendor's lien could be interpreted as denying D possession until she bore the burden of paying the purchase price. On the other hand, the reason that the law imposes an unpaid vendor's lien is to protect the unpaid vendor by entitling it to possession until the purchase price is paid. This reason does not require the purchaser to be the one who bears the burden of paying the purchase price.

In short, C bore the burden of discharging X's unpaid vendor's lien, but it is unclear whether this burden ought to have been borne by D, as opposed to her parents. It is therefore difficult to justify subrogation in *Menelaou*.

E. Beyond Debts

This chapter speaks of subrogation distributing the burden of 'debts', because that is the effect of subrogation in almost all cases. But the same principles are equally applicable to other obligations. In *Gebhardt v Saunders*, a landlord and tenant were both obliged to abate a nuisance.[126] The tenant abated the nuisance. The Court of Appeal held that he could recoup his expenses from the landlord because the

[124] *Menelaou* (n 122) [140].
[125] ibid [55] (Lord Clarke), [82] (Lord Neuberger).
[126] *Gebhardt v Saunders* [1892] 2 QB 452 (QB).

nuisance was caused by a structural defect rather than improper use by the tenant, so the landlord ought to have borne the burden of abating the nuisance. *Gebhardt* therefore shows that subrogation extends beyond cases where D was obliged to pay a debt, to cases where D was obliged to do something else.

VII. Chapter Summary

This chapter argued that subrogation is justified by properly distributing the burden of a debt. Where C bears the burden of a debt which should have been borne by D, subrogation lifts that burden from C and reinstates it upon D by giving C rights with prima facie the same content as X's extinguished rights. Subrogation therefore ensures that the burden of a debt falls where it should.

11

Marshalling

I. Introduction

This chapter addresses the controversy of the relationship between subrogation and marshalling. Consistent with the theme of this book, the key is to focus on form. Subrogation describes a particular form of rights, of which marshalling is an example. However, marshalling has a different justification to other instances of subrogation. The previous chapter argued that other instances of subrogation are justified by properly distributing the burden of a debt. Section II of this chapter argues that, in its core case, marshalling has a different justification: preventing a private party determining the distribution of assets on insolvency.

The remainder of the chapter then considers how this justification applies to more complicated instances of marshalling. Section III examines marshalling by appointment. Section IV argues that at least one case in which the court ordered marshalling is in fact better understood as an example of subrogation properly distributing the burden of a debt. Finally, section V examines the so-called 'surety exception' or 'extended' case of marshalling, in which the justification for marshalling interacts with the justification for other instances of subrogation.

II. The Core Case of Marshalling

To reiterate, the core case of marshalling can be illustrated by the following example. Say D owes £1m to X, secured over two properties, Whiteacre and Blackacre, which are each worth £1m. D also owes £1m to C who has security over Whiteacre, ranking behind X's security. However, C does not have security over Blackacre. This is illustrated by the following diagram.

WHITEACRE	**BLACKACRE**
Value £1m	Value £1m
X's first charge for £1m	X's first charge for £1m
C's second charge for £1m	

If D is solvent, then both creditors can be paid. The problem arises if D is insolvent.[1] If X chooses to realise its security over Blackacre, then C can realise its security over Whiteacre and so both creditors will be paid. However, if X chooses to realise its security over Whiteacre, then X's right to £1m will exhaust Whiteacre (which is only worth £1m), leaving C unsecured. C would then compete with D's unsecured creditors and so may not be paid in full. As such, X's choice of which security to realise can affect whether or not C will be paid.

Marshalling prevents X's choice prejudicing C, by giving C security over Blackacre with the same characteristics as X's extinguished security.[2] In other words, C is subrogated to X's extinguished security over Blackacre.

Even in this core case, marshalling is difficult to justify. C chose not to bargain for security over Blackacre, so why should marshalling give C more than it bargained for?[3] Why should marshalling favour C over the unsecured creditors?[4]

Unlike other cases of subrogation, marshalling cannot be justified on the basis that C bore the burden of a debt which should have been borne by D. In the core case of marshalling, D pays its debt to X; the burden of this debt is already properly distributed before marshalling.

One might change focus and argue that marshalling is justified because the burden of the debt to C should fall on Blackacre, instead of making Blackacre available to the debtor's unsecured creditors. However, there is no good reason why the burden of the debt to C should fall on Blackacre, and there is a good

[1] *National Crime Agency v Szepietowski* [2013] UKSC 65, [2014] AC 338 [32] (Lord Neuberger).

[2] *Aldrich v Cooper* (1803) 8 Ves Jun 382, 32 ER 402; *Ex p Kendall* (1811) 17 Ves Jun 514, 520, 34 ER 199, 201 (Lord Eldon LC); *Webb v Smith* (1885) 30 ChD 192 (CA) 200 (Cotton LJ); *Re Bank of Credit and Commerce International SA (No 8)* [1996] Ch 245 (CA) 271F–H (Rose LJ); *Re Bank of Credit and Commerce International SA (No 8)* [1998] AC 214 (HL) 230H–31B (Lord Hoffmann); *Szepietowski* (n 1) [1]–[2], [31]–[32] (Lord Neuberger). In Australia, C only acquires this security once there is a court order giving effect to marshalling: *Commonwealth Trading Bank v Colonial Mutual Life Assurance Society Ltd* (1970) 26 FLR 338 (Tas SC); *Chase Corporation (Australia) Pty Ltd v North Sydney Brick and Tile Co Ltd* (1994) 35 NSWLR 1 (NSWSC) 18G–21B (Cohen J); *Sarge Pty Ltd v Cazihaven Homes Pty Ltd* (1994) 34 NSWLR 658 (NSWSC) 664D–65G (Young J).

[3] C Mitchell, 'Book Review' [2000] *LMCLQ* 589, 591.

[4] C Rotherham, 'Subrogation' in S Hedley and M Halliwell (eds), *The Law of Restitution* (London, Butterworths, 2002) para 8.72.

reason to make Blackacre available to the unsecured creditors. Namely, C never bargained for rights over Blackacre. As Mitchell explains:

> It is also open to a junior creditor to protect himself by contracting with the debtor to take junior security over [Blackacre] as well as [Whiteacre], and if he chooses not to do this, but instead to charge the debtor at a higher rate reflecting the lower value of his security over [Whiteacre], then the law has no need to put him into a better position than the one he has bargained for[.][5]

Consequently, if marshalling is to be justified, one must look beyond the justification for other cases of subrogation. In the leading Supreme Court decision of *National Crime Authority v Szepietowski*, Lord Neuberger justified marshalling as follows:

> the right to marshal is an incident of the second mortgage when it is granted …. It is normally easy to imply a common intention on the part of the parties to the second mortgage (the mortgagor and the second mortgagee) that there should be a right to marshal where the second mortgage secures a debt due from the mortgagor, because such a right is to the manifest advantage of the second mortgagee and of no significance either way to the mortgagor.[6]

However, marshalling is an arcane doctrine and most parties are unlikely to be aware of it. If the contract is silent about marshalling, it seems fictitious to interpret this silence as agreement to marshalling.[7]

In his monograph on marshalling, Ali argues that marshalling is justified because:

> In the absence of such a device as security, which gives secured creditors preferential rights of recourse to the assets of a debtor, many debtors would be either unable to obtain credit on an unsecured basis or would only be able to do so at relatively high rates of interest, because of the risk of loss to the creditor. … Security reduces the risk of loss to creditors and, as a consequence, they are willing to lend funds at lower rates of interest. Under the conventional theory, the law accords secured creditors priority over unsecured creditors because it recognises that security allows debtors access to credit which might not otherwise have been available. … As a corollary …, the law will do all it can to protect security and preserve the preferential status of secured claims, for by so doing it protects the supply of credit to debtors. It is this policy imperative which underpins the doctrine of marshalling of securities.[8]

[5] Mitchell (n 3) 591.

[6] *Szepietowski* (n 1) [54] (citation omitted).

[7] C Hare, 'Marshalling Marshalling' in PS Davies, S Douglas and J Goudkamp (eds), *Defences in Equity* (Oxford, Hart Publishing, 2018) 244–46.

[8] PAU Ali, *Marshalling of Securities* (Oxford, OUP, 1999) paras 6.35–6.37.

However, this is not a justification for marshalling specifically; it is a general argument for giving advantages of any form to secured creditors in order to incentivise lending. The 'policy imperative' of allowing 'debtors access to credit' could equally justify giving C a floating charge over all D's rights, or a state compensation scheme for creditors in C's position. Thus, Ali's argument fails to justify the particular form of the rights creating by marshalling: giving C security over Blackacre with the same characteristics as X's extinguished security over Blackacre.

Neyers argues that marshalling is one manifestation of a prohibition on abuse of rights. He explains:

> the only point of [X] insisting on realising its security [over Whiteacre] can be to harm [C] without any gain for itself. [X] is not allowed to do this when its obligations can be met perfectly through the realisation of another security [over Blackacre].[9]

The problem with this argument is that it cuts both ways. One could deploy exactly the same argument for the opposite result:

> the only point of [X] insisting on realising its security [over Blackacre] can be to harm [the unsecured creditors] without any gain for itself. [X] is not allowed to do this when its obligations can be met perfectly through the realisation of another security [over Whiteacre].

Neyers' argument is therefore ambiguous about whether C should be given security over Blackacre, or whether the proceeds should be distributed between C and the unsecured creditors. It is therefore ambiguous as to whether marshalling should occur.

A better argument for marshalling focuses on the fact that, were it not for marshalling, X would have the ability to determine the distribution of the insolvent debtor's assets. On the one hand, if X chooses to realise its security over Blackacre, then C's security over Whiteacre allows it to be paid before D's unsecured creditors. On the other hand, if X chooses to realise its security over Whiteacre, then C loses its security and competes with the unsecured creditors for the proceeds of Blackacre. In effect, then, X's choice determines how the insolvent debtor's assets are distributed between C and unsecured creditors. However, it is the role of the

[9] JW Neyers, 'Explaining the Inexplicable? Four Manifestations of Abuse of Rights in English Law' in D Nolan and A Robertson (eds), *Rights and Private Law* (Oxford, Hart Publishing, 2012) 316.

state to determine how an insolvent debtor's assets are distributed. Allowing a private party to determine this would undermine the insolvency regime.

Furthermore, a private party could abuse their power. As Lord Neuberger explained:

> there are also good practical reasons for equity adopting the doctrine, namely the unattractive and adventitious benefit which would otherwise be accorded to [X]. If marshalling was not available to [C], [X]'s free right to choose the property against which he enforced could have substantial value. In effect, he could auction that right as between [C] (who would be prepared to pay him to enforce against [Blackacre]) and the unsecured creditors of the mortgagor (who, especially where the mortgagor was actually or potentially insolvent, would be prepared to pay him to enforce against [Whiteacre]).[10]

Consequently, the law should step in and determine how the insolvent debtor's assets are distributed between C and unsecured creditors, rather than leaving it to X's whim.

Marshalling achieves this. If X chooses to realise its security over Blackacre, then C's security over Whiteacre allows it be paid before the unsecured creditors. To take the power out of X's hands, the law must ensure the same result if X makes a different decision. Thus, if X chooses to realise its security over Whiteacre, marshalling gives C security over Blackacre with the same characteristics as X's extinguished security. This ensures that C and unsecured creditors end up in the same position, regardless of the decision that X makes.

III. Marshalling by Apportionment

The cases on marshalling by apportionment also support the idea that marshalling is justified by preventing a private party deciding the distribution of assets on insolvency. In these cases, the facts are the same as in the core case of marshalling, except that D also owes £1m to a fourth party, C2, who has security over Blackacre, ranking behind X's security.[11] This is illustrated by the following diagram.

[10] *Szepietowski* (n 1) [36]. See also JD Heydon, MJ Leeming and PG Turner, *Meagher, Gummow and Lehane's Equity: Doctrines and Remedies* (Chatswood NSW, Butterworths, 2015) para 11-180.

[11] *Barnes v Racster* (1842) 1 Y & C Ch 401, 62 ER 944; *Bugden v Bignold* (1843) 2 Y & C Ch 377, 63 ER 167.

WHITEACRE	BLACKACRE
Value £1m	Value £1m
X's first charge for £1m	X's first charge for £1m
C1's second charge for £1m	C2's second charge for £1m

Just as in the core case, if marshalling did not exist, then X would have the ability to determine the distribution of assets on insolvency. On the one hand, if X chose to realise its security over Blackacre, exhausting Blackacre, then C1 can realise its security over Whiteacre while C2 competes with the unsecured creditors. On the other hand, if X chose to realise its security over Whiteacre, exhausting Whiteacre, then C2 can realise its security over Blackacre while C1 competes with the unsecured creditors.

Furthermore, if marshalling operated in the same way as the core case, then X would still have the ability to determine the distribution of assets on insolvency. On the one hand, if X chose to realise its security over Blackacre, then C2 could marshal X's extinguished security over Whiteacre, so C2 recovers while C1 competes with the unsecured creditors. On the other hand, if X chose to realise its security over Whiteacre, then C1 could marshal X's extinguished security over Blackacre, so C1 recovers while C2 competes with the unsecured creditors.

Consequently, marshalling does not allow C1 or C2 to take the full benefit of X's unrealised security. Instead, the rights created by marshalling are capped in proportion to the value of each property.[12] This is called marshalling by apportionment.

In this example, Whiteacre and Blackacre have the same value, so the rights created by marshalling are capped at 50 per cent of X's unrealised security. On the one hand, if X chooses to realise its security over Blackacre, then C2 acquires new security over Whiteacre for £500,000, with the same content as the security X used to have. On the other hand, if X chooses to realise its security over Whiteacre, then C1 acquires new security over Blackacre for £500,000, with the same content as the security X used to have.

Marshalling by apportionment is therefore also justified by preventing a private party determining the distribution of D's assets on insolvency. It ensures the same result, whatever decision X makes. In this example, either way, C1 and C2 each have good security for £500,000 and must compete with the unsecured creditors to recover their remaining £500,000.

[12] *Barnes* (n 11); *Bugden* (n 11).

IV. Subrogation and Marshalling Confused

In *Re Stratton ex p Salting*, a controversial case on the fringes of marshalling, subrogation and marshalling were confused.[13] The case purported to apply the doctrine of marshalling, but it is better understood to be an instance of subrogation properly distribution the burden of a debt.

The facts were that the Warre Brothers sold some brandy to Salting. The Court of Appeal refers to the brandy as Salting's 'property' so title seems to have passed.[14] Meanwhile, the Warre Brothers owed a debt to their bank which was guaranteed by Stratton. Without Salting's consent, the Warre Brothers pledged Salting's brandy to their bank. The Warre Brothers then went into liquidation. The bank realised its pledge and sold the brandy. Salting, having lost his brandy, looked for someone to sue.

The Warre Brothers pledged Salting's brandy without Salting's consent, so Salting had a claim in conversion against the Warre Brothers. However, the Warre Brothers were in liquidation so this claim was practically worthless.

Furthermore, legislation provides that where a seller in possession pledges goods, the pledge is valid as if it were authorised by the owner of the goods.[15] Accordingly, the bank's pledge validly encumbered Salting's title and when the bank exercised its power of sale, Salting's title was extinguished. Consequently, Salting had no claim against the bank or the purchaser.

Instead, Salting pursued Stratton, who was the guarantor of the Warre Brothers' debts. The Court of Appeal held that marshalling allowed Salting to claim the benefit of Stratton's guarantee.

This was a radical expansion of marshalling. In other marshalling cases, marshalling gives C a security interest over Blackacre. But in *Re Stratton*, there was no 'Blackacre'. Stratton's personal guarantee took its place. Instead of giving C a security interest, marshalling gave Salting a personal claim against Stratton.

Meagher, Gummow, and Lehane criticises the result on three grounds:

> 1. treating the right of a party to marshall as analogous to that of a surety to subrogation to the rights of the principal creditor; whereas in the usual case there is no question that [C] is in any way secondarily liable for the debt [which is] the

[13] *Re Stratton Ex p Salting* (1883) 25 ChD 148 (CA).
[14] ibid 152 (Cotton and Lindley LJJ).
[15] Factors Act 1825, s 2; Factors Acts Amendment Act 1877, s 3. Superseded by the Factors Act 1889, s 8 and now the Sale of Goods Act 1979, s 24. For discussion, see A Televantos, *Capitalism Before Corporations* (Oxford, OUP, 2020) ch 4.

subject of [X]'s rights so as to succeed to them upon satisfaction of [X's] claim from [Whiteacre];

2. prejudicing [Stratton] by the unrelated claims of [Salting]; and
3. overlooking the effect of *Ex parte Kendall* [in which marshalling was denied because of the common debtor rule, which is discussed below in the next section.][16]

However, these problems disappear if the language of marshalling is jettisoned. Instead, *Re Stratton* is a case of subrogation properly distributing the burden of a debt. As between Salting and Stratton, the burden of the Warre Brothers' debt should be borne by Stratton (the guarantor) and not Salting (the innocent customer).

Furthermore, Salting could establish that it bore the burden of this debt. The previous chapter argued that C bears the burden of a debt where C can trace into the payment which discharged a debt.[17] It seems that there is no authority on whether a party in Salting's position can trace into the payment which discharged the debt, but reasoning from first principles suggests that he can do so. Tracing requires transactional links.[18] The meaning of this phrase is rarely defined, but Cutts persuasively argues that 'a legal transaction is the performance of an act that is intended to and does in fact change the legal rights and obligations of two or more persons, precisely because that is what is intended'.[19] Here, by exercising its power of sale, the bank intended and achieved three changes to legal rights and obligations:

1. title to the brandy passed from Salting to the buyer;
2. title to the purchase money passed from the buyer to the bank;
3. the Warre Brothers' debt to the bank was extinguished.

Consequently, there was a transactional link Salting's loss of title to the brandy (1) and the discharge of the debt (3), allowing Salting to trace from its title to the brandy and into the payment which discharged the debt.

Salting had therefore borne the burden of a debt which ought to have been borne by Stratton. Giving Salting rights against Stratton with the same content as

[16] Heydon, Leeming and Turner (n 10) para 11-155 citing *Kendall* (n 2).
[17] See ch 10, s IV(C) above.
[18] *Foskett v McKeown* [2001] 1 AC 102 (HL) 128B–C (Lord Millett); A Burrows, 'Proprietary Restitution: Unmasking Unjust Enrichment' (2001) 117 *LQR* 412, 417; A Burrows, *The Law of Restitution* (Oxford, OUP, 2011) 120; T Cutts, 'Tracing, Value and Transactions' (2016) 79 *MLR* 381.
[19] Cutts (n 18) 297.

the bank's extinguished rights against Stratton therefore properly distributed the burden of the debt. This accords with the reasoning of Cotton LJ:

> the bank have paid themselves by selling the property of Mr. Salting. In that state of circumstances he stands in the position of a surety, that is to say, his property has been taken to pay another person's debt, and, in my opinion, he is entitled to say that any other security, which the bank, who have thus applied his property, hold, should be applied for his benefit.[20]

In short, *Re Stratton* sails under false colours. The Court described it as a case of marshalling, but it is better understood as an example of subrogation properly distributing the burden of a debt.[21]

V. Interaction between the Two Justifications for Subrogation

Finally, the common debtor rule and its surety exception demonstrate the interaction between the justification for marshalling and the justification for other examples of subrogation. These rules apply to cases where Whiteacre and Blackacre have different titleholders, and can be illustrated by contrasting the cases of *Ex p Kendall*[22] and *Highbury Pension Fund Management Co v Zirfin Investments Ltd*.[23]

Simplified, the facts of *Kendall* were that D1 and D2 jointly owed a debt to X, secured over D1's property, Whiteacre, and D2's property, Blackacre. D1 also owed a debt to C who has security over Whiteacre, ranking behind X's security, but C has no rights against D2. This is illustrated by the following diagram.

<u>**D1's WHITEACRE**</u>	<u>**D2's BLACKACRE**</u>
X's first security	X's first security
C's second security	

[20] *Re Stratton* (n 13) 152.

[21] Ali (n 8) para 8.26 fn 25, para 8.27 fn 27, para 8.31 fn 33; C Mitchell and S Watterson, *Subrogation: Law and Practice* (Oxford, OUP, 2007) para 6.45, fn 65.

[22] *Ex p Kendall* (n 2).

[23] *Highbury Pension Fund Management Co v Zirfin Investments Ltd* [2013] EWCA Civ 1283, [2014] Ch 359.

Kendall established the common debtor rule: marshalling is only possible where C and X's debts are owed by the same debtor, and secured over rights of the same debtor.[24] Here, title to Blackacre is held by D2, who not C's debtor. D2 was not a common debtor of C and X, so the common debtor rule prevented C marshalling X's security over Blackacre.

However, if the debt to X was primarily owed by D2, and D1 merely stood surety, then the result changes and C will be able to marshal X's security over Whiteacre. That was what happened in *Highbury*,[25] and this is known as the '"surety exception" to the common debtor rule'[26] or the 'extended' case of marshalling.[27]

In both *Kendall* and *Highbury*, if marshalling did not operate, X would have a choice which could determine the distribution of assets on insolvency. On the one hand, if X chooses to realise its security over D1's Whiteacre, exhausting Whiteacre, then C is left unsecured and must compete with D1's unsecured creditors. Meanwhile, Blackacre will be available to pay D2's unsecured creditors. On the other hand, if X chooses to realise its security over D2's Blackacre, exhausting Blackacre, then no proceeds of Blackacre will be available to D2's unsecured creditors. Meanwhile, C retains their security over Whiteacre, so need not compete with D1's unsecured creditors. In effect, then, X's choice would determine distribution of assets between C, D1's unsecured creditors, and D2's unsecured creditors. The distribution of assets on insolvency should not be determined by a private party who could abuse their power. The justification for marshalling is therefore engaged in both of these cases. Why, then, did marshalling only succeed in the surety exception in *Highbury*, and not in *Kendall*?

The key is that, before marshalling, C has no rights against D2. Consequently, allowing marshalling would require D2 to hold their property on security for the debt of a third party (D1) owed to a stranger (C). In *Kendall*, this is a decisive objection to marshalling.[28] It is one thing for marshalling in the core case to recreate a security interest until D has paid a debt to another one of their creditors. But it is quite another for marshalling to recreate a security interest over D2's property in order to secure the debt of a third party owed to a stranger.

However, in the surety exception in *Highbury*, this objection is overcome. D1 stands surety for D2's debt to X so, as between D1 and D2, the parties have agreed that the burden of the debt should fall on D2. When X realises its security

[24] *Ex p Kendall* (1811) 17 Ves Jun 514, 520, 527, 34 ER 199, 201–02, 204 (Lord Eldon LC).
[25] *Highbury* (n 23).
[26] Ali (n 8) para 8.01.
[27] *Highbury* (n 23) [2] (Lewison LJ).
[28] Ali (n 8) paras 2.34, 7.18–7.19.

over D1's property Whiteacre, it is D1 who bears this burden. That burden needs to be lifted from D1 and reinstated upon D2. Thus, in *Highbury*, Lewison LJ justified marshalling on the basis that:

> as between [D1 and D2, D1] was entitled to ensure that [D2] bore ultimate liability for their own debts. … Where two persons are liable to a creditor for the same debt, but as between themselves one of them is primarily liable and the other is only secondarily liable, the debtor with the secondary liability is entitled to be exonerated from liability by the primary debtor.[29]

Here, unlike in *Kendall*, marshalling would not be imposing a security interest over D2's property in order to secure the debt of a third party owed to a stranger. Rather, marshalling reimposes a security interest to put burden of the common debt back on D2, where it ought to be.

In other words, in the surety exception, the two justifications work together. Without marshalling, X would be able to decide the distribution of assets on insolvency. This choice should be taken out of the hands of a private party who could abuse their power. Ordinarily, this cannot justify giving C rights against D2, a stranger. But in the surety exception this is justified to put the burden of D1 and D2's secured debt to X back onto D2, where the parties agreed it ought to be. Together, then, these arguments justify giving C new security over Blackacre, with the same content as X's extinguished security. This ensures that, whichever security X chooses to realise, C remains secured and does not need to compete with unsecured creditors.

VI. Chapter Summary

The key to understanding the relationship between subrogation and marshalling is, consistent with the theme of this book, to focus on form. Subrogation describes the creation of a distinctive form of rights: C's new rights have prima facie the same content as X's extinguished rights. Marshalling gives C security with the same characteristics as X's extinguished security. It therefore creates rights which fit the definition of subrogation; marshalling is an example of subrogation.

However, marshalling has a different justification to other instances of subrogation. Marshalling is justified by preventing a private party, X, determining the

[29] *Highbury* (n 23) [5], [19]. See also Ali (n 8) para 8.24.

distribution of an insolvent debtor's assets. There is certainly a familial resemblance between this justification and the idea in the previous chapter that subrogation is justified by properly distributing the burden of a debt. Both are concerned with preventing private parties changing how the benefit and burden of debts are distributed.[30] Ultimately, however, these are two distinct justifications which operate in two distinct sets of circumstances. The justification for marshalling is premised on X having a choice and an ability to decide the distribution of the debtor's assets. By contrast, subrogation can be justified to properly distribute the burden of a debt, even if C was not obliged to pay D's debt to X.[31] In these cases, X had no right against C; X had no choice to make and no ability to decide the distribution of assets.

Consequently, there is some truth in both views about the relationship between subrogation and marshalling. On the one hand, subrogation describes a particular form of rights, of which marshalling is an example. On the other hand, marshalling has a different justification, and so operates in different circumstances, compared to other instances of subrogation. As such, it is correct to analyse the availability of marshalling and other instances of subrogation separately. In the core case of marshalling, marshalling is justified to prevent a private party determining the distribution of assets on insolvency, but subrogation is not justified to properly distribute the burden of a debt. In *Re Stratton*, the court used the language of marshalling, but the case is better understood as an instance of subrogation properly distributing the burden of a debt. Finally, in the extended case, the two justifications work together to justify marshalling.

[30] L Smith, 'Book Review' (1995) 9 *TLI* 133, 134 fn 4.
[31] See ch 10, s IV(B) above.

12

Conclusion

I. Introduction

Chapter 1 argued that subrogation describes the creation of a particular form of rights: C's new rights have prima facie the same content as X's extinguished rights. Recognising this is the key to understanding subrogation, and to resolving six controversial questions surrounding subrogation, which were introduced in Chapter 2. This chapter summarises the book's answers to each of these questions.

II. Is Subrogation Redundant?

Part II considered whether, as the law stands, subrogation is redundant. Chapter 2 explained that, when writers make this suggestion, they slide between different ideas. Sometimes they endorse the narrow idea that subrogation to personal rights in common liability cases duplicates recoupment or contribution. In fact, recoupment and contribution are examples of subrogation, but it does not follow that subrogation is redundant.

In other places, writers endorse the broader idea that subrogation to personal rights and direct unjust enrichment claims are governed by the same rules, so they are available in the same circumstances and have the same effect. On this view, subrogation to personal rights is redundant in all cases. Furthermore, it is said that subrogation to proprietary rights is different only because it gives C proprietary rights; in all other respects subrogation to proprietary rights is governed by the same rules as direct claims.

Part II argued that none of the propositions in the previous paragraph are true.

- Chapter 3 showed that direct claims and subrogation do not reverse the same enrichment.

- Chapter 4 showed that direct claims require a (direct) transfer of value from C to D whereas subrogation does not.
- Chapter 4 also showed that direct claims are subject to an incidental benefits rule whereas subrogation is not.
- Chapter 5 showed that a defeated unilateral expectation about the future can render D's enrichment unjust in subrogation cases, but not in a direct claim.
- Chapter 6 showed that many direct claims are subject to the change of position defence, whereas there is no convincing authority for this defence applying to subrogation.
- Chapter 7 showed that direct claims reverse a transaction whereas subrogation does not.

In sum, subrogation is available when a direct claim is not. Consequently, subrogation does not always duplicate a direct claim and so subrogation is not redundant. Even where direct claims and subrogation are both available, the two have different effects. Consequently, subrogation is never redundant. Instead, it has a unique role to play.

This has four important implications. First, just because a rule applies to direct claims does not mean that it applies to subrogation. For example, in *Swynson*, C's loan to EMSL caused D's liability in negligence to be 'reduced to nil'.[1] C did not intend this, so Lord Mance characterised this as an incidental benefit for D, and he applied *ITC*'s incidental benefits rule to bar C's subrogation claim.[2] Lord Sumption and Lord Neuberger were sympathetic to this idea, though they did not decide the point.[3] However, Chapter 4 showed that subrogation is not governed by the incidental benefits rule. As such, the incidental benefits rule should not have been mechanically applied to the subrogation claim.

Second, just because a rule applies to subrogation does not mean that it applies to direct claims. Subrogation cases cannot be relied upon as authority for a broad causal test for whether an enrichment came at C's expense in direct claims.[4]

Third, the law can dispense with unsatisfactory reasoning which is used only to prop up the fallacy that subrogation is governed by the same rules as direct claims.

[1] *Swynson Ltd v Lowick Rose LLP* [2017] UKSC 32, [2018] AC 313 [89] (Lord Mance). For the facts, see ch 2, s V(C) above.

[2] ibid [67], [88]–[89] (Lord Mance).

[3] ibid [20] (Lord Sumption), [115] (Lord Neuberger).

[4] P Birks, *Unjust Enrichment* (Oxford, OUP, 2005) 96–98; S Watterson, '"Direct Transfers" in the Law of Unjust Enrichment' (2011) 64 *CLP* 435, 458–59, 464–66.

For instance, co-ordinated transactions reasoning is over-inclusive, under-inclusive, and uncertain.[5] Yet it has been applied only in subrogation cases: co-ordinated transactions reasoning exists only to ensure that subrogation cases satisfy *ITC*'s requirement of a direct transfer of value. Once it is recognised that direct claims and subrogation are governed by different rules, and that *ITC* governs direct claims but not subrogation, then there is no need to squeeze the subrogation cases into the *ITC* rules. The unsatisfactory co-ordinated transactions reasoning can be forgotten.

Finally, as direct claims and subrogation are governed by different rules, a direct claim may succeed where subrogation fails and subrogation may succeed where a direct claim fails. In *BFC*, *Anfield*, and *Menelaou* subrogation succeeded, whereas the *ITC* rules would now bar a direct claim.[6] In *Reversion Fund*, *Mayfair Estates*, and *Anfield* subrogation succeeded, whereas a direct claim would fail for want of an unjust factor.[7] As a result, Moses LJ was mistaken in *Menelaou* when he stated that there is 'no need to duplicate the reasoning in relation to both unjust enrichment and subrogation; the answer should be the same'.[8]

III. Is Subrogation Justified?

Part III then turned to consider whether subrogation is justified as a matter of principle. Chapters 8 and 9 cleared the ground by rejecting a number of previous attempts to justify subrogation, because they failed to justify the form of rights created by subrogation.

Instead, Chapter 10 argued that subrogation's distinctive form reflects a distinctive justification. Subrogation is justified by ensuring that the burden of debts are distributed as they should be. If C bears the burden of D's debt to X and this burden should have been borne by D, then the burden needs to be lifted from C and reinstated upon D. Subrogation achieves this by reinstating the debt and having D now owe the debt to C. Thus, the particular form of rights created by subrogation reflects subrogation's particular role in ensuring interpersonal justice. Subrogation gives C new rights against D with the same content as X's extinguished rights against D because this ensures that the burden of D's extinguished debt to X is distributed as it should be.

[5] See ch 4, ss III(C) and III(F) above.
[6] See ch 4 above.
[7] See ch 5 above.
[8] *Menelaou v Bank of Cyprus Plc* [2013] EWCA Civ 1960, [2014] 1 WLR 854 [59].

IV. When Should Subrogation Occur?

Chapter 10 then considered, in light of this justification, when subrogation should occur. Properly distributing the burden of a debt uncontroversially justifies subrogation where C and D share a common debt to X, and C pays X discharging both C and D. Chapter 10 pushed that justification further, arguing that it can also justify subrogation in two further scenarios. First, the justification applies where C pays D's debt to X, even though C was not obliged to do so. Second, the justification applies even where C did not pay X, so long as C can trace into the payment which discharged D's debt to X.

The availability of subrogation may then be cut back by countervailing considerations. A legal system may also choose to have a rule that a malicious intervenor cannot discharge D's debt, or a rule that a malicious intervenor can discharge D's debt but cannot be subrogated to it. Furthermore, insofar as C consents to bearing the burden of D's debt, subrogation will not come to its aid. A mistake, defeated expectation, or failure of basis shows that C did not consent to bearing the burden, even though they cannot justify subrogation on their own.

V. What Rights Should Subrogation Create?

Chapter 10 also argued that this justification has implications for the rights that subrogation should create. The quantum of the rights created by subrogation are rightly capped by C's loss. If X's rights were secured then, subject to the rules in previous paragraph, subrogation should give C security too. If X had legal security, then subrogation should give C legal security and not just equitable security. However, the awards of subrogation in *BFC* and *Menelaou* are difficult to defend.

VI. What is the Relationship between Subrogation and Marshalling?

Chapter 11 then considered the relationship between subrogation and marshalling. Marshalling gives C security with the same characteristics as X's extinguished security. It therefore creates rights which fit the definition of subrogation; marshalling is an example of subrogation. However, marshalling has a different justification to other instances of subrogation. Marshalling is justified by preventing a private party, X, determining the distribution of an insolvent debtor's assets. This justification operates, and so marshalling is available, in different circumstances, compared to other instances of subrogation.

VII. Is Subrogation a Remedy for Unjust Enrichment?

Together Parts II and III addressed the question of whether subrogation is a remedy for unjust enrichment. Cane writes that 'classifications in the law' can perform two functions.[9] The first is 'expository': 'to make it easier to understand, expound and teach the law, and to make it more user-friendly for lawyers seeking to solve real-life problems for clients'.[10] The second is 'dispositive': determining the 'criteria of success and failure in legal actions'.[11]

Part II showed that classifying subrogation as a remedy for unjust enrichment does not perform a dispositive function. Subrogation and direct unjust enrichment claims are governed by different rules; unjust enrichment does not supply the rules which govern subrogation; unjust enrichment does not determine the criteria for success and failure of subrogation.

Nor does unjust enrichment perform an expository function. Part III argued that, marshalling aside, subrogation is justified by properly distributing the burden of a debt. As Hilliard explains:

> This rationale is sufficient in itself both to determine the measure of relief and explain why such relief should be granted. It is unnecessary to go on to enquire as to the extent of [D]'s gain, whether such gain was at [C]'s expense and whether any defences are available: the rationale above takes care of everything. …
>
> Unjust enrichment … adds needless complexity, replacing a one stage process (Is the distribution of liability equitable?) with a four stage version (Is [D] enriched? Is this at [C]'s expense? etc.). Unjust enrichment is both unnecessary and undesirable here.[12]

[9] P Cane, *The Anatomy of Tort Law* (Oxford, Hart Publishing, 1997) 198. See also K Barker, 'Understanding the Unjust Enrichment Principle in Private Law: A Study of the Concept and Its Reasons' in JW Neyers, M McInnes and SGA Pitel (eds), *Understanding Unjust Enrichment* (Oxford, Hart Publishing, 2004) 84; C Webb, 'Treating Like Cases Alike: Principle and Classification in Private Law' in A Robertson and TH Wu (eds), *The Goals of Private Law* (Oxford, Hart Publishing, 2009); C Webb, 'What Is Unjust Enrichment?' (2009) 29 *OJLS* 215, 228.

[10] Cane (n 9) 198.

[11] ibid 198.

[12] J Hilliard, 'A Case for the Abolition of Legal Compulsion as a Ground of Restitution' (2002) 61 *CLJ* 551, 554 (footnote omitted). See also *Trades House of Glasgow v Ferguson* [1979] SLT 187 (IH)

Indeed, a poor expository classification leads to bad disposition of claims. Part II showed that it is all too easy to slip from the idea that subrogation cases are best *exposited* using the four unjust enrichment questions to the error that subrogation cases are *disposed* of by the rules which govern direct claims. This has misled the law. For instance, Chapter 10 showed that, by drawing an unsafe analogy to direct unjust enrichment claims, the courts have unjustifiably used subrogation to allow lenders to escape the consequences of their own negligence.[13] It also argued that the House of Lords in *BFC*, by applying rules applicable to direct unjust enrichment claims, made an award of subrogation which cannot be justified.[14]

Conversely, clear exposition and just disposition go hand in hand.[15] Where C bore the burden of a debt which should have been borne by D, that burden needs to be lifted from C and reinstated upon D. Subrogation achieves this by reinstating D's debt, and having D now owe that debt to C. Subrogation's form and its justification are therefore tied together. Other rights (including direct unjust enrichment claims) have a different form, so cannot share the same justification, and so are governed by different rules.

It is therefore dangerous to treat subrogation as a remedy for unjust enrichment. Subrogation creates rights of a distinctive form because it has a distinctive justification. Grouping subrogation with rights which take a different form obscures the important relationship between the form of rights and their justification.[16] It obscures the distinctiveness of each form of rights and the distinctiveness of each justification, creating a mirage of similarities which do not exist. It becomes easy to slip into to the error of thinking that subrogation cases are governed by the same rules as other unjust enrichment claims.

192 (Lord Justice-Clerk Wheatley); S Meier, 'No Basis: A Comparative View' in A Burrows and Lord Rodger of Earlsferry (eds), *Mapping the Law: Essays in Memory of Peter Birks* (Oxford, OUP, 2006) 359–61; NJ McBride, *The Humanity of Private Law: Part I: Explanation* (Oxford, Hart Publishing, 2019) 213; S Meier, 'Enrichment "at the Expense of Another" and Incidental Benefits in German Law' [2019] *Acta Juridica* 453, 460–61; N Whitty, 'Rights of Relief, Subrogation and Unjustified Enrichment in Scots Law' [2019] *Acta Juridica* 493, 509–10, 518; H Scott, 'Comparative/Civilian Perspectives' in E Bant, K Barker and S Degeling (eds), *Research Handbook on Unjust Enrichment and Restitution* (Cheltenham, Edward Elgar Publishing, 2020) 165.

[13] See ch 10, s V(E) above.

[14] *Banque Financière de La Cité SA v Parc (Battersea) Ltd* [1999] 1 AC 221 (HL) ('*BFC*'). See ch 10, s VI(C) above.

[15] E McKendrick, 'Taxonomy: Does It Matter?' in D Johnston and R Zimmermann (eds), *Unjustified Enrichment: Key Issues in Comparative Perspective* (Cambridge, CUP, 2002) esp 639.

[16] B McFarlane, 'Form and Substance in Equity' in A Robertson and J Goudkamp (eds), *Form and Substance in the Law of Obligations* (Oxford, Hart Publishing, 2019) 198; B McFarlane, 'Equity and the Justification of Private Rights' in S Degeling, M Crawford and N Tiverios (eds), *Justifying Private Rights* (Oxford, Hart Publishing, 2020) 222–23.

This has implications for the wider controversy over whether unjust enrichment creates personal and proprietary rights, or only personal ones.[17] Uncontroversial examples of unjust enrichment creating proprietary rights are difficult to come by.[18] Subrogation to proprietary rights is the only example which the courts have clearly recognised as a remedy for unjust enrichment.[19] However, if this book's argument that subrogation is not a remedy for unjust enrichment is accepted, then the central example of unjust enrichment creating proprietary rights is lost, making it harder to argue that unjust enrichment creates proprietary rights.

Ultimately, the key to understanding subrogation is form. Subrogation describes the creation of a unique form of rights: C's new rights have prima facie the same content as X's extinguished rights. This unique form is matched by unique justifications. As such, subrogation has a different form and justification compared to unjust enrichment claims. Subrogation is, and should be, disposed of by different rules compared to unjust enrichment claims. Classifying subrogation as a remedy for unjust enrichment performs neither an expository nor a dispositive function; rather, it is a dangerous distraction. Cases of a discharge of a debt raise unique considerations and are not simply another example of D being unjustly enriched.

[17] cf eg WJ Swadling; 'Property and Unjust Enrichment: From Genes to Pension Funds' in JW Harris (ed), *Property Problems* (London, Kluwer Law International, 1998); W Swadling, 'Policy Arguments for Proprietary Restitution' (2008) 28 LS 506; A Burrows, *The Law of Restitution* (Oxford, OUP, 2011) ch 8; A Burrows, *A Restatement of the English Law of Unjust Enrichment* (Oxford, OUP, 2012) 159–71; G Virgo, *The Principles of the Law of Restitution* (Oxford, OUP, 2015) 10; C Mitchell, P Mitchell and S Watterson, *Goff and Jones: The Law of Unjust Enrichment* (London, Sweet & Maxwell, 2022) ch 37.

[18] cf eg *Chase Manhattan Bank NA v Israel-British Bank (London) Ltd* [1981] 1 Ch 105 (Ch); *Neste Oy v Lloyds Bank Plc* [1983] 2 Lloyd's Rep 658 (QB); *Westdeutsche Landesbank Girozentrale v Islington LBC* [1996] AC 669 (HL); *Re Farepak Food and Gifts Ltd* [2006] EWHC 3272 (Ch), [2008] BCC 22; *Angove's Pty Ltd v Bailey* [2016] UKSC 47, [2016] 1 WLR 3179.

[19] *Boscawen v Bajwa* [1996] 1 WLR 328 (CA) 335C–F (Millett LJ); *BFC* (n 14) 228C–F (Lord Steyn), 231H (Lord Hoffmann), 238H (Lord Clyde); *Menelaou v Bank of Cyprus UK Ltd* [2015] UKSC 66, [2016] AC 176 [37], [49]–[50] (Lord Clarke), [78]–[99] (Lord Neuberger); *Investment Trust Companies v Revenue and Customs Commissioners* [2017] UKSC 29, [2018] AC 275 [49] (Lord Reed); *Swynson* (n 1) [19], [22], [30] (Lord Sumption), [55]–[90] (Lord Mance).

BIBLIOGRAPHY

Agnew S, 'The Meaning and Significance of Conscience in Private Law' (2018) 77 *CLJ* 479.

Agnew S and McFarlane B, 'The Paradox of the Equitable Proprietary Claim' in S Agnew and B McFarlane (eds), *Modern Studies in Property Law: Volume 10* (Oxford, Hart Publishing, 2019).

Ali PAU, *Marshalling of Securities* (Oxford, OUP, 1999).

Armstrong M and Cerfontaine A, 'Subrogation, Unjust Enrichment and Insolvency: A French View of *Banque Financière de la Cité SA v Parc (Battersea) Ltd*' in F Rose (ed), *Restitution and Insolvency* (London, Mansfield Press, 2000).

Ball E, 'At the Claimant's Expense' (2014) 130 *LQR* 13.

Barker K, 'Understanding the Unjust Enrichment Principle in Private Law: A Study of the Concept and its Reasons' in JW Neyers, M McInnes, and SGA Pitel (eds), *Understanding Unjust Enrichment* (Oxford, Hart Publishing, 2004).

Beatson J, *The Use and Abuse of Unjust Enrichment: Essays on the Law of Restitution* (Oxford, Clarendon Press, 1991).

Birks P, *An Introduction to the Law of Restitution* (rev edn, Clarendon Press 1989).

—— 'Equity in the Modern Law: An Exercise in Taxonomy' (1996) 26 *University of Western Australia LR* 1.

—— 'Misnomer', in WR Cornish and others (eds), *Restitution Past, Present and Future: Essays in Honour of Gareth Jones* (Oxford, Hart Publishing, 1998).

—— 'Annual Miegunyah Lecture: Equity, Conscience, and Unjust Enrichment' (1999) 23 *Melbourne University LR* 1.

—— 'Rights, Wrongs, and Remedies' (2000) 20 *OJLS* 1.

—— 'Receipt', in P Birks and A Pretto (eds), *Breach of Trust* (Oxford, Hart Publishing, 2002).

—— *Unjust Enrichment*, 2nd edn (Oxford, OUP, 2005).

Birks P and Beatson J, 'Unrequested Payment of Another's Debt' (1976) 92 *LQR* 188.

Bridge MG, 'Failed Contracts, Subrogation and Unjust Enrichment: *Banque Financière de la Cité SA v Parc (Battersea) Ltd*' [1998] *JBL* 323.

Burrows A, 'Proprietary Restitution: Unmasking Unjust Enrichment' (2001) 117 *LQR* 412.

—— 'We Do This at Common Law But That in Equity' (2002) 22 *OJLS* 1.

—— 'Absence of Basis: The New Birksian Scheme' in *A Burrows* and *Lord Rodger of Earlsferry (eds), Mapping the Law: Essays in Memory of Peter Birks* (Oxford, OUP, 2006).

—— 'The Relationship between Unjust Enrichment and Property: Some Unresolved Issues' in *S Degeling* and *J Edelman (eds), Unjust Enrichment in Commercial Law* (Lawbook Co 2008).

—— *The Law of Restitution*, 3rd edn (Oxford, OUP, 2011).

—— *A Restatement of the English Law of Unjust Enrichment* (Oxford, OUP, 2012).

—— '"At the Expense of the Claimant": A Fresh Look' [2017] *RLR* 167.

—— 'In Defence of Unjust Enrichment' (2019) 78 *CLJ* 521.

—— *Remedies for Torts, Breach of Contract, and Equitable Wrongs*, 4th edn (Oxford, OUP, 2019).

Cane P, *The Anatomy of Tort Law* (Oxford, Hart Publishing, 1997).

Chambers R, 'Tracing and Unjust Enrichment' in JW Neyers, M McInnes, and SGA Pitel (eds), *Understanding Unjust Enrichment* (Oxford, Hart Publishing, 2004).

—— 'Two Kinds of Enrichment' in R Chambers, C Mitchell, and J Penner (eds), *Philosophical Foundations of the Law of Unjust Enrichment* (Oxford, OUP, 2009).

Chambers R and Penner J, 'Ignorance' in S Degeling and J Edelman (eds), *Unjust Enrichment in Commercial Law* (Lawbook Co 2008).

Cleaver M, 'Equitable Subrogation in Australia and England' (2018) 29 *Journal of Banking and Finance Law and Practice* 34.

Cross R and Harris JW, *Precedent in English Law*, 4th edn (Oxford, Clarendon Press, 1991).

Cutts T, 'The Role of Tracing in Claiming' (DPhil thesis, University of Oxford 2015) ora.ox.ac.uk/objects/ora:12239.

—— 'Tracing, Value and Transactions' (2016) 79 *MLR* 381.

—— 'Modern Money Had and Received' (2018) 38 *OJLS* 1.

Day W, '"At the Expense of" in Unjust Enrichment: Causal, Direct or Intentional Transfers of Value?' [2017] *LMCLQ* 588.

—— 'Further Narrowing the Scope of Unjust Enrichment' (2019) 78 *CLJ* 24.

Derham SR, 'Set-off Against an Assignee' (1991) 107 *LQR* 126.

Dieckmann JA, 'Scots Influence on English Law: the Guarantor's Right to Derivative Recourse (Subrogation)' (2004) 8 *Edinburgh LR* 329.

—— 'The Normative Basis of Subrogation and Comparative Law: Select Explanations in the Common Law, Civil Law and in Mixed Legal Systems of the Guarantor's Right to Derivative Recourse' (2012) 27 *Tulane European & Civil Law Forum* 49.

—— 'The Province of Subrogation Determined: Some Corrections – A Functional Analysis of the Guarantor's Right to Derivative Recourse, Comprising a Critique of the Restitutionary Thesis' (2012) 20 *ERPL* 989.

Dixon M, 'Equitable Co-ownership: Proprietary Rights in Name Only?' in E Cooke (ed), *Modern Studies In Property Law, Volume 4* (Oxford, Hart Publishing, 2007).

Edelman J, 'Two Fundamental Questions for the Law of Trusts' (2013) 129 *LQR* 66.

Edelman J and Bant E, *Unjust Enrichment*, 2nd edn (Oxford, Hart Publishing, 2016).

English J and Hafeez-Baig MJ, *The Law of Tracing* (Alexandria NSW, Federation Press, 2021).

Evans M, *Equity and Trusts*, 4th edn (Chatswood NSW, LexisNexis Butterworths, 2003).

Friedmann D, 'Payment of Another's Debt' (1983) 99 *LQR* 534.

Grantham RB and Rickett CF, 'Property Rights as a Legally Significant Event' (2003) 62 *CLJ* 717.

Gregson R, 'Is Subrogation a Remedy for Unjust Enrichment?' (2020) 136 *LQR* 481.

—— 'Subrogation, Marshalling, and Property' in N Mrockova, A Nair, and L Rostill (eds), *Modern Studies in Property Law Volume 12* (Oxford, Hart Publishing, 2023).

Hare C, 'Marshalling Marshalling' in PS Davies, S Douglas, and J Goudkamp (eds), *Defences in Equity* (Oxford, Hart Publishing, 2018).

Havelock R, 'Rivalry over Liability for Defective Transfers' in P Devonshire and R Havelock (eds), *The Impact of Equity and Restitution in Commerce* (Oxford, Hart Publishing, 2019).

Hedley S, *A Critical Introduction to Restitution* (London, Butterworths, 2001).

—— *Restitution: Its Division and Ordering* (London, Sweet & Maxwell, 2001).

—— 'Rival Taxonomies Within Obligations: Is There a Problem?' in S Degeling and J Edelman (eds), *Equity in Commercial Law* (Pyrmont NSW, Lawbook Co, 2005).

Heydon JD, Leeming MJ, and Turner PG, *Meagher, Gummow and Lehane's Equity: Doctrines and Remedies*, 5th edn (Chatswood NSW, Butterworths, 2015).

Hilliard J, 'A Case for the Abolition of Legal Compulsion as a Ground of Restitution' (2002) 61 *CLJ* 551.

Jaffey P, *The Nature and Scope of Restitution* (Oxford, Hart Publishing, 2000).

Klimchuk D, 'Unjust Enrichment and the Forms of Justice' in E Bant, K Barker, and S Degeling (eds), *Research Handbook on Unjust Enrichment and Restitution* (Cheltenham, Edward Elgar Publishing, 2020).

Leeming M, 'Subrogation, Equity, and Unjust Enrichment' in J Glister and P Ridge (eds), *Fault Lines in Equity* (Oxford, Hart Publishing, 2012).

Letelier P, 'A Wrong Turn? Reconsidering the Unified Approach to Unjust Enrichment Claims' (2020) 136 *LQR* 121.

Leung J and Wong SY, 'Subrogation and Unjust Enrichment in the Supreme Court' [2016] *LMCLQ* 337.

Liau T and Leow R, 'Proprietary Restitution' in E Bant, K Barker, and S Degeling (eds), *Research Handbook on Unjust Enrichment and Restitution* (Cheltenham, Edward Elgar Publishing, 2020).

Lodder AM, *Enrichment in the Law of Unjust Enrichment and Restitution* (Oxford, Hart Publishing, 2012).
Maitland FW, *Equity: Also the Forms of Action at Common Law* (Cambridge, CUP, 1909).
McBride NJ, *The Humanity of Private Law: Part I: Explanation* (Oxford, Hart Publishing, 2019).
McBride NJ and McGrath P, 'The Nature of Restitution' (1995) 15 *OJLS* 33.
McFarlane B, *The Structure of Property Law* (Oxford, Hart Publishing, 2008).
—— 'Unjust Enrichment, Property Rights and Indirect Recipients' [2009] *RLR* 37.
—— 'Unjust Enrichment, Rights and Value', in D Nolan and A Robertson (eds), *Rights and Private Law* (Oxford, Hart Publishing, 2012).
—— 'Form and Substance in Equity', in A Robertson and J Goudkamp (eds), *Form and Substance in the Law of Obligations* (Oxford, Hart Publishing, 2019).
—— 'Equity and the Justification of Private Rights' in S Degeling, M Crawford, and N Tiverios (eds), *Justifying Private Rights* (Oxford, Hart Publishing, 2020).
McFarlane B and Stevens R, 'The Nature of Equitable Property' (2010) 4 *J Eq* 1.
—— 'What's Special about Equity?: Rights about Rights' in D Klimchuk, I Samet, and HE Smith (eds), *Philosophical Foundations of the Law of Equity* (Oxford, OUP, 2020).
McGee J, *Snell's Equity*, 1st supp, 34th edn (London, Sweet & Maxwell, 2020).
McKendrick E, 'Taxonomy: Does it Matter?' in D Johnston and R Zimmermann (eds), *Unjustified Enrichment: Key Issues in Comparative Perspective* (Cambridge, CUP, 2002).
McMeel G, *The Modern Law of Restitution* (London, Blackstone, 2000).
Meier S, 'Enrichment "At the Expense of Another" and Incidental Benefits in German Law' [2019] *Acta Juridica* 453.
—— 'No Basis: A Comparative View' in A Burrows and Lord Rodger of Earlsferry (eds), *Mapping the Law: Essays in Memory of Peter Birks* (Oxford, OUP, 2006).
Merkin R and Steele J, *Insurance and the Law of Obligations* (Oxford, OUP, 2013).
Midwinter SB, 'Subrogation Finds Some "Well-Settled Principles"' [2003] *LMCLQ* 6.
Millett P, 'Proprietary Restitution', in S Degeling and J Edelman (eds), *Equity in Commercial Law* (Pyrmont NSW, Lawbook Co, 2005).
—— '*Jones v Jones*: Property or Unjust Enrichment?' in A Burrows and Lord Rodger of Earlsferry (eds), *Mapping the Law: Essays in Memory of Peter Birks* (Oxford, OUP, 2006).
Milsom SFC, *Historical Foundations of the Common Law*, 2nd edn (London, Butterworths, 1981).
Mitchell C, 'The Law of Subrogation' [1992] *LMCLQ* 483.
—— *The Law of Subrogation* (Oxford, Clarendon Press, 1994).
—— Book Review [2000] *LMCLQ* 589.
—— *The Law of Contribution and Reimbursement* (Oxford, OUP, 2003).
—— 'Subrogation: Persistent Misunderstandings' in A Burrows and Lord Rodger of Earlsferry (eds), *Mapping the Law: Essays in Memory of Peter Birks* (Oxford, OUP, 2006).
—— 'Unjust Enrichment', in A Burrows (ed), *English Private Law*, 3rd edn (Oxford, OUP, 2013).
—— 'Unjust Enrichment', in A Burrows (ed), *Principles of the English Law of Obligations* (Oxford, OUP, 2015).
—— 'Current Issues in Unjust Enrichment: The "Time Value" of Money and Proprietary Remedies for Failure of Basis' (2017) ssrn.com/abstract=3055715.
—— 'End of the Road for the Overpaid Tax Litigation?' (2017–18) 9 *UKSCYB* 225.
—— 'Other Reasons for Restitution' in E Bant, K Barker, and S Degeling (eds), *Research Handbook on Unjust Enrichment and Restitution* (Cheltenham, Edward Elgar Publishing, 2020).
Mitchell C, Mitchell P, and Watterson S, *Goff and Jones: The Law of Unjust Enrichment*, 10th edn (London, Sweet & Maxwell, 2022).
Mitchell C and Watterson S, *Subrogation: Law and Practice*, rev edn (Oxford, OUP, 2007).
Nadler J, 'What is Distinctive about the Law of Equity?' (2021) 41 *OJLS* 854.
Neyers JW, 'Explaining the Inexplicable? Four Manifestations of Abuse of Rights in English Law' in D Nolan and A Robertson (eds), *Rights and Private Law* (Oxford, Hart Publishing, 2012).
Nolan R, 'Civil Recovery After Fraud' (2015) 131 *LQR* 8.

Oman NB, 'Why There is No Duty to Pay Damages: Powers, Duties, and Private Law' (2011) 39 *Florida State ULR* 137.
Palmer J, 'Unjust Enrichment, Proprietary Subrogation and Unsatisfactory Explanations' (2016) 28 *Singapore Academy of Law Journal* 955.
Penner JE, *Property Rights: A Re-Examination* (Oxford, OUP, 2020).
Raczynska M, *The Law of Tracing in Commercial Transactions* (Oxford, OUP, 2018).
Rotherham C, *Proprietary Remedies in Context* (Oxford, Hart Publishing, 2002).
—— 'Subrogation', in S Hedley and M Halliwell (eds), *The Law of Restitution* (London, Butterworths, 2002).
Sales P, 'The Future of Tracing: Practical and Conceptual Issues' [2017] *RLR* 183.
Scott H, *Unjust Enrichment in South African Law: Rethinking Enrichment by Transfer* (Oxford, Hart Publishing, 2013).
—— 'Comparative/Civilian Perspectives' in E Bant, K Barker, and S Degeling (eds), *Research Handbook on Unjust Enrichment and Restitution* (Cheltenham, Edward Elgar Publishing, 2020).
Shah R, 'Indirect Enrichment in the Supreme Court' (2017) 76 *CLJ* 490.
Smith HE, 'Equitable Defences as Meta-Law' in PS Davies, S Douglas, and J Goudkamp (eds), *Defences in Equity* (Oxford, Hart Publishing, 2018).
Smith L, Book Review (1995) 9 *TLI* 133.
—— *The Law of Tracing* (Oxford, Clarendon Press, 1997).
—— 'Unjust Enrichment, Property and the Structure of Trusts' (2000) 116 *LQR* 412.
—— 'Restitution: The Heart of Corrective Justice' (2001) 79 *Texas LR* 2115.
—— 'Tracing', in A Burrows and Lord Rodger of Earlsferry (eds), *Mapping the Law: Essays in Memory of Peter Birks* (Oxford, OUP, 2006).
—— 'Philosophical Foundations of Proprietary Remedies', in R Chambers, C Mitchell, and J Penner (eds), *Philosophical Foundations of the Law of Unjust Enrichment* (Oxford, OUP, 2009).
—— 'Security', in A Burrows (ed), *English Private Law*, 3rd edn (Oxford, OUP, 2013).
—— 'Defences and the Disunity of Unjust Enrichment', in A Dyson, J Goudkamp, and F Wilmot-Smith (eds), *Defences in Unjust Enrichment* (Oxford, Hart Publishing, 2016).
—— 'Restitution: A New Start?' in P Devonshire and R Havelock (eds), *The Impact of Equity and Restitution in Commerce* (Oxford, Hart Publishing, 2019).
—— 'Equity is Not a Single Thing', in D Klimchuk, I Samet, and HE Smith (eds), *Philosophical Foundations of the Law of Equity* (Oxford, OUP, 2020).
Smith SA, 'A Duty to Make Restitution' (2013) 26 *Canadian Journal of Law and Jurisprudence* 157.
—— *Rights, Wrongs, and Injustices* (Oxford, OUP, 2019).
Steel S and Stevens R, 'The Secondary Legal Duty to Pay Damages' (2020) 136 *LQR* 283.
Stevens R, 'Is there a Law of Unjust Enrichment?' in S Degeling and J Edelman (eds), *Unjust Enrichment in Commercial Law* (Pyrmont NSW, Lawbook Co, 2008).
—— 'When and Why does Unjustified Enrichment Justify the Recognition of Proprietary Rights?' (2012) 92 *BULR* 919.
—— 'Floating Trusts' in PS Davies and J Penner (eds), *Equity, Trusts and Commerce* (Oxford, Hart Publishing, 2017).
—— 'Set-Off and the Nature of Equity' in PS Davies, S Douglas, and J Goudkamp (eds), *Defences in Equity* (Oxford, Hart Publishing, 2018).
—— 'The Unjust Enrichment Disaster' (2018) 134 *LQR* 574.
—— 'Private Law and the Form of Reasons', in A Robertson and J Goudkamp (eds), *Form and Substance in the Law of Obligations* (Oxford, Hart Publishing, 2019).
—— *The Laws of Restitution* (Oxford, OUP, 2023).
Swadling W, 'Property and Unjust Enrichment: From Genes to Pension Funds' in JW Harris (ed), *Property Problems* (London, Kluwer Law International, 1998).
—— 'Ignorance and Unjust Enrichment: The Problem of Title' (2008) 28 *OJLS* 627.
—— 'Policy Arguments for Proprietary Restitution' (2008) 28 *LS* 506.
—— 'The Nature of "Knowing Receipt"', in PS Davies and J Penner (eds), *Equity, Trusts and Commerce* (Oxford, Hart Publishing, 2017).

—— 'In Defence of Formalism' in A Robertson and J Goudkamp (eds), *Form and Substance in the Law of Obligations* (Oxford, Hart Publishing, 2019).
Tamblyn N, 'Separating Unjust Enrichment and Subrogation' (2017) 44 *Exeter LR* 1.
Televantos A, *Capitalism Before Corporations* (Oxford, OUP, 2020).
Tettenborn A, 'Lawful Receipt – A Justifying Factor?' [1997] *RLR* 1.
—— *The Law of Restitution in England and Ireland*, 3rd edn (London, Cavendish, 2002).
Villiers T, 'A Path Through the Subrogation Jungle: Whose Right is it Anyway?' [1999] *LMCLQ* 223.
Virgo G, *The Principles of the Law of Restitution*, 3rd edn (Oxford, OUP, 2015).
—— 'Restitution and Unjust Enrichment in the Supreme Court: Reflections on *Bank of Cyprus UK Ltd v Menelaou*' [2016] University of Cambridge Faculty of Law Research Paper No 10/2016, https://ssrn.com/abstract=2724024.
—— 'Whose Conscience? Unconscionability in the Common Law of Obligations', in A Robertson and M Tilbury (eds), *Divergences in Private Law* (Oxford, Hart Publishing, 2016).
—— 'Unjust Enrichment', in W Day and S Worthington (eds), *Challenging Private Law: Lord Sumption on the Supreme Court* (Oxford, Hart Publishing, 2020).
Watterson S, '"Direct Transfers" in the Law of Unjust Enrichment' (2011) 64 *CLP* 435.
—— 'Modelling Subrogation as an "Equitable Remedy"' (2016) 2 *CJCCL* 609.
—— 'Subrogation, Priority Disputes and Rectification: Mapping a Route Through the Thicket' [2016] *RLR* 1.
—— 'Subrogation', in G Virgo and S Worthington (eds), *Commercial Remedies: Resolving Controversies* (Cambridge, CUP, 2017).
—— 'At the Claimant's Expense', in E Bant, K Barker, and S Degeling (eds), *Research Handbook on Unjust Enrichment and Restitution* (Cheltenham, Edward Elgar Publishing, 2020).
Watts P, 'Mistaken Payment of Another's Debt – A Brief Defence of the Orthodox View' [1993] *NZ Recent LR* 248.
—— 'Subrogation – A Step Too Far?' (1998) 114 *LQR* 341.
Webb C, 'Property, Unjust Enrichment, and Defective Transfers' in R Chambers, C Mitchell, and J Penner (eds), *Philosophical Foundations of the Law of Unjust Enrichment* (Oxford, OUP, 2009).
—— 'Treating Like Cases Alike: Principle and Classification in Private Law' in A Robertson and TH Wu (eds), *The Goals of Private Law* (Oxford, Hart Publishing, 2009).
—— 'What is Unjust Enrichment?' (2009) 29 *OJLS* 215.
—— *Reason and Restitution: A Theory of Unjust Enrichment* (Oxford, OUP, 2016).
Weinrib EJ, *Corrective Justice* (Oxford, OUP, 2012).
Whitty N, 'Rights of Relief, Subrogation and Unjustified Enrichment in Scots Law' [2019] *Acta Juridica* 493.
Wilmot-Smith F, 'Failure of Condition' (DPhil thesis, University of Oxford 2013) ora.ox.ac.uk/objects/uuid:93ab182a-be71-489a-88e8-1479d9b8efb3.
—— 'Taxing Questions' (2015) 131 *LQR* 531.
—— 'Should the Payee Pay?' (2017) 37 *OJLS* 844.
—— 'A Prudent Decision' (2019) 135 *LQR* 195.
Winterton D, 'Unjust Enrichment and Rough Justice' [2016] *RLR* 164.
Winterton D and Pilkington T, '*Mann v Paterson Constructions Pty Ltd*: The Intersection of Debt, Damages and *Quantum Meruit*' (2020) 44 *Melbourne LR* 679.
Worthington S, 'Subrogation Claims on Insolvency', in F Rose (ed), *Restitution and Insolvency* (Mansfield Press 2000).
—— 'Justifying Claims to Secondary Profits' in EH Schrage (ed), *Unjust Enrichment and the Law of Contract* (London, Kluwer Law International, 2001).
—— 'The Myth of Common Law Tracing', in C Mitchell and S Watterson (eds), *The World of Maritime and Commercial Law: Essays in Honour of Francis Rose* (Oxford, Hart Publishing, 2020).
Zakrzewski R, *Remedies Reclassified* (Oxford, OUP, 2009).

INDEX

www.ingramcontent.com/pod-product-compliance
Ingram Content Group UK Ltd.
Pitfield, Milton Keynes, MK11 3LW, UK
UKHW020816290926
15470UKWH00003B/1195

9 781509 969227